A Celebration of
ANGLO-SCOTTISH
FOOTBALLERS

A Celebration of
ANGLO-SCOTTISH
FOOTBALLERS

DAVID STUART AND
ROBERT MARSHALL

pitch

First published by Pitch Publishing, 2025

1

Pitch Publishing
9 Donnington Park,
85 Birdham Road,
Chichester, West Sussex,
PO20 7AJ

www.pitchpublishing.co.uk
info@pitchpublishing.co.uk

A CIP catalogue record is available for this book
from the British Library.

ISBN 978 1 80150 953 4

Typesetting and origination by Pitch Publishing

Printed and bound in India by Thomson Press

Contents

Introduction. 7

Prologue 9

1. 1945/46–1959/60. 13

2. 1960/61–1969/70. 47

3. Seaside Celebrities. 94

4. 1970/71–1979/80. 106

5. 1980/81–1989/90. 147

6. The Alternative Cult Heroes. 185

7. 1990/91–1999/2000 191

8. Early 21st Century. 215

Appendix 1 261

Appendix 2 270

Appendix 3 275

Appendix 4 278

Epilogue. 283

Acknowledgements. 286

Bibliography. 287

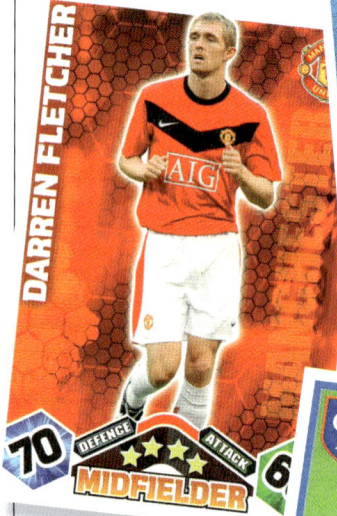

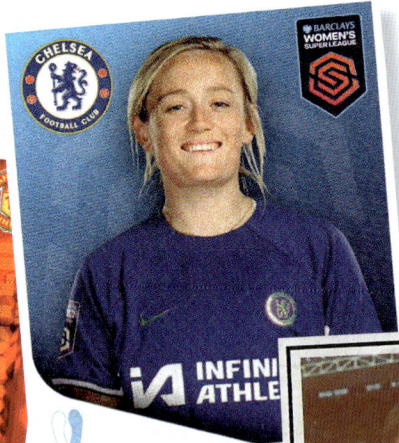

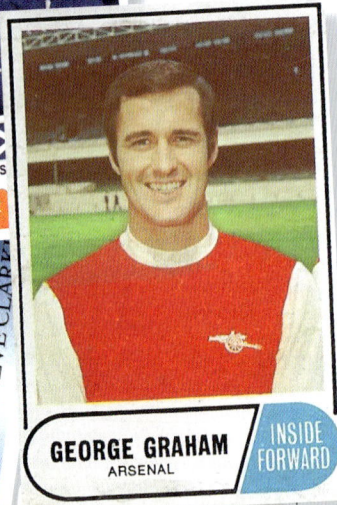

Introduction

There is no point in trying to deny it: most aficionados of Scottish football, including the two authors of this book, also enjoy, and are regularly envious of fitba played south of the border. It then follows that many Scots are also pleased when we see some of our fellow countrymen (or women) excelling in what has always been one of the best leagues in the world. For us, the exploits of Anglo-Scots are to be admired and applauded, and not lambasted because of petty jealousies and prejudices. Watching Scottish footballers scoring goals and lifting trophies at Wembley, Anfield, Old Trafford, Villa Park, Elland Road et al makes for great viewing and can help lift the spirits.

Throughout our school years in Glasgow during the 1960s and 1970s we savoured rare TV highlights of the English game via programmes such as *Sportscene* and *Scotsport* plus the midweek 'dream date' of *Sportsnight with Coleman*. Large atmospheric crowds, unusual strips (Crystal Palace throughout the 70s), quirky stadia (Derby County's Baseball Ground was a particular favourite – plus a muddy pitch beats red blaes every time) and even the funny-shaped helmets of the English policemen all added to the allure.

Knowledge of the English game was enhanced via the collecting of trading cards, matchday programmes and magazines such as *Goal* and *Shoot!*. Pin badges, posters and pennants then became must-haves with the latter two competing for bedroom wall space with images of the likes of Mud, Slade, Wizzard and Suzi Quatro.

Favourite 'Sassenach clubs' were identified – Aston Villa, Chelsea (the white vertical stripes down the sides of the blue shorts were the epitome of cool), Leeds United for their sizeable Scottish contingent, Norwich City and Southampton. Players hero-worshipped included Bruce Rioch, Charlie Cooke, Peter Lorimer, Jimmy Bone, Peter Osgood and Mick Channon – yes, we even liked and admired some of our near neighbours' own homegrown talent. Some of us even mimicked Channon's trademark 'windmill' goal celebration by swinging one arm round and round until it hurt! A headed goal in the school playground was often labelled an 'Alan Gilzean' while any powerful shot from distance, i.e. more than six yards, was a 'Peter Lorimer special'. Some of us also regularly tried to recreate the iconic Dave Mackay v Billy Bremner 'confrontation' from the mid-60s, with torn shirts and bruises testimony to us being a wee bit over-enthusiastic at times.

Of course, that was then and this is now, and to a large extent favourite clubs have been replaced with enjoying seeing so-called 'unfashionable' clubs such as Brentford, Brighton and Bournemouth making it into the mega-bucks top flight, staying there and occasionally sticking it to the big boys in the process.

Furthermore, that old saying springs to mind – that you don't fully appreciate what you have until you no longer have it – and we no longer have a substantial Scottish influence on football in England. There is still a Caledonian contribution to be savoured, however, and we shouldn't be afraid to shout, or at least speak loudly, about it.

So here is our homage to successful Scottish exports as well as English-born Scots, *A Celebration of Anglo-Scottish Footballers* (and managers), with the word 'celebration' being both a verb as well as a collective noun. We hope you enjoy it.

David and **Robert**

Prologue

So just what is (or who is) an Anglo-Scot? For the purposes of this book, it is a term often used to describe Scottish footballers who were based in England or played for English clubs at some point in their careers. By and large, these are footballers who were born and bred in Scotland before heading south for a new challenge and/or a larger salary and other financial benefits. However, Anglos also include English-born footballers who are considered Scottish through the birthplace of their parents or grandparents. A notable, groundbreaking example would be Bruce Rioch who was capped 24 times for Scotland between 1975 and 1978, and who played for several English clubs, but who was born in Aldershot, Hampshire, where his father – who was from Aberdeenshire – was serving with the Scots Guards. His mother was from the Isle of Skye.

Unfortunately, the modern-day rule allowing youth internationals to change their allegiances tends to muddy the waters a bit as well as creating irritating anomalies among match programmes and other football collectables!

Of course, Scots involved in the world of 'entertainment' have done rather well in England for donkeys' years now – Harry Lauder, Jack Buchanan, Alastair Sim, Gordon Jackson, Lulu, Stanley Baxter, Ronnie Corbett, Billy Connolly, Midge Ure, Annie Lennox and David Tennant to name but a few – but none of those star names ever picked up a league winners' medal, played in a Wembley cup final or helped stick it to Real Madrid, Argentina, the Netherlands and, er, England, so we'll concentrate on the footballers. As an aside though, does having a Sussex-based publisher make the two Glaswegian authors of this book literary Anglo-Scots – or just a couple of chancers?

Anyway, the Scottish Football Association was founded in 1873 and throughout those 150-plus years a vast amount of Scottish footballing talent has been exported to our wealthier, and usually warmer, next-door neighbour. That said, it was April 1896 before Anglo-Scots played for the national team when five pioneers – goalkeeper Ned Doig of reigning champions Sunderland plus Thomas Brandon of Blackburn Rovers, James Cowan of Aston Villa, Stoke City's Tommy Hyslop and Everton's John Bell made it into the team that defeated England 2-1 at Celtic Park to clinch the British Championship. It would be 1905, however, before Anglos played in games against sides other than England (i.e. Wales and Ireland).

The Anglos' first overall majority in the national team came about in April 1903 when six 'southerners' – three from defending champions Sunderland, two from Newcastle United plus skipper Alex Raisbeck of Liverpool – headed to Bramall Lane in Sheffield to help Scotland defeat England 2-1. Fast-forward to September 1977 when Ally MacLeod's Scotland lost 1-0 to East Germany in a friendly match in East Berlin – no fewer than 12 of the 13 players who got game time were Anglos, with Celtic's Danny McGrain the only home Scot who played behind the Iron Curtain that evening. Thirteen months later, the Anglos had a full set as Jock Stein's XI defeated Norway 3-2 in a Euro qualifier at Hampden Park with Kenny Dalglish of Liverpool netting a brace and Nottingham Forest's Archie Gemmill hitting the penalty winner three minutes from time.

Quite often though there have been problems getting English clubs to release their Scottish players for international duty, the nadir coming in December 1965 when some Scots were made to play for their clubs on the Saturday just three days prior to a decisive World Cup qualifier in Italy. An injury-depleted Scotland lost 3-0 in Naples and so missed out on the opportunity to triumph at the finals in England.

It has been suggested by peers, press and public (but not the authors of this book) that over the years some Anglos may not be sufficiently motivated to play for Scotland perhaps because they are earning more than enough in England thank-you-very-much, and furthermore do not wish to risk an injury upsetting the cosy economics of it all. However, surely you cannot question the commitment of the likes of Denis Law and Billy Bremner to the national cause in the 1960s and 70s, and more recently by Andy Robertson, John McGinn, Lyndon Dykes and co.

When Scotland lost 5-0 to England in the February 1973 SFA Centenary match (aka the St. Valentine's Day massacre) ten of the 12 players fielded were Anglo-Scots with five coming from Tommy Docherty's Manchester United. Suffice to say, the 'shellshocked ten' would have suffered a dose (or ten) of the 'verbals' from their English club-mates upon their return to Old Trafford, Maine Road, Bramall Lane, Elland Road and Highfield Road.

Conversely, some Anglos have complained about unfair treatment and discrimination against them by the SFA and the Scottish press with regard to team selection and the reporting of individual performances – and they may have a point. Anglos are, however, an integral part of Scottish teams and that's the way it should be. Simples.

Scores of Scottish footballers, and a fair number of managers, have done really well for themselves south of the border both in English domestic competitions as well as European tournaments, which is what this book is mostly about. Old Trafford hero Denis Law is arguably the best-known example having, regrettably, never played for a Scottish club – what could his hometown team Aberdeen have achieved with the Lawman up front? Over the decades Manchester United have also utilised the services of a great many Scots such as Pat Crerand, Jim Holton, Brian McClair and Darren Fletcher.

Meanwhile, what about Montrose-born John McGovern who, with Derby County and Nottingham Forest combined, won two European Cups, two First Division titles and two League Cups, but couldn't get a game for Scotland?!

There was ex-Shawfield Juniors midfielder Frank McLintock who in 1970/71 became only the second player that century to captain a double-winning side as skipper of Arsenal, while East of Scotland trio Bill Brown, Dave Mackay and John White had helped Tottenham Hotspur to the double ten years previous. Don Revie's physical but successful Leeds United team of the late 1960s and early 70s *without* the so-called 'Scottish Mafia' and Stirling's Billy Bremner skippering them to glory and not a little controversy? Unthinkable! And then there is Liverpool's trophy-laden 'Tartan Trinity' of Alan Hansen (Sauchie), Kenny Dalglish (Glasgow) and Graeme Souness (Edinburgh) which in season 1983/84 became a Tartan Fab Four with the addition of Steve Nicol (Ayrshire). These are just some of the more obvious examples of successful Scottish exports.

Managerially speaking, Matt Busby and Alex Ferguson (Manchester United) and Bill Shankly (Liverpool) were extra special leaders who changed the course of English football while the likes of George Graham (Arsenal *and* Tottenham), Doug Livingstone (Newcastle United), Les McDowall (Manchester City), Matt Gillies (Leicester City) and Tommy

Docherty (various) also made a significant impact. Again, these are just some examples.

Even in the fictional world of comic-book heroes, Anglo-Scottish footballers have made their mark and none more so than at Melchester Rovers. Andy McDonald was the club captain when Roy Race made his debut in the late 1950s and was described as 'a great mentor and natural leader of men who would go on to become the assistant coach'. Another example was Duncan MacKay, the 'rampaging Scottish international left-back'. In the real world, a Glasgow-born Duncan Mackay played right-back for Scotland, Celtic and Third Lanark before heading to Australia (as opposed to England) in 1965.

This book, in its own relatively small way, seeks to recognise and celebrate the achievements of the Anglo-Scots – our heroes in a 'foreign' land. From the end of the Second World War to the end of the first quarter of the 21st century – an 80-year snapshot in which the game of football, everyday technology and our general way of life has changed immeasurably.

Now if you will indulge us, let's end the prologue with a 'What if?' scenario. London Scottish Football Club were founded in 1878 and did not go 'open' until 1996 and while the Exiles are of course a rugby union side, their soccer contemporaries also gave it a try (no pun intended). United London Scottish FC were founded in 1883 and competed in the London Senior Cup as well as the FA Cup before disbanding in 1887. London Caledonians existed between 1885 and 1887 and also competed in the London Senior Cup.

So what if? So what if Dunfermline-born American millionaire industrialist and large-scale philanthropist Andrew Carnegie had thrown some of his wealth at creating an Anglo-Scottish super-team in the Football League in the late 19th or early 20th century? Would the site of 'Watkin's folly' now house a 100,000-capacity Robert the Bruce Arena, home to Carnegie Caledonians FC, ten times winners of the UEFA Champions League? All we can say for certain is that you should not drink several cans of Younger's Tartan Special Ale when you are drafting a prologue! Slainte!

1

1945/46–1959/60

Overview

The Second World War had a two-part ending – victory in Europe was declared on 8 May 1945 while victory over Japan was announced on 15 August 1945. For a period of six years throughout the hostilities, national football competitions in England were suspended and replaced with regional tournaments with a 50-mile limit for travelling implemented by the government.

Many footballers were enlisted in the armed forces and several were killed in the conflict, including Greenock-born Private James 'Jumbo' Gilliespie who played for Luton Town and Portsmouth (killed 1940 during the fighting retreat to Dunkirk); Sapper Thomas Alexander Douglas who turned out for Motherwell, Blackpool, Burnley, Witton Albion and Rochdale (killed in action in North Africa in 1943); and Flight Sergeant Edwin Watson, a forward with Partick Thistle, Huddersfield Town and Bradford Park Avenue (his aircraft was downed following an encounter with a German U-boat off the coast of France in 1944). Sad reminders that peace came at a price.

The first peacetime competition, the 1945/46 FA Cup, got under way on 1 September with a preliminary qualifying round and then the first round proper commenced on 17 November. However, the league championships did not return until season 1946/47 to give the country a much-needed boost in terms of providing the masses with access to a 'rare luxury'.

Attendances soared and the development of midweek floodlit matches, especially against overseas opposition, added to the magic. Floodlight pylons became an instantly recognisable and often much-loved piece of British football architecture. Improvements in stadium design, facilities and safety came at a relatively slow pace although a significant

Billy Steel who joined Derby from Morton for £15,500 in 1947. He returned north to Dundee in 1950 for £22,500.

development was the building of a new generation of grandstands – the propped cantilever stand – at clubs such as Birmingham City and Leeds United, resulting in improved all-round vision for spectators.

In season 1958/59 league reconstruction took place as the Third Division North and Third Division South were replaced with the non-geographical Third and Fourth Divisions. English football had since 1950 possessed the original 'Fab Four', encompassing 92 clubs in total. 'Got to do the 92' would become a groundhopping mantra in the 1980s, however road travel to and from football stadia in the 1950s was not so speedy. It was 1958 before the UK's first stretch of motorway opened – the eight-mile-long Preston bypass. The M1, Britain's first full-length motorway, opened in 1959.

On the international front and the world's oldest competition, the British Championship, resumed in season 1946/47. In 1946 the four home nations also rejoined FIFA and England competed at the 1950, 1954 and 1958 World Cup finals. Scotland also competed at the latter two tournaments with Anglos well represented in the playing squads.

The late 1940s and early 1950s was a time of austerity though – dreary, make-do-or-mend years with shortages of goods and services. Rationing for the likes of food, petrol and paper (the latter having a detrimental effect on the production of newspapers, books, match programmes and souvenir cigarette and trading cards), which had been introduced during the war, did not fully end until 1954.

As an aside, FA Cup Final programmes would have a cover price of one shilling (5p) from 1948's Blackpool v Manchester United fixture until 1969 when Leicester City met Manchester City – it doubled to 10p. The £1 FA Cup Final programme would arrive in 1985 as Everton faced Manchester United, while the £10 version first appeared in 2000 for Aston Villa v Chelsea. The £10, 2024 tome, when Manchester City met Manchester United, extended to 112 pages, while in the 1950s, 20 pages was the norm.

Back to the 1940s and on the plus side Clement Attlee's postwar Labour government laid the foundations for the 'modern-day' welfare state which included the creation of the National Health Service in 1948. As the 1950s progressed, personal austerity faded away and lifestyles improved with new housing and increased car and television ownership. Consumerism boomed and the concept of the British teenager grew in terms of a sense of identity as well as in economic importance. Even the look of our footballers improved in the 1950s as heavy shirts and baggy shorts gave way to modern lightweight kits as fashioned by our trendy European neighbours.

Like organised football, the British movie industry did its bit to lift the nation's spirits by producing comedy classics such as *Passport to Pimlico* (1949) which poked fun at the aforementioned rationing and bureaucracy; *The Love Match* (1955) starring Arthur Askey as a football-mad train driver with some filming done at Bolton Wanderers' Burnden Park; and *Carry On Sergeant* (1958) a mickey-take of national service which lasted until 1960 and which interrupted many a peacetime football-playing career.

The UK music singles charts were inaugurated in 1952 with Elvis Presley first charting in 1954 and Cliff Richard doing similar in 1958 but with football novelty records and drunken appearances by Scottish footballers on *Top of the Pops* still more than a decade away.

The Independent Television (ITV) network was launched in 1955 and in season 1955/56 the advent of the European Champions Clubs' Cup competition plus the introduction of a BBC TV regular Saturday night football highlights programme, in monochrome, called *Sports Special* (the forerunner to *Match of the Day*), all combined to stimulate an ongoing increase in the coverage of football on television. Live football, however, continued to be a rare treat.

It would be January 1961 before the maximum wage cap for professionals would be abolished in England – a policy that had been in place for 60 years. In 1939 the footballers' maximum weekly wage of £8 was approximately double the average industrial wage but by 1960 the gap had narrowed to £20 and £15 respectively.

In terms of player transfers, the first postwar British transfer record was set in September 1947 when Derby County splashed out £15,500 on Billy Steel to bring Greenock Morton's international inside-left to the Baseball Ground. In March 1960 Manchester City signed Scottish international Denis Law from Huddersfield Town for a British record fee estimated to be £55,000. In the summer of 1961, however, the Lawman would leave Manchester City for Italian side Torino for £110,000, a record for a transfer involving a British player.

For the seasons 1945/46 to 1959/60, the 29 major domestic trophies up for grabs were spread among 17 clubs with Arsenal, Manchester United and Wolverhampton Wanderers all triumphing in both league and cup –

A young Denis Law in his Huddersfield Town days before big money moves to Manchester City, Torino and Manchester United.

the West Midlands outfit bringing home five trophies in total. European silverware would start arriving in England from 1963 onwards.

Thirteen of the 14 championship winning-squads contained at least one Scot – Matt Busby's Manchester United of 1955/56 were the ironic exception – while in the FA Cup, no fewer than 26 of the 30 finalists contained at least one Scotsman in their starting line-up. Eight of the finalists were managed by Scots including future Rangers manager Scot Symon of Preston North End who fielded five of his countrymen against West Bromwich Albion in the 1954 final. To paraphrase the words of the British Prime Minister Harold McMillan in 1957 – 'We had never had it so good!'

Trophy winners 1945/46 to 1959/60

Successful clubs	League	FA Cup	Total
Wolverhampton Wanderers	3	2	5
Manchester United	3	1	4
Arsenal	2	1	3
Newcastle United	-	3	3
Portsmouth	2	-	2
Burnley	1	-	1
Chelsea	1	-	1
Liverpool	1	-	1
Tottenham Hotspur	1	-	1
Aston Villa	-	1	1
Blackpool	-	1	1
Bolton Wanderers	-	1	1
Charlton Athletic	-	1	1
Derby County	-	1	1
Manchester City	-	1	1
Nottingham Forest	-	1	1
West Bromwich Albion	-	1	1
TOTALS	**14**	**15**	**29**

What the above table doesn't show was that Tottenham's first four postwar league seasons were spent in the old Second Division – indeed, prior to 1950/51 when they were crowned champions, Spurs' most recent season in the top flight had been in 1934/35.

In the 1950s Everton spent three successive seasons in the Second Division from 1951/52 to 1953/54, while Liverpool, champions in 1946/47, were relegated at the end of 1953/54 and did not return to the top flight until 1962/63 just in time for the 'Birth of the Beatles'.

One-off relegation shocks would come to both Manchester United and Tottenham Hotspur in the 1970s while Aston Villa, Chelsea, Leeds United, Manchester City and Newcastle United have all 'yo-yoed' between divisions, to varying degrees since the end of the Second World War. Blessed are the Arsenal!

Domestic competitions

NB: Player appearances statistics are for league games only unless stated otherwise

The war had seen the end of many careers due to players aging but it also saw the peak for some too. Such a player was Jock Dodds. Born Ephraim Dodds in Grangemouth in 1915, by the time he was 12 Jock was living in Durham and a few years later he would sign on at Huddersfield Town. He failed to make an impression there and likewise in the one season at Lincoln City, however a transfer to Sheffield United saw Jock begin to flourish.

Jock scored 113 goals in 178 league matches for the Blades and was also part of the side that lost 1-0 to Arsenal in the 1936 FA Cup Final. In March 1939 he moved to Blackpool for a fee of £10,000. His official figures for the club show 15 league games and 13 goals.

And yet Jock is a Blackpool 'Hall of Famer'. During the war years he joined the RAF as a PT instructor and continued to play for his team. Overall, Jock is recognised as the second-top scorer in the war years with a total of 221, only five behind Albert Stubbins of Newcastle but nine ahead of Everton great Tommy Lawton.

All eight of Jock's Scotland appearances were during the war period and included a hat-trick v England in a 5-4 victory at Hampden in 1942. After the war Jock was sold to Everton to replace Lawton. He hit 36 goals in 55 games before finishing his career back at Lincoln.

1945/46

Although there was to be no league competition for this season, the FA Cup was competed for with each round over two legs until the semi-final stage. The semi-finals saw Scots among the goals as winger Chris Duffy scored a brace to win the tie for Charlton Athletic v Bolton Wanderers at Villa Park. At Hillsborough, Jock Mulraney of Birmingham City hit the equaliser to take their match with Derby County to a replay. The replay at Maine Road saw Derby romp home 4-0 to reach the final.

Jock Dodds who netted 221 goals for Blackpool during the war.

Chris Duffy was a losing finalist in 1946 but returned to Wembley a year later to score the only goal to give Charlton Athletic their only FA Cup success.

At Wembley, Derby ran out 4-1 winners after extra time. Three Scots took part in the contest with Jim Bullions and Dally Duncan showing for the Rams and Duffy the lone Charlton Scot.

Bullions, from Dennyloanhead, signed with Derby in 1946 after two years as a youth. Although his time at Derby was short (17 appearances, no goals), he remained a supporter of the club up until his death in 2014. November 1947 saw him move to Leeds (35/0) and by 1950 he was at Shrewsbury (131/2). Jim then spent the rest of his career in non-league football.

Aberdonian Douglas 'Dally' Duncan had been a stalwart in the Derby team (261/63) after signing from Hull City (111/47) in 1932 and was part of the side that finished runners-up in the First Division to Sunderland in 1935/36. Duncan later played for and managed Luton Town (32/4) then managed Blackburn Rovers. He led Luton into the top tier for the first time as Second Division champions in 1955/56 and Blackburn to the 1960 FA Cup Final.

Charlton's Chris Duffy would see victory in the following season's FA Cup.

1946/47

When the season finally concluded in mid-June due to a decimated winter schedule, Liverpool emerged as champions. They finished on 57 points, one ahead of both Manchester United, with newly appointed manager Matt Busby, and Wolverhampton Wanderers.

Captaining the Liverpool side that year was forward Willie Fagan. Starting out at Celtic (12/9), Willie joined Preston North End in 1936 (35/6) and played in the 1937 FA Cup Final alongside the likes of Bill Shankly and Andy Beattie. Seven Scots turned out for Preston that day but lost 3-1 to a Sunderland side only containing a mere five. Both clubs were also managed by Scots in Johnny Cochrane and Tommy Muirhead. Willie joined Liverpool in 1937 and remained with the Reds until 1952 (158/47).

Full-back Jim Harley, from Methil, joined Liverpool straight from Fife Junior side Hearts of Beath in 1934. He remained with the Reds until 1948 (115/0) when he retired from football.

The third Scot in the championship-winning side was the great Billy Liddell. Winger Liddell joined Liverpool as a 16-year-old in 1938. However, it was to be in 1946 that he was to make his official debut for the club. He was already an established favourite by this time having made over 150 wartime appearances, scoring 82 goals.

Before his time with Liverpool ended in season 1960/61, Billy made 492 league appearances which at the time was a club record. However, it was not a successful period for Liverpool for in the next few seasons after their 1947 title win, eighth was their highest placing. In season 1953/54 they suffered the ignominy of relegation and did not return until 1962/63.

Billy is still well revered down Anfield way despite the lack of honours his tenure brought.

Once again, Charlton Athletic reached the FA Cup Final to face Burnley, runners-up in the Second Division that season. The match was goalless after 90 minutes and it was to be the lone Scot in Chris Duffy who would score the only goal in the 114th minute to give Charlton their solitary FA Cup success. Outside-left Chris had guested for Charlton during the war and for a modest fee of over £300 transferred from Leith Athletic to the London club. He remained with Charlton until 1953 after which he hung up his boots (162/33).

1947/48

Arsenal won the title with 59 points, seven ahead of Manchester United with four Scots involved.

Edinburgh-born Jimmy Logie had signed for Arsenal in June 1939 from Lochore Welfare. The inside-forward remained with them until 1955 (296/68), winning two championships as well as the FA Cup in 1950. Jimmy ended his career in non-league football with Gravesend & Northfleet. In season 1947/48 Jimmy played 39 games, scoring eight times.

Joining him at the club in 1946 was Glaswegian Ian McPherson, signed from Notts County. Winger McPherson played 29 games, scoring five. He left Arsenal in 1951 (152/19), heading back to County (50/7), and later had spells at Brentford, Bedford Town and Cambridge United.

Playing in 40 matches without netting that season was wing-half Archie Macaulay. Falkirk-born Archie had played for Rangers (36/7), West Ham (83/29) and Brentford (26/2) before moving to Highbury for £10,000 in 1947. Macaulay was a regular in the side over the next few seasons (103/1) before joining Fulham in June 1950 for a few seasons more (48/4).

Dundee-born Alex Forbes had joined Sheffield United (61/6) in 1944 after playing Junior football with Dundee North End. Signed in March

*Jimmy Logie, winner of two
championships with the Gunners
and the FA Cup too.*

Liverpool legend Billy Liddell. Billy played over 500 games for the club but only ever won the league title in 1946/47 with them.

Jimmy Delaney of Manchester United who won the FA Cup in 1948.

1948, he played in 11 games of the title-chasing run, scoring twice. He also won the FA Cup in 1950 and was part of the side that clinched the 1952/53 Championship

The 1948 FA Cup Final was contested between Manchester United and Blackpool, with the Reds winning 4-2. Outside-right Jimmy Delaney was among Matt Busby's first signings at Old Trafford. Winger Jimmy, who was in his early 30s, had been playing with Celtic for 13 years (143/68) when Busby secured his signature for £4,000. Jimmy left United in 1950 (164/25) for Aberdeen (31/7) before turning out for Falkirk (40/20), Derry City, Cork Athletic and finally Elgin City in the Highland League in 1956/57.

On the Blackpool side were three Scots. Fifer Hugh Kelly was signed in 1944 at age 20 having been with Junior side Jeanfield Swifts. Left-half Hughie also played in the losing 1951 final but a broken ankle kept him out of the victorious 1953 final. He remained at the club until 1960 (428/8).

Forward Alex Munro was bought from Hearts in 1936, staying with Blackpool until he retired in 1950 (136/17). Alex later served the club in a coaching capacity and as a scout for several years.

George Dick had been signed following a trial in 1946 and made an immediate impact, netting 11 league goals in 30 games that season. In 1947/48 he was played less, and the final was to be his last game for the Seasiders (47/13). George had spells at West Ham (14/1), Carlisle (52/23), Stockport (25/12) and Workington (56/16) before moving into management with Racing Club Ghent, Danish club Boldklubben 1909, and Turkish side Galatasaray.

1948/49

Livingston Station-born Jimmy Scoular was one of two players alongside goalkeeper Ernest Butler to play in all 42 of Portsmouth's championship-winning matches. The fiery Scot had signed for Portsmouth in 1945 while based with the Royal Navy in the town. Pompey won the league five points clear of Manchester United, once more in second place. Jimmy played 36 games in the following season's league triumph. He left Pompey (247/8) to play for Newcastle United in 1953 where he won the FA Cup in 1955.

Born in West Kilbride, Ayrshire, Duggie Reid signed for Stockport in 1936 (84/23). Sold to Portsmouth in 1946 for £7,000, he was to become a regular scorer for the south coast outfit before leaving the club in 1956 (307/129).

Leading scorer in the top flight that year was fellow Scot Willie Moir for Bolton Wanderers, who finished 14th, netting 25 of the Trotters' 59 goals. Aberdeenshire-born Moir signed for Bolton in 1945 and captained the side in the 1953 FA Cup Final.

The 1949 FA Cup Final saw Leicester City lose 3-1 to Wolves. Foxes forward Kenny Chisholm's postwar career looks more typical of a player in the modern era as he flitted from one team to another every couple of years. Starting out as a fresh 16-year-old with Pollok Juniors in 1941, he moved to Queen's Park, Partick Thistle (34/13), Leeds United (40/17), Leicester City (42/17), Coventry City (68/34), Cardiff City (63/33), Sunderland (78/33) and finally Workington (39/15) before a short spell at Glentoran as manager in 1958.

Fellow Glaswegian Charlie Adam had been at Strathclyde Juniors before signing for Leicester in 1938 and remained with the club until 1954 (158/22). After a short spell at Mansfield (94/7) he returned to Filbert Street as a youth coach in 1960 until 1976.

Kingbarns-born defender Sandy Scott signed from Lochgelly Albert in 1947. He spent a few years at Filbert Street (31/0) before heading to Carlisle where he ended his career in 1953 (200/4).

Remarkably, manager Johnny Duncan started his days at Lochgelly but with United and not Albert before playing for Raith Rovers and then Leicester. Johnny was controversially sacked by the club in 1930 as he refused to give up management of the Turk's Head public house in the city. However, in an about-turn from the club he took up management of the side from 1946 to 1949 before leaving once more to continue running his ale house until the mid-60s.

As to the winning Wolves side, Edinburgh-born Jimmy Dunn in lifting the cup emulated his father Jimmy Snr. who had done so with Everton in 1933. Forward Jimmy had joined Wolves in 1942 and spent ten years at the club (123/33). He signed for Derby in 1953 for £15,000 for three seasons (57/21) before moving on to non-league football.

1949/50

Portsmouth retained their title by the slimmest of margins, winning on goal average over Wolves with both on 53 points and Sunderland only a point below. A Duggie Reid hat-trick in a 5-1 final-day win over Aston

Villa at Fratton Park helped clinch it in style. Duggie netted 16 goals over the season in total.

Alongside Reid and Scoular was Glaswegian wing-half Bill Thompson who made nine appearances over the season and three the one before. The three other Scots 'Jimmys' at the club – Elder, Stephen and Dawson – all made one appearance in the 1949/50 title run.

Arsenal won the FA Cup, 2-0 in the final against Liverpool with Alec Forbes and Jimmy Logie playing their part. The two 1947/48 championship winners, Archie Macaulay and Ian McPherson, were both still at the club but not selected.

Liverpool's Billy Liddell had been subject to rough tackling by Forbes and faded out of the game. Willie Fagan, as in 1937 with Preston, would once more be on the losing side at Wembley.

1950/51

Tottenham won the Second Division in 1949/50 and lifted the First Division title a year later with 60 points, four ahead of Manchester United. Kirkcaldy-born Alex Wright had signed from Barnsley (84/31) in September 1950 for £12,000 but only played two league games for the club. The following season he moved to Bradford Park Avenue (131/25) until he joined Falkirk in 1955 (95/20). At Brockville he was part of the side that won the 1957 Scottish Cup. He was the only Scot in the Tottenham team.

Newcastle United were to win the FA Cup in 1951, 1952 and 1955. Centre-half Frank Brennan was to play in the first two and left-winger Bobby Mitchell all three. Local hero Jackie Milburn was to net a double in the first of the three successes.

Born in Lanarkshire, Brennan moved from Airdrieonians in 1946 and was to spend ten years on Tyneside (318/3). In his book *Newcastle United Cult Heroes*, Dylan Younger suggests that 'Big Frank is widely regarded as the finest defender in Newcastle United's history', such was the esteem he was held in at St James'.

Left-winger Bobby Mitchell, nicknamed 'Bobby Dazzler' by the Newcastle fans, had been top scorer in Scotland in season 1946/47 with Third Lanark (70/42). A fee of £16,000 in February 1949 saw him move south. Bobby was to remain with the Magpies until 1961 (367/95). He played one more season in Scottish football for Berwick Rangers (51/10) before finishing up at Gateshead as player-manager for a short time.

Hugh Kelly was joined in the Blackpool team that lost 2-0 to the Magpies in the 1951 final, with two fellow Scots who would play for the club throughout the 1950s: goalkeeper George Farm and forward Jackie Mudie.

Farm only played a handful of senior games before moving to Bloomfield Road on a free transfer in 1948 from Hibs (7/0) and remained firmly between the sticks until 1960 (461/1). He moved into management in 1960 while still playing for Queen of the South (119/0) and proved to be quite adept, taking them into the Scottish top tier. Later he was to manage Dunfermline Athletic to Scottish Cup glory and the semi-finals of the European Cup Winners' Cup. Jackie was to become a prolific scorer for the Seasiders after a move to centre-forward in the mid-50s, ending his days at the club in 1960 (324/144). He left Blackpool to join Stoke and enjoyed promotion with them in 1962/63 with Stanley Matthews playing alongside him once more (89/32). Jackie finished his career at Port Vale (54/9) before playing in non-league football with Oswestry Town.

1951/52

After several years of being runners-up, Matt Busby's Manchester United claimed the title on 57 points, four clear of Spurs and Arsenal. Only a couple of Scots made appearances during the season and like Busby they were both Lanarkshire men.

Inside-forward Johnny Downie was bought from Bradford Park Avenue (86/33) in 1947 for a club record of £18,000. During the title-winning season he played 31 matches, netting on 11 occasions. Johnny left Old Trafford in 1953 (110/35) and had spells at Luton (26/12), Hull City (27/5), Mansfield (18/4) and Darlington (15/2) as well as a host of non-league clubs.

Outside-left Harry McShane was more of a bit-part player in the United success of 1951/52 as he was only to make 12 appearances, although his one goal was to prove the winner against Manchester City at Maine Road. Holytown-born Harry stayed with the club for four years (56/8) having joined from Bolton in 1950 (93/6). McShane had also previously turned out for Blackburn (2/0) and Huddersfield (15/1) and left United for Oldham in 1954 (41/5). His son is the actor Ian McShane of *Lovejoy*, *Deadwood* and *John Wick* fame.

As stated, Newcastle returned to Wembley to triumph once more in the FA Cup. Chilean George Robledo scored the game's only goal to

Left winger Bobby Mitchell who won three FA Cups with Newcastle.

give the Magpies victory. Brennan and Mitchell were still integral to the side and were joined by goalkeeping legend Ronnie Simpson. Having started aged 14 with Queen's Park in 1945 (78/0), he was part of the 1948 Great Britain Olympic side before turning professional in 1950 at Third Lanark (21/0). Ronnie signed for Newcastle for £8,750 in February 1951. He won two FA Cups in his time on Tyneside (262/0) before heading to Hibernian (123/0) in 1962. Two years later he joined Celtic (118/0) where he was to amass numerous trophies including the European Cup before retiring in 1970.

On the losing Arsenal side were Jimmy Logie and Alex Forbes.

1952/53

Arsenal won their seventh title on the final day of the season. They had to beat Burnley at home to surpass Preston North End on goal average. Forbes and Logie, who had both played in over 30 games, each scored to give Arsenal a 3-2 victory and secure the championship. Forbes left Highbury in 1956 (240/20) and after short spells with Leyton Orient (8/0) and Fulham (4/0) he coached in South Africa, Israel and Kuwait.

Blackpool and Stanley Matthews finally won the FA Cup with the famous comeback to snatch a 4-3 victory over Bolton. Joining George Farm and Jackie Mudie in the Blackpool side was Ewan Fenton. Dundonian Ewan signed in 1946, and though it took him a while to break into the team he began to establish himself by the 1951/52 season and was named captain by 1956. He was to leave in 1959 (195/20) for Wrexham (24/0) for a season before moving into Irish football as a player and then as a manager.

The losing Bolton team was captained by Willie Moir, the first Scot to captain a side in the FA Cup Final since Jimmy Guthrie did so in Portsmouth's win against Wolves in 1939. Moir was the leading scorer in the top flight in season 1948/49 with 25 goals and also netted Bolton's second in the final.

After ten years at the club (325/118), Willie then ended his career at Stockport (70/26).

1953/54

Wolves won the league for the first time, four points clear of West Brom in second place. The only Scot involved was Methil-born Billy Baxter who played in just a handful of games. Bill had been part of the ground staff as an apprentice at Molineux in 1939 and finally signed professionally in 1946. He was never a regular in the side (43/1) and moved on to Aston Villa in 1953, joining their backroom staff after a few seasons (98/6). Bill returned to Scotland for two short terms in charge of East Fife and Raith Rovers.

The FA Cup Final was played between West Brom and Preston. West Brom were to win with Gartcosh-born Jimmy Dudley the only Scot in their ranks. Jimmy signed professionally with the Baggies in 1945 and remained with them until 1959 (285/9). His record of 166 consecutive appearances for the club was finally broken by fellow Scot Ally Robertson in 1979. The wing-half moved to Walsall for five years (167/3) and won the Fourth Division title with the Saddlers before playing non-league football for a few years after that.

Preston's English manager Will Scott announced his retirement in March 1953 and Scot Symon, who had been successful with East Fife, took over. They had just missed out on the title and in what would prove to be his only full season with the Lilywhites, Symon took them to the FA Cup Final. He then went on to manage Rangers quite successfully for 13 years before being sacked in 1967. Symon put out five Scots in his side for the final.

Right-back Willie Cunningham was born in the Fife village of Hill of Beath, as was 1960s Rangers legend Jim Baxter, and 21st-century Celtic hero Scott Brown also grew up in the village. Willie started out at Dunfermline in 1946 (3/0) but soon moved to Airdrie (93/9) and then to Deepdale in 1949 for a fee of £5,000. It was money well spent as Cunningham stayed with the club until 1963 (437/3) before becoming player-manager at Stockport for a short stint (12/0).

Glaswegian Tommy Docherty had joined Preston from Celtic (9/2) in 1949. He left Preston (324/5) to join Arsenal for £28,000 in 1958. At Highbury (83/1), 'the Doc' played for three years before moving to Chelsea as player-coach (4/0) in 1961 where he was to begin his long and varied managerial career.

The other three Scots involved were all good servants to the club. Glaswegian Willie Forbes had a brief spell at Dunfermline (6/0) before moving to Wolves in 1946, playing for three years (71/23). The left-half then moved to Deepdale in December 1949, remaining until 1956 (192/7) before ending his career at Carlisle (26/0).

Jimmy Baxter was Willie Cunningham's cousin and like Willie he turned out for Dunfermline before heading south to Barnsley in 1946

Keepers Bill Robertson who played 26 games in Chelsea's 1954/55 title win and Chic Thomson who played the final 16 matches. Chic went on to win the FA Cup in 1959 with Nottingham Forest.

(222/54). Jimmy moved to Preston in 1952, staying for seven years (245/65) before returning to Oakwell. The move back to Barnsley (26/3) saw him reach a league appearance total of 493 games for the two clubs, scoring 122 goals.

Angus Morrison was born and bred in Dingwall and started out with hometown team Ross County, but was bought in 1944 by Derby County for a box of cigars. Given wartime rationing it probably wasn't as cheap as it sounds. He played two seasons with Derby (52/21) before a transfer to Preston in 1948 for a monetary fee. Angus scored an equalising goal in the final, but West Brom ran out 3-2 winners. Leaving Deepdale (262/70) in 1957, he finished his league career with Millwall (15/4) before moving into non-league football.

1954/55

Chelsea emerged as title winners for the first time in their history, four points clear of Wolves, Portsmouth, and Sunderland.

It was a tale of two goalkeepers over the course of the season and both were Scots. Bill Robertson was the first choice for a few years at Stamford Bridge having joined the club from Arthurlie in 1946, aged 17. It wasn't until season 1951/52 he became established, but after playing in the first 26 matches of 1954/55 injury kept him out of the final 16 games.

Charlie 'Chic' Thomson signed from Clyde (19/0) in 1952 as backup to Robertson and proved a more than capable replacement for the final matches of the title-winning run. By the next season though he was unable to retain his place with Robertson once more taking over. Robertson remained with Chelsea (199/0) until 1960 and moved to Leyton Orient (47/0) for a few seasons. Thomson was to join Nottingham Forest in 1957 and achieved success in the FA Cup with them in 1959.

In defence was centre-half John Harris. His career was to span from 1932 up to 1957 as a player. Prewar, John had spells with Swindon Town, Swansea Town (as they were known back then), Spurs and Wolves without accumulating too many appearances. During the war he played most of his football at Southampton. Chelsea signed him in 1946, and he was to play 31 matches in the championship victory. Leaving the club in 1957 (326/14) he joined Chester (27/1) where he moved into management. Apart from the 1968/69 season, John managed Sheffield United from 1959 to 1973, overseeing two promotions.

Up front, Chelsea had Kilmarnock-born Johnny McNichol. He had joined Newcastle from Junior club Hurlford in 1946 but was unable to break through to the first team. A move to Brighton & Hove Albion of the Third Division in 1948 saw Johnny play more regularly (158/37). He moved to Chelsea for £12,000 in 1952, playing 40 games in the title run and netting 14 goals to boot. Leaving Chelsea in 1958 (181/59) for Crystal Palace followed for a five-year period (189/15). In total John made 528 league appearances, scoring 111 goals, before ending his career in non-league football with Tunbridge Wells Rangers as player-manager.

Newcastle United won the FA Cup for the third time in five years that season with Simpson, Scoular – as captain this time – and Mitchell all still part of the side. United were managed by Doug Livingstone at the time. Livingstone had played with Celtic, Everton, Plymouth, Aberdeen and Tranmere in the 1920s. After he hung up his boots, he moved into management.

Starting out at Sparta Rotterdam for a year before taking over managing the Republic of Ireland side from 1951 to 1953, he then took Belgium to the World Cup finals in 1954 before heading to Tyneside later that year. Although he won the cup with the Magpies, he soon moved on to Fulham for a spell and then Chesterfield.

Bobby Mitchell scored in the 3-1 cup final victory over Manchester City with fellow Scot Bobby Johnstone hitting the reply for City, who were managed by Les McDowall. In 1956 McDowall, Johnstone and Dave Ewing returned to Wembley and claimed the trophy for themselves.

1955/56

Manchester did the double in 1955/56 with United winning the First Division and City the FA Cup. Matt Busby's United side contained no Scots. His young team finished 11 points clear of Blackpool.

Top scorer in the Second Division was Willie Gardiner. Willie had spent four years with Rangers (25/16) from 1951. He cost Leicester £4,000 in 1955 and proved good value with a goal return of 48 in 69 games including 34 that year. An injury-plagued period in 1958/59 at Reading (8/2) saw him finish his time at Sudbury Town.

Glaswegian Bob Crosbie topped the scoring charts in the Third Division North, hitting 36 of champions Grimsby's total of 76. Bob's career started at Bury (9/5) in 1947, then Bradford Park Avenue (139/72),

Hull City (61/22) and Grimsby (65/45) before heading back to Scotland with Queen of the South (21/11) in 1957/58.

Manchester City returned to Wembley to lift the FA Cup, beating Birmingham City 3-1. Manager Les McDowall was born in India but was of Scottish heritage and had joined Sunderland in 1934. He remained at Roker Park for three years, rarely featuring in the first team, and joined City. The war was to interrupt his playing career, but he was to continue to play for City until 1949 when a switch to Wrexham took place as player-manager. However, within a year he was back at Maine Road at the helm of the club. He was to oversee City's promotion back to the First Division in 1950/51 and took them to two FA Cup finals. Relegation in the early 60s saw Les leave Maine Road and manage Oldham for a couple of seasons before retiring.

Defender Dave Ewing signed as a 20-year-old for City from Perthshire Junior side Luncarty in 1949. He made his debut in January 1953, remaining with the club until 1962 (279/1). Dave then played with Crewe Alexandra (48/0) before finishing up at non-league Ashton United. In the early 70s he was to manage Hibernian before returning to City as a coach for several years.

Bobby Johnstone was a member of the Hibernian 'Famous Five' forward line and the only one who was to ply his trade in England. Bobby joined Hibs from hometown team Selkirk in 1946 but didn't make his first appearance until April 1949. This friendly v Nithsdale Wanderers was the first match that the 'Five' appeared in together. Bobby won two championships with the Hibees (168/88) before moving to Manchester City in 1955 for £22,000. Johnstone netted one of his team's three goals in the final and in doing so became the first player to score in consecutive Wembley finals. Leaving Maine Road in 1959 (124/42), he rejoined Hibs for the lower fee of £6,000 and spent a couple of years back at Easter Road (31/17). He moved to Oldham (143/36) in 1961, retiring in 1965.

On the losing side for Birmingham was outside-left Alex Govan. Glaswegian Alex joined Plymouth in 1944 and remained with them until 1953 (110/28), winning the Third Division South title with the Pilgrims in 1950/51.

A fee of £6,500 and the promise of a house brought Alex north from Devon to Birmingham in 1953. Alex was to spend five years at St Andrew's with the FA Cup Final being the pinnacle (165/53). The season after the final, Govan was Birmingham's top scorer with 30 goals in all

Malcolm Finlayson who won two titles and the FA Cup with Wolves but was never considered for the Scotland team.

competitions; his eventual league tally would be 53 goals in 165 games. He joined Portsmouth for a short period in 1958 (11/2) before heading back to Home Park and Plymouth (32/8), where another Third Division title was added before retiring in 1960.

1956/57

Sir Matt Busby's United team retained their title once more, with Alex Dawson the only Scot to be involved at any stage. Forward Alex was given three appearances at the end of the season after the championship had been won but even so managed to score a goal in each game. United had won the league with a total of 64 points, eight better than the runners-up, Tottenham.

Dawson, due to the Munich air disaster, was to make a greater impact in the following season, reaching the FA Cup Final with the Reds. Outwith Matt Busby there were no Scots involved in the FA Cup Final as United lost 2-1 to Aston Villa.

1957/58

Wolves were to clinch the title this season, five points clear of Preston North End with 64. Goalkeeper Malcolm Finlayson from Alexandria (West Dunbartonshire not Egypt) had joined Millwall in 1946 as a 17-year-old and quickly established himself as the first choice, staying at the Den until 1956 (230/0) before moving to Wolves for £3,000. He was initially seen as a backup keeper but by the 1957/58 season he made the position his own. Malcolm would also win the title with Wolves the following year and the FA Cup in 1960 too. He retired in 1964 (179/0) and in the early 80s was briefly vice-chairman of the club.

Glaswegian striker Jackie Henderson joined Wolves in March 1958 for £16,000 from Portsmouth (217/70). Jackie only ever played a few games for Wolves (9/3) at the end of this season and the start of the next before moving to Arsenal. The Gunners paid £20,000 for Jackie where he enjoyed a good few seasons (103/29) then in 1962 he moved to Fulham for £14,000. He spent a couple of seasons at Craven Cottage (45/7) prior to moving into non-league football with Poole Town.

Top scorer in the Second Division was Tommy Johnston of Leyton Orient and Blackburn Rovers with 43 goals. Johnston had started out at Kilmarnock (19/17) in 1949. From there he headed to Darlington (27/9), then on to Oldham (5/3), Norwich (60/28), and Newport (63/46), joining

Leyton Orient in 1956 where he was to become a club legend. In 1957/58 he hit 36 goals with the club (87/70). Blackburn had tried to buy him a few times with Orient finally relenting in March 1958 for a sum of £15,000. He scored a further seven goals for Rovers to end the season on 43.

His goal return at Ewood Park was 22 in 36 games but Orient bought him back in February 1959 for £6,000. Tommy still stands as Leyton Orient's all-time top scorer with 121 league goals in two spells with the club (93/51 for his second spell). He also has a stand named after him at Brisbane Road. Tommy finished his playing days at Gillingham for a final season in 1961 (35/10). He is one of only nine Scots to have scored over 200 goals in English league football, sitting fourth behind Hughie Gallacher, Ted MacDougall and Dave Halliday with 238 in total.

Sitting ninth on that table with 212 goals is Alex Dawson, the only playing Scot in the FA Cup Final of 1958 with Manchester United. Irishman Jimmy Murphy was caretaker manager for United with Matt Busby still recovering from his injuries sustained in the Munich plane crash that had taken so many young lives. Dawson was among those thrust into the first team decimated with loss.

Alex had scored a couple of goals in the early rounds of the cup, but it was in the semi-final that he was to make his mark. After a 2-2 draw with Fulham at Villa Park, the replay at Highbury saw Alex hit a hat-trick in a 5-3 victory to send United to Wembley. United lost the final 2-0 to Bolton with Nat Lofthouse hitting a double. However, the following season Alex struggled to maintain a first-team place and although he was given more games in the years after that, he left (80/45) for Preston North End for £20,000 in 1961. He was to be part of the Preston side that reached the 1964 FA Cup Final.

1958/59

Malcolm Finlayson continued in goal for Wolves, playing in 39 of the 42 games as they won consecutive titles. Manchester United were second with 55 points, six adrift of the Molineux outfit.

The FA Cup Final was won by Nottingham Forest, beating Luton Town 2-1 with five Scots in their ranks. To this day centre-half Bob McKinlay still holds the record for appearances for Forest. Signed in 1951, Lochgelly-born Bob went on to play 614 league games for the club with nine goals before hanging up his boots in 1969. His paternal uncle Billy also played for Forest, making 337 appearances from 1927 to 1937.

Adding on cup ties, Bob and Billy were to play over 1,000 games for Forest between them.

In between the sticks was former Chelsea (46/0) title winner Chic Thomson. Chic spent four years at the City Ground from 1957 to 1961 (121/0), ending his career at non-league Rugby Town.

Blantyre-born defender Joe McDonald had started out at Falkirk in 1951 (79/0) before moving south to Sunderland in 1954. Joe spent a few years at Roker Park (137/1) before moving to Forest in 1958. He stayed with Forest until 1961 (109/0) and finished his playing days at non-league Wisbech Town.

Although signed by Celtic, Govan-born Johnny Quigley was farmed out to local club St Anthony. Let go by the Parkhead club, he joined another Junior side in Ashfield before being scooped up by Forest in 1957. He quickly established himself in the team and spent seven seasons at the City Ground (237/51), scoring the winner v Aston Villa in the semi-final. Transfers to Huddersfield (67/4), Bristol City (66/7) and Mansfield Town (105/2) followed before moving into coaching. Johnny amassed over 470 English league games despite having not signed for Forest until he was 22.

Outside-left Stewart Imlach started out at his hometown team Lossiemouth FC before a move south to Bury beckoned in 1952 (71/14). Two years later he moved to Derby County for a season (36/2) and then on to the City Ground with Forest. He spent five years with Forest (184/43). In the final he assisted in the first goal, laying a pass on to Roy Dwight. After Forest, Imlach played for Luton Town (8/0), Coventry City (73/11), Crystal Palace twice (35/2 and 16/1) with spells at non-league Dover and Chelmsford in between.

On the losing side, the sole Scottish Hatter was Allan Brown. Allan had enjoyed Scottish League Cup success with East Fife (62/20) in 1950 six years after joining the club but soon left to sign for Blackpool. The fee of £26,500 was the highest received by a Scottish club at that time. However, he didn't have much luck in the cup in England. He missed Blackpool's 1951 final appearance due to a knee injury and two years later he also missed out, having broken his leg scoring the winner in the quarter-finals against Arsenal.

Allan spent six years with the Seasiders (158/68) before moving to Luton in 1957 for £8,000. En route to the final Allan scored five goals including the winner over Blackpool in the fifth round. He left Kenilworth Road (151/51) for Portsmouth in 1960 for a couple of years (69/8) before playing with Wigan Athletic for a similar period as player-manager. He went on to manage Luton, Torquay, Bury and Forest plus Southport and Blackpool for two spells each.

1959/60

Burnley were the champions, pipping Wolves by a point after a win in their final match, topping the table for the first time that season. Aberdonian Adam Blacklaw was the man between the sticks for 41 of the 42-game league campaign. Adam had signed for the Clarets in 1956 (318/0). He left for Blackburn in 1967 (96/0) before a one-game spell with Blackpool in 1970/71.

Interestingly, with Malcolm Finlayson still retaining his place at Wolves, Bill Brown at Spurs and future Rangers manager Jock Wallace playing for West Brom, the top four English clubs that season all had Scottish goalkeepers.

Coatbridge-born Bobby Seith had signed as a 16-year-old at Turf Moor in 1948, making his debut in 1953. During the title run a defensive mistake against Wolves saw him dropped from the side after playing in 27 games and he did not feature again. He left Burnley (211/6) that summer, moving to Dundee, and was to play a large part in Dundee's championship win in the 1961/62 season and their European exploits the following year (134/5).

He returned to England for a couple of years as manager of Preston North End and went on to take charge of Hearts for four years in the early 70s.

Despite his Caledonian-sounding name, and despite his appearance in the 1970/71 A&BC Scottish Footballers set of trading cards, Burnley right-back John Angus was not Scottish but an English international.

The consolation for Wolves losing out on achieving a third consecutive league title was to be victory in the FA Cup Final. Malcolm Finlayson was the only Scot in the team that beat Blackburn Rovers 3-0.

In the Rovers side at outside-left was Ally 'Noddy' MacLeod. Future Tartan Army legend Ally had started out at Third Lanark for six years from 1949 to 1955 (112/17) before a brief stop at St Mirren (22/3). Signed in 1956 by fellow Scot Dally Duncan who had won the FA Cup with Derby in the first postwar final, MacLeod was to leave the club in 1961 (193/47), heading back to Scotland for Hibs (52/6), followed by a return to Thirds (24/1) and then to Ayr where his playing days would end (17/0), and his management ones were to begin. Duncan was to fall foul of the Blackburn directors and was sacked from the club by July 1960. He would not return to football management and for a while ran a guest house in Brighton.

* * *

European and international competitions

Two major European club competitions got under way in the 1950s – the European Champions Clubs' Cup and the Inter-Cities Fairs Cup.

The Union of European Football Associations (UEFA) was founded on 15 June 1954 in Basel, Switzerland, although it was Jacques Ferran and Gabriel Hanot, two journalists for the French sports newspaper *L'Équipe*, who were the driving force behind the creation of the European Cup, which UEFA approved in April 1955. *L'Équipe* were the initial organisers of the competition and participating clubs were selected on the basis that they were both representative and prestigious.

The inaugural competition comprised 16 clubs but with no English representation, as champions Chelsea, who had initially agreed to compete, withdrew following pressure from the Football League who viewed the competition as a distraction to domestic football. Thus, Stamford Bridge's Anglo-Scottish quintet of goalkeepers Charlie Thomson and Bill Robertson, defender 'Gentleman' John Harris, inside-forward John McNichol and centre-half Bill Livingstone were denied the opportunity for a groundbreaking European adventure.

Matt Busby's Manchester United, as reigning English champions, had two goes at the new competition however – in 1956/57 and 1957/58 – losing out at the semi-final stage on each occasion, to Real Madrid, who would win the trophy, and AC Milan respectively. In 1958/59 UEFA invited Manchester United to enter the competition after eight of the club's players were killed in the Munich air tragedy while returning from a European Cup tie in Belgrade the previous season; however, the Football League refused to allow the Old Trafford outfit to participate.

League winners Wolverhampton Wanderers then had two consecutive attempts at the European Cup in 1958/59 and 1959/60 but were eliminated at the first round and quarter-final stages respectively. The former Renfrew Juniors goalie Malcolm Finlayson was between the sticks in some of the matches against Schalke 04, Vorwärts Berlin, Red Star Belgrade and Barcelona.

The Inter-Cities Fairs Cup was a competition set up in 1955 to promote international trade fairs and as such was initially only open to teams from cities that hosted such events. The tournament was organised by a Fairs Cup Committee (future FIFA president Stanley Rous was its chairman) and eventually competitions featured a 'one city, one team' rule which meant qualification could be determined by geography instead of success on the football field.

The first tournament took three seasons to complete and a representative side – London XI – reached the final before being overcome by Barcelona. While the London Select were managed by Joe Mears – the chairman of Chelsea! – in the first leg of the final at Stamford Bridge, come the second leg in Spain, Scotsman Billy Milne, Arsenal's first-team trainer, took over the managerial reins. As a wing-half earlier in his career, Milne had played for his local club Buckie Thistle before joining the Gunners in 1921 and playing over 100 times for them before a leg break ended his playing days in 1927. During the war he was an air raid precautions warden at Highbury and was in attendance the evening the stadium was hit with incendiary devices but was able to help put out the resulting fire, saving the stadium from even more serious damage.

Birmingham City competed in the first four editions of the Inter-Cities Fairs Cup, thus becoming the first English club side to compete in Europe, and reached the finals in 1960 and 1961 before losing to Barcelona and Roma respectively. In the first leg of the 1961 final the Midlands side fielded former (and future) Celtic player Bertie Auld at outside-left. European Cup glory, however, would await Bertie and Matt Busby either side of the border in the late 1960s.

* * *

International glory for Anglo-Scots was primarily achieved in the shape of Scotland being crowned outright British champions in 1948/49 and 1950/51 with maximum points on both occasions. With goal difference not counting back then, it meant that several British titles were shared.

In October 1948 Scotland opened with a 3-1 win over Wales at Ninian Park, Cardiff, in front of a crowd of 59,911. The Scots' line-up included no fewer than nine players from north of the border while the 'foreigners' were inside-left Billy Steel of Derby County, winning his eighth cap, and outside-left John Kelly of Second Division Barnsley who was making his international debut. Kelly was the Yorkshire club's first Scot to be capped for his country – loanee Oli McBurnie would be the second, in 2018. Paisley-born Kelly would make over 200 league appearances for Barnsley, who allowed him a five-day, expenses-paid visit to the family home in Barrhead, Renfrewshire each month.

Kelly would win his second and final cap in November 1948 in the 3-2 victory against Northern Ireland (having trailed 2-0 after just four minutes) at Hampden Park, Glasgow, with 93,182 watching on. Again, Billy Steel was his only team-mate from down south. In the decisive game against England at Wembley in April 1949, the official attendance of 98,188 saw the visitors triumph 3-1 with lone Anglo Steel netting the second goal.

The 1950/51 campaign began in October with another 3-1 victory against Wales at Ninian Park where 50,000 saw Liverpool's Billy Liddell net the third goal. Incidentally, the winger who hailed from the Kingdom of Fife served as a Royal Air Force navigator during the war. The only other Anglo in the side that day was wing-half Alex Forbes of Arsenal. Dundee-born Forbes would play 14 times for Scotland and also represented his country at ice hockey.

Liddell and Forbes teamed-up again at Hampden Park in November 1950 as Northern Ireland were crushed 6-1 in front of 83,142. Liddell and Forbes had of course faced off against one another in the FA Cup Final back in April with the Arsenal man taking home a winners' medal. As they did two years previous, the Scottish Selection Committee opted for only one Anglo-Scot against an England side which included Alf Ramsey, Billy Wright, Stanley Matthews, Stan Mortensen and Tom Finney at Wembley in April 1951. Billy Liddell was the man and his goal, Scotland's third, made all the difference as his side took the title thanks to a 3-2 win with 98,000 in attendance.

In the 1950s Scotland would also appear at two World Cups – Switzerland 1954 and Sweden 1958 – having declined to participate in the 1950 finals in Brazil.

For the 1954 pantomime the SFA decided that only 13 players of the 22-man squad would actually travel to Switzerland, the other nine remaining at home on reserve. Yes really. Of the 13, four were Anglo-Scots from across three Lancashire clubs: Willie Cunningham and Tommy Docherty from Preston North End, Jock Aird of Burnley and Allan Brown of Blackpool. The reserve Anglos were Alex Wilson and Jackie Henderson, both of Portsmouth.

The 'Lancashire Four' played in both of Scotland's matches – losing 1-0 to Austria in Zurich and 7-0 to Uruguay in Basel. Cowdenbeath man Cunningham skippered Scotland in the two games, which were painful experiences in more ways than one as he damaged a shoulder in the first, while Docherty quipped that against Uruguay, 'Scotland were lucky to get the nil!' Allan Brown's 14-cap run ended with the battering in Basel.

Jock Aird was a full-back who joined Burnley from Perth Junior side Jeanfield Swifts in 1948 and went on to make around 150 appearances for the top-flight outfit before leaving for New Zealand in 1955. His compact 1954 Scotland 'career' comprised four games – home and away World Cup warm-up matches against Norway on 5 and 19 May followed by the two World Cup defeats on 16 and 19 June.

For the 1958 tournament there were six Anglos in the squad – goalkeeper and captain Tommy Younger (Liverpool); defenders Alex Parker (Everton) and John Hewie (Charlton Athletic); midfielder Tommy Docherty (Preston North End); and forwards Jackie Mudie (Blackpool) and Stewart Imlach (Nottingham Forest).

Matt Busby was due to manage the Scotland team but was unable to do so as he was still recovering from injuries sustained in the Munich air disaster. Busby did of course manage the strictly amateur Great Britain football team at the 1948 Olympic Games in London, losing out to Denmark for a bronze medal.

In Scotland's opening match in Sweden, a creditable 1-1 draw against Yugoslavia in Västerås was achieved with Younger, Hewie, Imlach and Mudie all playing their part and with the Dundee-born Blackpool player having a perfectly good goal disallowed for a foul on the Yugoslav goalie.

Three days later in Norrköping, however, Scotland, fielding Younger, Parker and Mudie, lost 3-2 to Paraguay, the supposedly weakest team in the group, with two errors from Liverpool man Younger ending up in the back of the net. Sadly, it was to be Younger's 24th and final appearance for his country – an unbroken sequence which began with his debut in a 3-0 friendly win over Portugal at Hampden in May 1955. Alex Parker also bowed out from international football against Paraguay having won 15 Scotland caps. A goal from Mudie had made it 1-1 in a bitterly disappointing game in which Scotland were never in front.

In the qualifying campaign Scotland had recorded a memorable 4-1 win over Spain at Hampden with Mudie hitting a hat-trick and Hewie netting the other goal. Mudie also scored in the home and away wins

Nottingham Forest winger Stewart Imlach who played at the 1958 World Cup in Sweden and won the FA Cup a year later.

Tommy Docherty of Preston North End who played in the 1954 World Cup and was part of the 1958 squad too.

against Switzerland. Against France in the third group match, in Örebro, the Blackpool centre-forward drew a blank though as Scotland went down 2-1 (Raymond Kopa and Just Fontaine the scorers for France). It was Mudie's 17th and final Scotland appearance. Also featuring were Hewie, whose penalty hit the post, and Imlach, with the Forest winger winning his fourth and final cap.

South Africa-born John Hewie (he had Scottish emigrant parents) came to the UK when he was 21 and turned professional with Charlton Athletic – the First Division outfit had already signed several other South African-based players. Hewie would make over 500 appearances for the London club between 1949 and 1966, and the versatile left-back/utility player (he even had a four-game spell in goal for the Addicks) would win a total of 19 Scotland caps between 1956 and 1960, scoring two goals.

Squad player Tommy Docherty didn't get any game time in Sweden but won his final three caps in the 1958/59 British Championship against Wales, Northern Ireland and then England. Against Wales, Scotland's first match after the World Cup, Denis Law of Bill Shankly's Huddersfield Town made his international debut aged 18, and netted in the 3-0 win in Cardiff. Against England, Docherty won his 25th and final cap and also earning his final cap that day was Hibernian's outside-left Willie Ormond who would succeed Docherty as Scotland manager in 1973.

2

1960/61–1969/70

Overview

With the abolition of football's maximum wage in early 1961, which was £20 per week at the time (God bless PFA chairman Jimmy Hill!), the genie emerged from the narrow-necked container and soon thereafter Fulham's England captain Johnny Haynes became the first footballer in Britain to earn £100 per week. By 1968, Manchester United's Northern Ireland striker George Best was on £1,000 a week. An additional source of income for the clubs, however, came about following a copyright test-case victory against Littlewoods Pools in 1959 whereby pools companies now needed to pay for the privilege of printing the fixtures on their coupons. Staying with the economics, Tottenham Hotspur created a couple of notable British record transfer fees when they signed striker Martin Chivers from Southampton in January 1968 for £125,000 and then midfielder Martin Peters from West Ham United for £200,000 two years later.

More and more footballers would also become 'TV stars' with television coverage of the game improving considerably throughout the 1960s. ITV showed highlights in the 1961/62 season, only to its own regions, but in August 1964 a new Saturday evening football highlights programme called *Match of the Day* was launched on the new BBC2 channel – which was initially only available in the London area although come December 1964 it extended into the Midlands via new transmitters in the Birmingham area. In 1966 action replays were introduced, in 1967 David Coleman was an *MOTD* presenter for the first time, and by 1969 colour had fully arrived. In 1968 ITV launched *The Big Match* across its network on Sunday afternoons.

On Saturday nights in Scotland, the BBC had introduced *Sportsreel* in 1958 which then became *Sportscene* in 1974 with both also regularly broadcasting an edit of one of the main games from *MOTD*. Over on ITV,

Scottish Television gave us *Scotsport* from 1957 to 2008 – a mostly football highlights show which had Arthur 'Disaster for Scotland' Montford at the helm for 32 years. A largely Sunday afternoon programme, it too eventually showed top-flight games from south of the border.

Stadia-wise, the trend at the big clubs was to increase seating capacities while at Old Trafford in 1964, Manchester United introduced private boxes, the first to be installed at any European football ground. Chelsea followed suit in 1965 and by 1986 a total of 34 British clubs had private boxes in one shape or another.

British movies continued to give a supporting role to the beautiful game with the classic 1962 'kitchen-sink' drama *A Kind of Loving* starring Alan Bates and June Ritchie again having footage from Burnden Park featured as Bolton Wanderers played Sheffield United in a First Division match. Meanwhile, the 1968 comedy-drama *Charlie Bubbles* had Albert Finney and his on-screen son watching a Manchester United match from one of the glass-fronted private boxes and included footage of Bobby Charlton and Denis Law in action.

Of course, the biggest blockbuster movies of the 1960s were arguably the initial James Bond films, most of which starred Edinburgh-born Sean Connery, one of the most successful Anglo-Scots of modern times. Back in the early 1950s, however, Connery was an impressive-looking outside-right with junior outfit Bonnyrigg Rose (about 70 years later the Rose would move up the grades to join the Scottish Professional Football League). In 1954, Manchester United manager Matt Busby offered a two-year contract to the former milkman/artist model/lifeguard/coffin-polisher who declined it on the basis that a successful actor's career would have greater longevity than that of a successful footballer.

The 1960s though were all about swinging, so to speak: a youth-driven cultural revolution which stimulated creativity in fashion, music and the arts from which football was not immune. The music, particularly that of the bands, was sublime – Liverpool gave us the Beatles, the Searchers and Gerry & the Pacemakers, whose version of Rodgers and Hammerstein's 'You'll Never Walk Alone' topped the UK singles charts in 1963 and quickly became the signature tune of Liverpool and Celtic.

Manchester pitched in with the Hollies and Herman's Hermits; the Animals hailed from Newcastle; the Spencer Davis Group from Birmingham. From the 'Big Smoke' came the Rolling Stones, the Kinks, the Who and the Small Faces – which begat the Faces featuring Rod

Stewart, possibly the most recognisable/successful Anglo-Scot ever – though not as cherished as Denis Law. The USA, meanwhile, concentrated much of its efforts on putting a man on the moon.

In the 1960s the UK experienced a period of low unemployment and relative economic prosperity. Capital punishment and theatre censorship were abolished, divorce laws were relaxed and birth control liberalised. Unlike with the Korean War in the previous decade, Britain managed to avoid becoming embroiled in the Vietnam War but 'troubles' were brewing just across the water in Northern Ireland.

In 1960/61 a new competition was introduced in England – the Football League Cup, taking its inspiration from the Scottish version which had been inaugurated in 1946/47. The first six finals were two-legged affairs on a home and away basis before moving to a one-match Wembley final from 1967 onwards. Initially several of the big clubs declined to participate, however the allure of Wembley and the winners securing a place in European competitions eventually won everyone over.

By the end of the decade, the 30 major domestic trophies up for grabs had been shared among 16 clubs, five of which also won a European trophy. Only Manchester City managed to win all three domestic competitions, doing so over three successive seasons – 1967/68 (First Division), 1968/69 (FA Cup) and 1969/70 (League Cup). Tottenham Hotspur won a total of four domestic trophies earlier in the decade – First Division and FA Cup 1960/61, plus two more FA Cup successes in 1961/62 and 1966/67.

Again, Anglo-Scots made their presence felt with all ten championship-winning squads having at least one Scot among their ranks; Liverpool in 1963/64 had seven, four of whom were regulars. In the FA Cup, 17 of the 20 finalists contained Scots with the 1965 final particularly notable as both Liverpool and Leeds United fielded four apiece plus the successful Mersey club also had a Scottish manager in Bill Shankly. In the 1963 final involving Manchester United and Leicester City there were seven Scottish footballers and two Scottish managers – Matt Busby and Matt Gillies respectively. Like the FA Cup, 17 of the 20 League Cup finalists contained Scots with Leicester fielding six to Chelsea's three in the first leg of the 1965 final. Furthermore, both managers were Scots – Matt Gillies was still at Filbert Street while Tommy Docherty was in charge at Stamford Bridge.

Seven English clubs each brought home a European trophy – Matt Busby's Manchester United won the European Cup; Tottenham Hotspur,

West Ham United and Manchester City the Cup Winners' Cup; Leeds United, Newcastle United and Arsenal the Inter-Cities Fairs Cup. Anglo-Scots contributed to five Euro trophy wins with West Ham and Manchester City's successes being all-English affairs.

Trophy winners 1960/61 to 1969/70

Successful clubs	League	FA Cup	League Cup	European	Total
Tottenham Hotspur	1	3	-	1	5
Manchester United	2	1	-	1	4
Manchester City	1	1	1	1	4
Everton	2	1	-	-	3
Liverpool	2	1	-	-	3
Leeds United	1	-	1	1	3
Chelsea	-	1	1	-	2
West Bromwich Albion	-	1	1	-	2
West Ham United	-	1	-	1	2
Ipswich Town	1	-	-	-	1
Aston Villa	-	-	1	-	1
Birmingham City	-	-	1	-	1
Leicester City	-	-	1	-	1
Norwich City	-	-	1	-	1
Queens Park Rangers	-	-	1	-	1
Swindon Town	-	-	1	-	1
Arsenal	-	-	-	1	1
Newcastle United	-	-	-	1	1
TOTALS	**10**	**10**	**10**	**7**	**37**

Despite having an extensive pool of talented players to choose from, Scotland were unsuccessful in three World Cup and one European Championship qualifying campaigns. There were near-misses and some notable scalps though plus the consolation of three outright British Championship titles. In 1966, however, England successfully hosted and won the World Cup – which was a great comfort to Scots living either side of the border!

* * *

Domestic competitions
1960/61

Tottenham Hotspur completed a famous double in the 1960/61 season, the first club to do so since Aston Villa in 1896/97, with Preston North End being the first in 1888/89. Although the League Cup was in its inaugural season, Spurs opted out of the tournament along with five other clubs – Arsenal, Sheffield Wednesday, Wolves and West Brom – so a treble was not possible.

The First Division was won with 66 points, eight clear of runners-up Sheffield Wednesday. Bill Brown continued in goal, playing in 41 of the 42 league games. Arbroath-born Bill had played for Dundee (215/0) for ten years when Spurs manager Bill Nicholson laid out £16,500 for him. Brown won the league, two FA Cups and the Cup Winners' Cup with Spurs before a young Pat Jennings began to establish himself in the side (225/0). He spent the 1966/67 season with Northampton Town (17/0) before emigrating to Canada in 1967.

Dave Mackay was another with a great deal of experience when Nicholson paid £32,000 for him from Hearts in March 1959 (135/25). Mackay had won the league, Scottish Cup and League Cup with Hearts before his move south. In the title run Dave played in 37 games. His trophy tally would be one more than Brown at Spurs with the 1967 FA Cup also being won. Dave spent nine years at the club (268/42) but had two spells out, recovering from broken legs. A move to Derby at the start of 1968/69 (122/5) under Brian Clough saw him lift the Second Division championship that season. A leader on the park, Mackay would soon lead off the park, first as player-manager with Swindon (26/1) in 1971/72, then Nottingham Forest before taking Derby to the First Division title in 1974/75.

John White was to play in all 42 league games as well as the seven FA Cup ties, scoring 13 goals in the title run to boot. Bill Nicholson had been reluctant to sign White due to his slight build but had been convinced by Mackay and club captain Danny Blanchflower to do so.

John had started out with Alloa (68/26) in 1955 before moving to Falkirk in 1958 (30/8). Bought for £22,000 in 1959, John's life would tragically end aged 27 in July 1964 after being struck by lightning. However, he achieved 183 appearances for Spurs, scoring 40 goals, winning the league, FA Cup twice and the European Cup Winners' Cup in the time that was allotted to him. Nicknamed 'the Ghost' by Spurs fans for his ability to slip into goalscoring positions almost unseen by the opposition, who knows what his club and country could have achieved had he lived longer.

The FA Cup was won with a 2-0 victory over Leicester City, a side with a fair smattering of Scots and a Scottish manager.

West Lothian-born Matt Gillies had joined Bolton in 1942, remaining with the club until 1952 (145/1). It was then the defender began his long-term relationship with Leicester (103/0). Matt was part of the Foxes team that won the Second Division title in season 1953/54.

After hanging up his boots in 1955, he returned to Filbert Street as a coach a year later and became manager in 1958. In the 60s he was to oversee an exciting Leicester team that challenged for trophies, reaching two FA Cup finals, achieving several top-four league placings, and competing in two League Cup finals, lifting that trophy in 1964.

The sacking of his coach and assistant after a run of poor results led him to resign after ten years in the post. Matt went on to manage Nottingham Forest for four years but never achieved the same level of success with them and left the club and indeed football in 1972.

The most famous Scot to play for Gillies's 'Ice Kings' as they were dubbed was centre-half Frank McLintock. Frank joined the large Scottish contingent at Leicester as a 17-year-old in 1956, debuting in the 1958/59 season.

At Leicester (168/25), Frank was to experience two losing FA Cup finals before moving to Arsenal in 1964. His Wembley hoodoo would continue there as two League Cup finals were to be lost in the 60s also, but fate would be kinder as the 70s came in.

Alongside Englishman Colin Appleton and McLintock in the half-back line for Leicester was former Arniston Rangers player Ian King. King had joined the side in 1957, playing his first game that year too. Leaving Leicester (244/6) to play for Charlton in 1965, Ian spent three years at the Valley (63/0) and ended his playing days with the then non-league club Burton Albion.

Captain of the Leicester side was Glaswegian forward Jimmy Walsh. Starting out at Bo'ness United, Jimmy joined Celtic in 1949 (144/59). He moved to Leicester in 1956 and is among the club's all-time top ten scorers (176/80). Leaving in 1964, Jimmy finished off his career with non-league Rugby Town.

Striker Hughie McIlmoyle was thrown in at the deep end for the Wembley final. Hughie joined City from his hometown team of Port Glasgow Juniors in 1960 and had only played seven games by the time of the final. However, four goals in those matches swayed Gillies to choose Hughie over the more experienced Ken Leek. McIlmoyle was to have a nomadic career, rarely settling at any one club. Leaving Filbert Street in 1962 (20/5), he would also play with Rotherham (12/4) and then Carlisle where his goalscoring exploits saw him emerge as the Fourth Division's top scorer in season 1963/64.

Aston Villa were to win the first League Cup Final, played over two legs against Second Division Rotherham. However due to fixture congestion these matches were played in August and September of 1961. Three Scots played in the first leg for Villa at Millmoor.

After spells with Arbroath and Raith Rovers (209/53), winger Jimmy McEwan joined Villa aged 30 and was to spend seven years with the club (143/28). Leaving Villa in 1966, he had one season with Walsall (10/1), before coaching at the club until 1973.

Dundee-born Bobby Thomson had spent a fruitless five years with Wolves, only achieving the one league appearance in 1957. Villa were to spend £8,000 on him in 1959, which he repaid immediately by scoring 22 goals in their promotion-winning season of 1959/60. Bobby was also part of the Villa side that lost to Birmingham in the 1963 League Cup Final and moved to the Blues the following September (140/70). Bobby stayed at St Andrew's before moving to Stockport for the 1967/68 season and finished his days at non-league Bromsgrove Rovers.

Glaswegian Ron Wylie played in the first leg of the final, which Villa lost 2-0. He started out as an inside-forward at Notts County at the start of the 50s (227/35), moving to Villa in 1958 (196/16). He joined Birmingham in 1965, remaining there until 1970 (128/2). Ron spent many years coaching at Villa as well as Coventry City before taking over as manager at West Brom for almost two seasons from 1982 to 1984.

Although there were no Scots players in the Rotherham side, they were managed by Tom Johnston from Coldstream in the Scottish Borders. As a player Tom joined Peterborough (30/23) from St Bernard's just before war broke out. As hostilities were ending, Tom moved to Nottingham Forest (64 /26) then flitted 300 yards to Meadow Lane, the home of Notts County, from 1948 to 1956 (267/88). Tom then moved into management with Rotherham before heading to Grimsby and Huddersfield where he would eventually become general manager too and occasionally caretaker as well at York City.

As to the final, Villa recovered from being 2-0 down in the first leg to win the cup with a 3-0 win at Villa Park after extra time.

1961/62

Ipswich Town had won the Second Division championship in 1960/61 and in their first season in the top flight they won the title, three points clear of Burnley. Manager Alf Ramsey was reputed to be not very fond of Scots, but he had a few in his team.

Full-back Ken Malcolm joined Ipswich in 1954 after five years at Arbroath (111/7). In the Second Division title season, he played in 41 of the 44 matches with the younger John Compton of London playing in the other three. However, the following season it was Compton who played 39 times and Ken only three. Ken retired by 1964 (274/2).

Centre-back Billy Baxter joined from Broxburn Juniors in 1960 and made 19 appearances in the 1960/61 title run then 40 of the 42 in the top flight. Billy captained the side to the Second Division championship in 1967/68. A fall-out with Bobby Robson saw him leave the club in 1971 (409/21), going on to play with Hull City (21/0), Watford (11/0), Northampton as player-manager (41/4) finishing at Nuneaton Borough (64/2).

Jimmy Leadbetter, from Edinburgh, signed for Chelsea in 1949 but couldn't break into the first team (3/0). He was sold to Brighton (107/29) in a deal that saw Chelsea pay £12,000 plus Leadbetter for John McNichol in 1952. McNichol went on to win the championship with Chelsea in 1954/55 and Jimmy began his football career in earnest.

Moving to Ipswich in 1955 saw him soon working under the newly appointed Alf Ramsey. Originally a left winger, it is often said that Jimmy was the prototype for England's 1966 World Cup triumph. Ramsey brought him inside from the wings, encouraging him to play to the forwards through the middle rather than the traditional 'hit the byline and cross' tactic.

Jimmy played in 41 games in winning the First Division, netting eight times. He remained with Town until 1965 (334/43), moving into management with Sudbury Town before returning to live out his days in Scotland.

On the right of midfield was Musselburgh-born Doug Moran who began his career at Hibernian (3/0) but moved to Falkirk (135/75) in 1956. At Brockville, Doug won the 1957 Scottish Cup, scoring the winner in extra time against Kilmarnock. Doug is one of only three players to have scored over 100 competitive goals for Falkirk. Bought for £12,300, he was to be Ramsey's only signing as Ipswich prepared for their first season in the top tier. He played in all 42 league games, contributing 14 goals to the cause. He didn't remain long at Ipswich (104/31), moving to Dundee United in 1964 (3/1). Doug headed back to Falkirk for a few years (78/7), finishing his days at Cowdenbeath (8/1) and Gala Fairydean.

The FA Cup Final was between the clubs that finished second and third in the league that year: Burnley and Tottenham. It was Spurs with Brown, Mackay and White all playing who lifted the trophy with a 3-1 win. The sole Scot for the Clarets was Adam Blacklaw, still ensconced between the sticks from the title-winning team of 1959/60.

The League Cup Final was competed by two unfancied clubs in Norwich City of the Second Division and Rochdale from the Fourth Division. City were to win the first leg 3-0 at Spotland and the second leg 1-0 at home at Carrow Road.

Rochdale full-back Doug Winton had signed for Burnley as a youth from Junior side Jeanfield Swifts in 1947, making his debut in 1951/52. He left Burnley in 1959 (183/1) just before their league title success and joined Villa for two seasons (31/0) before moving to Rochdale in June 1961, retiring in 1964 (119/0).

Norwich were managed by Willie Reid. As a player Willie had been part of the Cowdenbeath team that won the Second Division championship in 1938/39 (55/17). After the war Willie turned out for St Mirren before taking over as manager in 1954 (116/18).

He took the Saints to the 1955 League Cup Final, losing 2-1 to Aberdeen, but his Paisley team beat the Dons 3-1 in the 1959 Scottish Cup Final. Willie took over at Carrow Road in December 1961 but only lasted six months as he wished to return home to Scotland to be with his family.

In the Canaries' playing ranks for the final was winger Bill Punton. Although born in Ormiston, East Lothian, Newcastle United (23/1) signed him from Portadown in 1954. He transferred to Southend United (38/6) for a season before joining Norwich in 1959 (219/24). Bill scored the third goal in the first leg of the final at Spotland. He left in 1967 to have spells with Sheffield United (16/1) and Scunthorpe (45/2).

1962/63

Everton, managed by Harry Catterick, won the title with five Scots in their ranks, three of whom were named Alex. The Toffees were champions with 61 points, six points clear of Tottenham.

David Herd, the forgotten Scot at Old Trafford. Herd scored twice in the 1963 FA Cup Final and netted 114 goals in 202 league games for the club.

Everton hero Alex Young who won the title in 1962/63 and the FA Cup in 1966.

Alex Young played in all 42 league games, bagging 22 goals, two behind the club's top scorer Roy Vernon. Alex had joined Everton in 1960 from Hearts (155/71) having won the Scottish title twice and the Scottish Cup and League Cup. He was to be dubbed the 'Golden Vision' by Danny Blanchflower for his stylish play, and this name stuck with the Everton fans too. Alex would win the 1966 FA Cup with Everton as well.

Young had been bought for £55,000 along with defender George Thomson from Hearts (117/14). George played in 17 games in the title run but left Everton (73/1) the following season for Third Division Brentford (162/5) where he spent just over four years before retiring.

Defender and Scottish Cup winner Alex Parker joined Everton from Falkirk (121/2) along with Bairns team-mate Eddie O'Hara (95/8) for £10,000 in 1958. Eddie left Everton in 1959 (29/2) for Rotherham (20/3). He then headed to Morton (29/5) before spending three years at Barnsley (127/36). Eddie emigrated and finished his career in South Africa.

As for Alex Parker, he played 33 games in the 1962/63 season and left in 1965 (198/5), joining Southport (76/0) for a few seasons before finishing his career in Ireland with Ballymena and Drumcondra.

Alex Scott also came from Scotland with a haul of medals having played with Rangers (216/57) since 1954 where he won four league titles, one Scottish Cup and two League Cups. His move to Goodison Park came in February 1963 for £39,000. Alex played 17 games in the remaining part of the season, contributing four goals and like Alex Young also won the FA Cup in 1966.

Unlike his compatriots, Jimmy Gabriel was relatively inexperienced when the then Everton manager Johnny Carey bought the 19-year-old from Dundee (55/0) for £27,000 which was then the highest fee paid for a player from Scotland. A defensive midfielder, Jimmy played in 40 of the 42 games in the 1962/63 season, netting five times. He too was to be part of the 1966 FA Cup-winning side.

The 1963 FA Cup was won by Matt Busby's Manchester United, beating Matt Gillies's Leicester 3-1. Denis Law, who had arrived from Torino at the start of the season, scored the opening goal, but it was the oft-forgotten David Herd who scored the other two in the second half who secured the victory.

There are only three Scots in the top 20 scorers of top-flight goals in English football; nestling at number ten is the great Hughie Gallacher with 246 goals, while Dave Halliday who like Gallacher played in the 1920s and 30s sits at 20, and the other is not Denis Law but David Herd.

Although born in Hamilton, Herd was brought up in Manchester as his father Alex was playing for City at the time. After starting his career with Hamilton (85/41), Alex moved to City in 1933, winning the title with them in 1936/37. Like his son, Alex was quite a prodigious scorer (257/107) and moved to Stockport County (111/35) in 1948. He was to witness his son's debut there as a team-mate in 1951.

David scored in that debut, but national service hampered his burgeoning career, although not so much to prevent Arsenal from swooping for his signature in 1954 for £10,000. At Arsenal (166/97), the goals started flowing quickly and for four straight seasons he emerged as their top scorer. David made his Scotland debut in October 1958, as did Law, then of Huddersfield. Managing the national side that day was Matt Busby.

Busby paid £35,000 for Herd in 1961. Never seen in the same light as the likes of Best, Charlton or Law, in his six years with the club, Herd hit 114 goals in 202 appearances. He moved to Stoke in 1968 (44/11) and finished his career with Irish club Waterford. His top-flight total is 222 goals, and he nestles at 15 in the all-time list for now.

As to Denis Law, he of course started out as a scrawny youngster at Huddersfield (81/16) under Bill Shankly, making his debut aged 16 in 1956. Although Busby had tried to buy him from Huddersfield, it was Manchester City (44/21) he signed for after a British record transfer fee of £55,000 was agreed in March 1960. His stint at Maine Road was short and he was off to Italy and Torino (27/10) in the summer of 1961.

His time in Italy was not a happy one and he was 'rescued' by Busby and United in July 1962. It had taken a British record fee of £110,000 for him to move to Turin, and it took a fee of £115,00 to bring him back to the UK. Like Herd he was to win the First Division twice with United and like Herd he also missed the 1968 European Cup Final.

Overall, Denis netted 171 times for United in 309 appearances before being ousted through the door by Tommy Docherty in 1973. Law joined Manchester City on a free transfer and played one more season, hitting a decent return of nine goals in 24 matches including an infamous back-heel against United at Old Trafford in April 1974.

Pat Crerand was the other Scot in United's FA Cup-winning side of 1963. Pat had been brought south after five years at Celtic (91/5) in

February of 1963 and had only been at the club for a few months before picking up his first major honour at Wembley. A tenacious, hard-tackling player, it was often said that if Paddy played well so did United. He was also known for his range of passing and indeed set up Law for the first goal in the final. Pat also played in the 1968 European Cup Final at Wembley.

Crerand played with United until 1971, accumulating 304 appearances and scoring ten goals. He was assistant manager to Tommy Docherty for a short spell after retiring and did have a managerial career with Northampton too. However, Pat has always enjoyed a media presence, notably with ITV and often around the environs of Old Trafford.

FA Cup runners-up Leicester still had Scots on their books: Matt Gillies as manager and players Frank McLintock and Ian King from the team that also lost the FA Cup Final of 1961. Aberdonian John Sjoberg joined Leicester from then Scottish Junior side Banks o' Dee in 1958. Full-back John was to remain at Filbert Street for 15 years and was to win the League Cup with the Foxes in 1964 (336/15). John ended his career with a six-game run with Rotherham.

Inside-forward Dave Gibson had six years at Hibs (41/6) before Leicester signed him up for a reported fee of £40,000 early in 1962 despite the fact he was still on national service. Gibson would win the League Cup in 1964 with the Foxes and play for them in the losing FA Cup Final of 1969.

The 1963 League Cup Final was an all-Birmingham affair with City playing Aston Villa. The Blues were to win it 3-1 over two legs.

On the winning side was one lone Scot, a future Lisbon Lion in Bertie Auld. Bertie signed for the Blues from Celtic (74/17) in May 1961 and left St Andrew's (126/26) for a return to the Parkhead club in January 1965. During his second stint at Celtic (102/36) Bertie would win the European Cup, five titles and numerous cups before finishing his time at Hibs (11/3) in 1973. He then went on to manage Partick Thistle, Hibs, Hamilton and Dumbarton.

On the losing Villa side, Cammie Fraser, Charlie Aitken and George Graham joined 1961 winners Bobby Thomson and Ron Wylie.

Right-back Fraser had signed for Villa in October 1962 for £24,000 from Dunfermline (80/0) where he had won the 1961 Scottish Cup. A falling out with the Villans in April 1964 (33/1) saw him out of football until February 1965 when Birmingham (39/0) took him on, paying Villa

£9,000 in compensation. He signed for Falkirk in 1967/68 but never played a league game before quitting football altogether.

The left-back for Villa on the other hand played more games for the club than any other in their history. Charlie Aitken signed as a youth in 1959 and went on to play 660 times, netting 16 goals until the end of the 1975/76 season. Although his time at Villa would not be highly successful as they would plummet to the Third Division by the early 70s, he was part of the climb-back under Ron Saunders and won the League Cup in 1975.

Like Aitken, George Graham signed as a youth in 1959 but was to make very few appearances as a Villan, playing in both legs of the final plus a meagre eight league games. George was to move to Chelsea for just under £6,000 in 1964 where he was to have more game time and indeed success in the League Cup Final of 1965.

1963/64

Legendary Liverpool manager Bill Shankly led his Scots-sprinkled side to the title with 57 points, Manchester United trailing four behind. Outwith the war years, Shankly played all his football in the English leagues, starting out briefly with Carlisle United (16/0). He moved to Preston North End in 1933 for a fee of £500. He was to remain with the Lilywhites until 1949 (297/13).

His first stop on the managerial ladder was at Carlisle, and in the years that followed he moved on to Grimsby Town, Workington, and Huddersfield before accepting the job at Liverpool in 1959.

Having been relegated in 1953/54, Liverpool had been unable to gain a quick promotion although Shankly led them to third place twice. Finally in 1961/62 they topped the table with 62 points, eight clear of second-placed Leyton Orient. In his time with Liverpool, Shankly was to win three championships, two FA Cups and the UEFA Cup but more than that, he left his stamp on the club that still stands today in many ways.

Captain Ron Yeats was bought from Dundee United (96/1) in 1961 for £20,000. In the title-winning season Ron played in 36 of the 42 games and by the time he left in 1971 he had won two First Division championships and the FA Cup (358/13). Yeats moved to Tranmere in 1971 as player-manager for three seasons (97/5). He spent the next few years in non-league football as well as spells in US soccer.

Playing in 40 games in goal was Tommy Lawrence, nicknamed 'the Flying Pig' by the Kop due to his stocky build coupled with his agility as a keeper. Ayrshire-born Tommy was brought up in Lancashire and signed with Liverpool in 1959. Making his debut in the promotion-winning season of 1961/62, Tommy remained between the sticks by and large for the rest of the 60s. Ultimately, the arrival of Ray Clemence would see him lose his place (306/0). A move to Tranmere to work under Ron Yeats in 1971 followed (80/1) and he wound his career down playing at non-league Chorley.

Willie Stevenson had won the league and Scottish Cup at Rangers (72/1) but began to lose out on a place in the side to Jim Baxter and moved to Anfield in October 1962 for £20,000. Willie played on the left side of midfield in 38 of the title-run matches, also winning two championships and the FA Cup with the Reds (188/15). In 1967 he moved to Stoke City (94/5) before teaming up with Yeats and Lawrence at Tranmere (20/0). Stevenson only had the one season there before spells at Limerick, Vancouver Whitecaps and non-league Macclesfield.

Ian St John had been a prolific scorer with Motherwell (113/80) when Shankly signed him in May 1961 for £37,500. He hit 18 goals in his first season, helping Liverpool gain promotion to the top flight. In the championship-winning year his tally was 21 in 40 games. St John was to score the winner in the following year's FA Cup Final.

Full-back Bobby Thomson was bought by Liverpool from Partick Thistle (3/0) for £7,000 in December 1962. He was to make two appearances in the title chase, but an unfortunate leg break saw him reduced to only a few more games for the Reds. In August 1965 he moved on to Luton Town (74/0) before emigrating to Australia in the late 60s.

Lanark-born – but Wales-reared – Gordon Wallace made just the one appearance that season. Although he was to play in only 20 league games for Liverpool, scoring three goals, he still has his place in history at Anfield for scoring the opening goal in the 1964 Charity Shield match, and he is also the scorer of Liverpool's first European Cup goal, as they beat KR of Reykjavík in August 1964. Wallace moved to Crewe Alexandra (93/22) in 1967 and helped them win promotion that year but a leg break in September 1968 effectively killed his career and he left the game in 1972.

Port Glasgow-born Hughie McIlmoyle was top scorer in the Fourth Division in 1963/64, netting 39 goals for Carlisle United and helping them to promotion behind champions Gillingham. Hughie played in the 1961 FA Cup Final for Leicester and had three spells with Carlisle, playing

174 games and scoring 74 times. He is so revered in the Cumbrian town that a statue of him sits outside Brunton Park. Hughie also turned out for Wolves (90/35), Bristol City (20/4), Middlesbrough (70/19), Preston (60/10) and Morton twice (35/9).

The all-England side of West Ham took the FA Cup, beating Preston North End 3-2 in the final with a winning goal in the 90th minute. Three Scots featured in the losing Preston XI.

Full-back George Ross from Inverness had joined Preston as a youth in 1960 and played 386 games for the Deepdale club, working with them on matchdays well beyond his playing career. He spent season 1973/74 with Southport (31/0) before a short period with Washington Diplomats. George also had a short stint managing Southport in 1983.

Arbroath-born Jim Smith signed in 1956 and broke into the first team a couple of seasons later. Centre-half Jim was with Preston (314/13) until moving to Stockport County in 1969 (78/2) where he finished his career.

Up front for the Lilywhites was the 'Black Prince of Deepdale' – Alex Dawson. So called for his jet-black hair, Alex had lost the 1958 FA Cup Final with Manchester United and moved to Preston in 1961 (197/114). Alex scored Preston's second goal in the final. His time at Deepdale was followed up with Bury (50/21), Brighton (57/26) and Brentford (10/6). Overall, Alex hit 212 league goals in 394 matches. He finished his career at non-league Corby Town.

The manager of Preston was Jimmy Milne, who had a brief spell playing with Dundee United before joining Preston in 1932. Milne played 230 games for the Lancashire club before the outbreak of war. After the war he started his managerial career at Wigan Athletic, then moved to Morecambe before heading back to Deepdale in 1961. Jimmy left football in 1967. His son Gordon played 14 times for England as he was born in Preston.

Matt Gillies's 'Ice Kings' were at last to lift a trophy after beating Stoke City 4-3 over two legs in the 1964 League Cup Final. Leicester still had John Sjoberg, Ian King and Dave Gibson in their ranks with Gibson scoring a goal in each match against the Potters.

Playing in both legs also was Max Dougan, a defender who had signed from Queen's Park (33/0) in September 1963. The former Scottish amateur international spent three years at Leicester (9/0), moving on to Luton Town (118/0) in 1966. He won the Fourth Division title in 1967/68 with the Hatters before he had a couple of years at Bedford Town (46/1). He then finished his career with Dunstable Town.

Ian St John who netted the winner in the 1965 final to give Liverpool their first ever FA Cup triumph.

In between the sticks for Stoke in the first leg was Lawrie Leslie. He had started out with his hometown club Hibernian (75/0) in 1956 and moved to Airdrie (42/0) in 1959. He transferred to West Ham in 1961 for £14,000 and in his two years there made 57 appearances. In 1962 he won the Hammer of the Year award and is still the only Scot to have done so; £14,000 was also the fee that Stoke (78/0) paid for Lawrie's services in October 1963. Lawrie moved to Millwall in 1966 (67/0) and had a final season with Southend United (13/0) in 1968.

Midfielder George Kinnell scored in the 90th minute of the second leg for Stoke. He had joined them from Aberdeen (130/20) in November 1963. Leaving Stoke (91/6) for a brief spell with Oldham (12/8), George then moved to Sunderland (69/3), and his final term in England was with Middlesbrough (13/1). George then headed to Juventus – albeit Brunswick Juventus in Australia, and finished his career down under.

1964/65

Manchester United topped the table on goal average with Leeds finishing on the same points (61). Leeds drew their last match with Birmingham allowing United the luxury of losing their final fixture to Villa two days later. Leeds were to lose the FA Cup Final a few days afterwards, too.

Denis Law was top scorer for the title winners, hitting 28 in 36 matches, while David Herd bagged 20 in 37 appearances. Pat Crerand played 39, scoring a more modest three goals. Scots John Fitzpatrick and Ian Moir played minor parts in the season. Like Law they were both born in Aberdeen.

Moir had joined United (45/9) as a youth player in 1958, graduating to the first team by 1960. In the 1964/65 season Moir made one appearance before joining Blackpool (61/12) in February 1965. Ian also played with Wrexham twice (165/20) and Shrewsbury (25/2) before a spell in South Africa, finishing his career in non-league football with Oswestry Town and Colwyn Bay.

John Fitzpatrick joined United in 1962 and for the next few years was a peripheral player at the club, initially deputising for the likes of Crerand and Nobby Stiles at wing-half. He only played in two league games in 1964/65. However, towards the end of the decade John began to play regularly at right-back, but was often troubled with cartilage issues in his knee. John eventually retired aged 26 after playing 117 matches, scoring eight goals.

In the Second Division, George O'Brien of Southampton finished top scorer with a tally of 34 goals. George began his professional career with hometown club Dunfermline (95/25) in 1952 before a move to Leeds in 1957 (44/6). Joining Southampton in July 1959, George helped the Saints win the Third Division that season and remained at the Dell until 1966 (244/154). George ended his career with stints at Leyton Orient (17/3) and Aldershot (41/8).

Liverpool were to win the FA Cup for the first time in their history, beating Leeds 2-1 after extra time. Ron Yeats captained Bill Shankly's side with fellow Scots Tommy Lawrence, Willie Stevenson and Ian St John playing. St John was to hit the winner in the 117th minute.

Captaining Leeds was the 'Wee Barra', Bobby Collins, who had joined them in 1962 aged 31. Don Revie had described Collins as one of his best signings. Govanhill-born Bobby had started off with Celtic in 1949 (220/81). These were at times fallow years for Celtic in comparison to later eras. However, Collins was part of the side that won the Coronation Cup and would go on to win the league the following season.

Collins left in 1958 to play for Everton (133/42) for a reported £23,000. He spent four years at Goodison before his move to Leeds, who were struggling at the bottom of the Second Division when he joined them, but they emerged as champions in 1963/64. It was said that Bobby brought a win-at-all-costs mentality to the side and that it imprinted itself on the young players around him, becoming the formula for the success of the Leeds team in the 1960s and 70s.

In October 1965 Bobby suffered a fractured thigh bone in a tackle v Torino in the Fairs Cup. At the age of 34 many a player might have thought about retiring but Bobby fought back to return to the side. Leaving Leeds in 1967 (149/24), he moved on to Bury (75/6). Bobby still had a lot of football in him and had spells with Morton (55/3), Oldham (7/0) and Shamrock Rovers (11/1) and a stint in Australia in between before hanging up his boots aged 43. Bobby tried his hand at management but never reached the same heights as he had done as a player.

Billy Bremner scored the Leeds goal in the 100th minute after Roger Hunt had put Liverpool ahead seven minutes earlier. From Raploch in Stirling, Bremner joined Leeds as a youth in 1959 and made his first-team debut aged 17. He was to eventually captain Leeds throughout their time under Don Revie.

At left-back was Willie Bell, who had joined Leeds (204/15) in 1960 from Queen's Park (54/2). There's a biography of Willie called *Willie Bell – Hewn from Scottish Granite* which suggests he was the archetypal Leeds player of that era. The emergence of Terry Cooper saw Willie move on to Leicester City in 1967 (49/0) for a couple of seasons. He finished his playing career at Brighton in 1969/70 (44/1). Willie went on to manage Birmingham City and then Lincoln, before moving to the States.

After four years with Airdrieonians (48/89), Jim Storrie transferred to Leeds for £15,000 in June 1962. However, Jim's time with Leeds (126/58) was marred by injuries and he returned to Scotland in 1967 for a short period with Aberdeen (13/3). He then headed back south, spending a few seasons with Rotherham (71/19) and Portsmouth (43/12), where he went on loan to Aldershot (5/1). Jim then headed to Paisley for a short period with St Mirren (9/3) in 1972/73. After a spell as player-manager of non-league Waterlooville, Jim took over the reins of St Johnstone from 1976 to 1978 and coached at Airdrie before retiring from the game.

The League Cup had a new name engraved on it in Tommy Docherty's Chelsea; the Doc had taken over from Ted Drake in 1961. As with his Manchester United side in the 70s, Chelsea were relegated before gaining promotion the following season and coming back stronger with a vibrant young side. Docherty's teams were quite flamboyant but too often there was an undercurrent of disharmony among the players regarding his treatment of certain individuals.

His Chelsea side had a great season in 1964/65, finishing third in the table, losing out in the FA Cup semi-final to Liverpool and winning the League Cup by beating Leicester 3-2 in the final. Playing up front in the first leg of the final, at Stamford Bridge, was Eddie McCreadie who normally slotted into the left-back position. An injury to Barry Bridges saw Eddie not only play further forward but score the winner in the 81st minute in the 3-2 first-leg victory. Eddie played at left-back for the goalless second leg at Filbert Street. He joined Chelsea from East Stirling (29/1) in 1962 for £5,000 and over the next ten years became a regular in the side (331/4). Eddie also won the FA Cup with the club in 1970. Hanging up his boots, in 1973 he joined the coaching staff and stepped into the manager's chair in 1975. Although he won promotion to the top flight with the Blues in 1977, a fall-out over a company car saw him leave Stamford Bridge. Eddie then headed across the Atlantic and coached Memphis Rogues and Cleveland Force and still resides in the US.

Born in Motherwell, John Boyle started his career as a youth player with Chelsea in 1961. His first-team debut came in the League Cup semi-final against Aston Villa, retaining his place for both legs of the final. An oft-forgotten player of the Chelsea side of the 1960s and early 70s (198/10), John missed out on the FA Cup victory in 1970 but was part of the side that lifted the Cup Winners' Cup the following season. In 1973 John had a short-term loan at Brighton (10/0) before moving to Orient (18/0) for a couple of seasons and finished his career in the US with Tampa Bay.

George Graham had been part of Villa's defeated League Cup Final team of 1963, joining Chelsea in July 1964. He only played in the first leg of the final and didn't remain long at Stamford Bridge (72/35). George was one of the eight first-team players along with McCreadie dropped by Docherty after breaking curfew in Blackpool. He was more than happy to move to Arsenal in 1966.

The curfew game against Burnley, that Chelsea lost 6-2 in April 1965, saw two Scots play their only match in English league football: Billy Sinclair and Jimmy Smart. Both had been youth players with Morton apparently. Sinclair was to play a lot of football in Ireland although he did have a ten-match stint with Kilmarnock in 1968. As to Smart, he just dropped off the radar but may have emigrated to Australia at some point.

Leicester started the first leg of the 1965 League Cup Final with six Scots in place. John Sjoberg, Ian King and Dave Gibson were joined in Matt Gillies's side by the trio of Billy Hodgson, Jimmy Goodfellow and Tom Sweenie.

Winger Billy Hodgson started out at St Johnstone (61/20) and moved to Sheffield United in 1957. He spent six years at Bramall Lane (152/32) before joining Leicester in 1963 (46/10). Billy then had spells at Derby County (78/17), Rotherham (9/0) and York City (98/3) before leaving England for a handful of games with Hamilton in 1971.

Centre-forward Jimmy Goodfellow started out at Tranent Juniors before joining Third Lanark in 1958 (117/30). Joining Leicester in May 1963 (98/26), Jimmy scored the second goal for the Foxes in the first leg of the final. In 1968 he moved to Mansfield Town (99/14) before drifting into non-league football and playing with several clubs.

Tom Sweenie started out in Junior football with Johnstone Burgh and joined Leicester in 1963 (51/11). He was badly injured in February 1967 and never really recovered. In July 1968 he joined Arsenal on trial, a month later he was at Huddersfield and by October he was playing at

York City (6/1) with Billy Hodgson who was coaching there at the time. He never appeared for the former two in the league.

Sweenie and Ian King dropped out of the team for the second leg and in came Bobby Roberts. Midfielder Bobby had joined from Motherwell (91/26) in September 1963 for a fee of over £40,000. He would also play for Leicester in the 1969 FA Cup Final.

1965/66

Liverpool finished top on 61 points, six clear of runners-up Leeds. Still in place for Shankly's side were keeper Tommy Lawrence, captain Ron Yeats and striker Ian St John. Yeats and Lawrence played in all 42 matches with St John missing the one and contributing ten goals over the season.

The end of 1970/71 saw Ian leave Liverpool (336/95) and over the summer he spent time with South African club Hellenic alongside former Anfield team-mates Roger Hunt and Willie Stevenson plus England goalkeeper Gordon Banks. On his return Ian moved to Coventry (18/3) and then Tranmere (9/1) with Yeats and Lawrence for a short period. He went on to manage at Motherwell and Portsmouth but in his later years he became more well known for the comedic ITV football punditry show *Saint and Greavsie* with ex-England striker Jimmy Greaves, which ran from 1985 to 1992.

Bobby Graham had been signed as a youth in 1961 but with Roger Hunt and St John in the side he found it hard to get any game time at Anfield. Bobby only played one match in the title run but he featured more as the decade ended (101/31). He then had brief spells at Coventry (19/3) and Tranmere (10/3) over the 1972/73 season before heading up to play for his hometown team Motherwell (132/37). At Fir Park he developed a striking partnership with a young Willie Pettigrew. He then moved to local rivals Hamilton in 1977 (118/42) where he spent four years, finishing his playing days for Junior side Shotts Bon Accord.

The 1966 FA Cup Final saw Everton come back from 2-0 down in the 57th minute to emerge as 3-2 winners against Sheffield Wednesday when the final whistle eventually blew. Jimmy Gabriel, Alex Scott and Alex Young all played in the final for the Toffees.

Young left Everton in 1968 (228/77) for a spell in Ireland with Glentoran (6/1) and then finished his career with Stockport County (23/5) by 1969. He then moved back to Edinburgh to run the family business after hanging up his boots.

Scott remained with the Toffees until 1967 (149/23), heading back up to Scotland and Hibernian (40/2). His fee of £13,000 was funded by the sum that Hibs received from Newcastle for his brother, Jim. Alex played for Hibs for a couple of seasons before joining his hometown team Falkirk (23/0), where he would play a few games alongside his sibling.

Jimmy Gabriel left Everton in 1967 (256/33) for Southampton (191/25). After departing the Dell, Jimmy then played for Bournemouth (53/4), Swindon (6/0) and Brentford (9/0). He finished his playing career in the US but returned to coach in England with both Bournemouth and Everton (where he had two spells as caretaker manager). He finally retired from the sport in 2005 having worked with Seattle Sounders for many years.

Losing side Sheffield Wednesday had young Jim McCalliog in their line-up. Jim had started out in the Leeds youth team before joining Tommy Docherty's Chelsea (7/2) a few months later in 1963. Despite McCalliog only playing a handful of games, Wednesday were happy to fork out £37,500, a then British record transfer fee for a teenager.

Jim netted a goal in the 90th minute of the semi-final as Wednesday dispatched Chelsea 2-0 at Villa Park. In the final itself he opened the scoring in the fourth minute. Jim stayed with the Owls until August 1969 (150/9) when Wolves paid £70,000 for his services and eventually he headed to Southampton and FA Cup success in 1976.

The last two-legged League Cup Final was contested by the Wests of Ham and Bromwich Albion. West Ham started with an all-English line-up as they had done in the 1964 FA Cup Final. West Brom, who were to win 5-3 on aggregate, had one lone Scot playing in the first game: Doug Fraser.

Full-back Doug started out at his hometown team Aberdeen (64/1), before he moved to the Baggies in 1963 for £23,000. Doug was to play in all four cup finals of this era for Albion (257/8), before leaving for Nottingham Forest in 1971. From Forest (85/3), Fraser moved to Walsall (27/0) at the start of the 1973/74 season, before moving into the manager's seat there from 1974 to 1977.

Taking part in the second leg of the final was Bridge of Allan-born Bobby Hope. Forward Bobby signed on as a youth with West Brom in 1959, graduating to the first team in 1960. He had a long career at the Hawthorns (336/33), playing until the end of the 1971/72 season, and like Fraser he was to experience two cup wins and two losses with Albion.

When he left, he moved five miles across the city to St Andrew's and Birmingham City. Bobby spent four years with the Blues (34/5), often playing for Philadelphia Atoms and Dallas Tornado too. This pattern was to continue when Bobby joined Sheffield Wednesday (42/7) in 1976 with two loans to the Dallas side. Bobby finished his career with non-league Bromsgrove, whom he was to manage on two separate occasions with a spell at Burton Albion in between.

1966/67

Manchester United were to top the league, giving Matt Busby his fifth title. However, it would be another 26 years until the Old Trafford outfit won the championship again. Crerand, Herd and Law all played their parts. Pat played in 39 of the matches, scoring three goals, David hit 16 in 28 with Denis adding 23 in 36. John Fitzpatrick only made three appearances altogether.

Stirling-born Jimmy Ryan featured in four of the matches. Jimmy came through the youth ranks in 1963, rarely playing in a seven-year spell (24/4). He transferred to Luton (184/21) in April 1970, staying until 1976. Jimmy then headed Stateside to play with Dallas Tornado and then Wichita Wings. He remained in the US until the opportunity of managing Luton's reserves was offered to him and he soon found himself taking over the vacated first-team manager's chair in 1990. After being sacked by Luton in 1991, Alex Ferguson invited Jimmy to take over the reserve side at Old Trafford. Jimmy would also be given the role of assistant towards the end of the 90s and again just after the turn of the century. His last position was as director of youth football at United before retiring in 2012.

Tottenham won the FA Cup, defeating Chelsea 2-1 at Wembley. Joining captain Dave Mackay in the Spurs line-up were Jimmy Robertson and Alan Gilzean.

Winger Robertson, from Glasgow, had started as a youth with Middlesbrough and Cowdenbeath before making his mark with St Mirren (54/12). Spurs bought him for £25,000 in March 1964 (157/25). Jimmy scored the opening goal in the final against Chelsea and later moved to Arsenal in 1968 in a straight swap for forward David Jenkins. After two years with the Gunners (46/7), Jimmy moved to Bobby Robson's Ipswich (87/10) for £50,000. Two years later Stoke City offered £80,000 for his services in 1972. Jimmy remained with the Potters for five years (114/12). Robertson, like a lot of his compatriots at the time, headed Stateside for a season with Seattle Sounders in 1976/77. This was followed with brief periods at Walsall (16/0) and Crewe Alexandra (33/0) before retiring. Overall, Jimmy made 453 appearances in English league football, hitting 54 goals.

By the time Spurs paid out £72,500 for Alan Gilzean in December 1964, he was already assured legend status at Dundee (190/169). Gilzean was part of the Dundee side that won the 1961/62 league title, hitting 24 goals in the run-in including four away to Rangers. He was also part of the team that reached the semi-finals of the European Cup the following year.

With Tottenham he was to team up with Jimmy Greaves and their lethal strike partnership was dubbed the 'G-Men'. Alan was to win the FA Cup, League Cups in 1970/71 and 1972/73, and the 1972 UEFA Cup in his time at Spurs (343/93). Known among the fans as the 'King of White Hart Lane', he was renowned for his headed goals but also his head flicks that laid on many a goalscoring opportunity for Greaves and latterly Martin Chivers. He left in 1974 and after a disappointing few months playing in South Africa, Gilzean returned to the UK. Other than a brief stint managing Stevenage in 1975/76 he was not involved in football again.

After Dundee agreed the fee for Gilzean in December 1964, within days they paid out £40,000 for winger Charlie Cooke from Aberdeen (125/27). Although Cooke's time with the Dens Park side was just under 18 months, he was quite revered by supporters of that era (44/11). Cooke was in the Chelsea team for the 1967 FA Cup Final alongside Eddie McCreadie and John Boyle; Tommy Docherty had splashed out £72,000 for him in May 1966. He soon established himself as a favourite among the Chelsea fans at a time when the likes of Peter Osgood, Alan Hudson and Ian Hutchinson were also all playing (212/15).

Charlie moved on to Crystal Palace in 1972 (44/0), spending a couple of years with them before Chelsea realised their mistake in letting him go too early and brought him back to Stamford Bridge. Although the team was a pale imitation of its former self, for Cooke it was a bit of a renaissance as he won two Scotland caps in 1975, his first in four years. Charlie left the Blues for good in 1978 (87/7) and ended his career in the US playing for several NASL sides including Los Angeles Aztecs, Memphis Rogues and California Surf and he still resides in the US.

As for Docherty, by the following October he was to resign as Chelsea manager following a 28-day suspension from the FA for his conduct during a tour of Bermuda that summer. Several stops down the road he was to return to Wembley with Manchester United in 1976.

The League Cup Final was played at Wembley as a one-off game for the first time. It saw an all-English Queens Park Rangers side defeat West Brom 3-2 with Rodney Marsh among the scorers for the victors. Doug Fraser and Bobby Hope from the 1966 victorious West Brom team were joined by non-playing sub Ken Foggo.

Perth-born Foggo started out as a youth at the Hawthorns, signing professionally in 1960. Remaining with Albion (129/29) until moving to Norwich in 1967, as a winger he was an integral part of the team that won the 1971/72 Second Division, gaining promotion to the top flight for the first time in the club's history. He left Carrow Road in 1973 (185/54). Ken went on to play with Portsmouth (60/3), Southend (30/6) and finished his footballing days playing with non-league Chelmsford City.

1967/68

Two years after clinching the Second Division title, Manchester City won the First Division, two points clear of Matt Busby's United. City greats such as Colin Bell, Tony Book, Mike Summerbee and Francis Lee all played their part with wing-half Bobby Kennedy as the lone Scot.

Kennedy started out at Kilmarnock in 1957 (85/1), spending four years at the club before City paid out £45,000 for his services. In the Second Division title win of 1965/66 he played in 35 games, scoring once. However, he was rarely utilised in 1967/68, only playing in four games. He left the Citizens in March 1969 (254/9) for a player-manager role with Grimsby Town (84/1) for just under two years. Later, he was to have a three-year spell in charge of Bradford City.

Aberdeen-born Les Massie of 11th-placed Halifax Town was equal top scorer in the Fourth Division with 25 goals. Les joined Huddersfield as a youth signing in 1953 from then Junior side Banks O' Dee. He made his debut in September 1956 and over the next three seasons he was top scorer for the club in a team that had a young Denis Law playing in it too. Les lies fifth on the all-time scoring list for Huddersfield (335/100). Leaving Huddersfield in 1966, Les went to Darlington (20/2) before heading to Halifax (89/41). Stints at Bradford Park Avenue (41/2) and Workington (62/15) followed before finishing up with Drogheda in Ireland.

Returning to Wembley for another final were the West Brom pair of Doug Fraser and Bobby Hope as their team beat the all-English line-up of Everton 1-0 thanks to a goal from Jeff Astle. This currently stands as Albion's last appearance in an FA Cup Final.

The League Cup Final had a lot more Scottish involvement as Leeds beat Arsenal 1-0 through a Terry Cooper goal. The three Scots in the winning team ended their careers with a combined league appearance tally of 1,567 for the Yorkshire club – we are of course talking about Billy Bremner, Peter Lorimer and Eddie Gray. Bremner epitomised the Leeds team of that era in being tenacious and uncompromising but also not without some undoubted skill.

Born in Dundee, midfielder Peter Lorimer made his debut aged 15 years and 289 days in September 1962, making him Leeds' all-time youngest player. Well known for his thunderous shot and goalscoring exploits with an overall total of 238 in all competitions, Peter is Leeds' all-time top scorer too.

Left-winger Eddie Gray, from Castlemilk, Glasgow, signed on at Leeds as a 16-year-old in 1965 and within a couple of years was an established player in the team. Eddie was a classic winger with the ability to take on and beat players with ease and like Jimmy Johnstone of Celtic he often came in for the heaviest of ill treatment from opposing full-backs. It is telling that in his time with Leeds, injury blighted his appearances, often missing ten to 15 games a season.

Frank McLintock, George Graham and Ian Ure were all involved for Arsenal. McLintock, since his £80,000 move from Leicester in 1964, had become the Gunners' captain, but his Wembley woes were to continue with this defeat.

Centre-half Ure, like Alan Gilzean of Spurs, had been part of the Dundee side that won the Scottish title in 1961/62. Arsenal paid £62,500 for him at the start of the 1963/64 season; Ure played in 41 of the 42 league matches that year but after that was to suffer from injuries and loss of form.

George Graham had already lost one League Cup Final with Aston Villa and won one with Chelsea in 1964/65. Arsenal had paid £50,000 plus Tommy Baldwin for George in October 1966 and he finished as top scorer that season and the one that followed. Like McLintock, he played his part in the double achieved in 1970/71.

1968/69

Leeds were to win the league for the first time in their history, six points clear of Liverpool in second place. Billy Bremner appeared in all

42 matches of the campaign as would Gary Sprake, Paul Reaney and Norman Hunter. Billy netted six goals in the title chase. Eddie Gray would compete in 33 of the games, scoring six goals, and Peter Lorimer played in 29 with a goal return of nine.

The FA Cup Final was won by all-English side Manchester City beating Leicester with Neil Young scoring the only goal. Among the four Scots in the Leicester line-up were two familiar faces, Dave Gibson and Bobby Roberts.

Gibson played in four finals with the Foxes (280/41) before moving to Aston Villa (19/1) in 1970. A couple of seasons with Exeter City (71/3) saw out his career.

Roberts left Leicester (230/25) for Mansfield (80/4) in 1970 and then moved into coaching with Coventry (2/0). This was followed by managing at Colchester, Wrexham and finishing with Grimsby Town in 1987/88. Roberts then moved into scouting for various clubs in England.

Andy Lochhead had been on the books with Burnley when they won the title in 1959/60, having signed in 1957 and broken into the side the following year. In the glut of goals scored in the English top flight on Boxing Day 1963, Andy hit four in a 6-1 win over Manchester United. Andy moved from Burnley in October 1968 (266/101) and scored the winner at Anfield as the Foxes knocked Liverpool out of the FA Cup in the fifth round.

Andy didn't stick around too long at Filbert Street (44/12), moving to Aston Villa in 1970. At Villa he became a cult hero to the fans and was to play in the 1971 League Cup Final with the club.

Centre-half Malcolm Manley came on as a sub in the 70th minute of the final. Malcolm had started out at his hometown club Johnstone Burgh and signed on at Leicester in January 1967. He spent six years with the Foxes (120/5), which included winning the Second Division title in 1970/71. Manley moved on to Portsmouth in 1973, but his career was ended in his 11th game for Pompey as he severed a cartilage in his knee.

The 1969 League Cup Final was won by Swindon Town from the Third Division. Most of the opposing Arsenal side were suffering from flu and as the match went into extra time on the heavy pitch, the Gunners languished. Swindon took advantage to score two more goals and win 3-1.

In goals for Arsenal was Bob Wilson, one of the first players to help change the definition of what is an Anglo-Scot. Scotland manager Tommy

Docherty took advantage of the newly established rules allowing players to represent the country of their parent's birth in October 1971 and capped Bob twice.

Born in Chesterfield, Bob signed as an amateur for Wolves as he was still involved in further education. He was playing in the reserves when the Gunners paid £7,500 in 1963 for him. Making his breakthrough towards the end of the 1967/68 season, Bob was first choice for the Gunners until he retired aged 32 in 1974 (310/0). Bob was a big part of the team that achieved the double in 1970/71.

As well as Bob, Ian Ure and Frank McLintock were in the Arsenal team with George Graham making an appearance as a substitute in the 70th minute. A defensive mistake in the final from Ure would see his time at Highbury come to an end (168/2) and he moved to Manchester United in 1969. He left United in 1971, moving back to Scotland to join St Mirren, but only played three games before retiring.

In the Swindon team at centre-half was Larkhall-born Frank Burrows. Starting out at Raith Rovers (76/1) in 1962, Frank moved to Scunthorpe (106/4) in June 1965. Swindon paid £12,000 for him in July 1967. He was a permanent fixture in the Swindon side (297/9) as they won promotion to the Second Division as well as the League Cup in 1968/69. Swindon and Frank went on to win the Anglo-Italian Cup in successive seasons following their Wembley triumph. Frank had a short loan spell at Mansfield (6/0) in his later years with Swindon.

Frank moved into coaching and by 1979 was at the helm of Portsmouth where he would manage twice and likewise with Cardiff with a spell at Swansea too. Promotions were won with Portsmouth and Cardiff and the Football League Trophy in 1994 with Swansea. Frank also worked alongside the likes of Harry Redknapp at West Ham and Gary Megson at West Brom.

Coming on in the 77th minute was forward Willie Penman. Fifer Willie had won the Scottish Junior Cup with St Andrews United and soon signed with Rangers. However, he was unable to break into the first team (3/0) and was sold to Newcastle United for £11,500 in April 1963. Willie was part of the Newcastle side that won the Second Division title in 1964/65.

After three years (63/18) he joined Swindon (98/18). Willie then went on to play for Walsall (123/6) before spending some time with Dundalk and then Seattle Sounders.

Bonnie Prince Charlie Cooke of Chelsea, who won the FA Cup in 1970 and the European Cup Winners' Cup a year later.

1969/70

Everton were to win the league with 67 points, nine clear of second-placed Leeds. In the era of three points for a win Everton would have been champions with 95 points, and Leeds would still be second on 78.

Sandy Brown had joined Everton from Partick Thistle in September 1963 (105/6) for £38,000. Although a regular in the side at the time, Sandy did not feature in the 1966 FA Cup win. Sandy is perhaps best known for a flying header he scored in the Merseyside derby in December 1969. Unfortunately, it was into his own net. Sandy left Goodison in May 1971 (209/9) for Shrewsbury Town (21/0). Further moves to Southport (19/0) and then non-league Fleetwood Town saw out his career.

The FA Cup was won by Chelsea in a torrid 2-1 replay victory against Leeds. The first meeting at Wembley saw Eddie McCreadie and Charlie Cooke turn out for Chelsea as well as the trio of Billy Bremner, Peter Lorimer and Eddie Gray for Leeds. The match ended 2-2 with Houseman and Hutchinson scoring for the Blues and Jack Charlton and Mick Jones for the Whites. Eddie Gray had been the chief tormentor of Chelsea and was the man of the match. The replay at Old Trafford was shown on both BBC and STV in Scotland and is one of the first matches we remember seeing broadcast around this time.

Leeds did make one change to their line-up in that reserve goalie David Harvey replaced Gary Sprake for the replay. Leeds-born Harvey had been with the club as a youth in 1963 and signed professionally in 1965. He found himself as backup to Sprake and was on the bench for some of Leeds' previous finals and never got any game time in their successful title race in 1968/69. It was to take David a couple of years to establish himself as the Whites' first choice.

The League Cup was won by Manchester City, beating West Brom 2-1 with goals from Mike Doyle and Glyn Pardoe. Jeff Astle netted for Albion.

City signed Falkirk-born Arthur Mann from Hearts (32/0) in November 1968 for £65,000. In his three years at Maine Road, he only made 35 league appearances without scoring, however a consistent place in the side may have been hindered by his fear of flying meaning he missed out on several European away ties. Mann had a three-game loan spell at Blackpool in 1971 but soon left City for Notts County in 1972, where he spent seven years (253/21). A brief spell at Shrewsbury (8/1) followed before finishing his career with Mansfield (116/3) from 1979 to 1982.

As for West Brom, fellow Scots Ray Wilson and Asa Hartford joined usual suspects Doug Fraser and Bobby Hope. Grangemouth-born Ray signed with Albion in May 1964 aged 17 and was to become a regular in the side at left-back. However, aged 28 he had to give up his career after his kneecap was shattered at the start of the 1975/76 season. Ray made 232 appearances for the club, scoring three goals.

Clydebank-born Asa Hartford began at Drumchapel Amateurs, who count the likes of Sir Alex Ferguson, Andy Gray and John Wark among their alumni. Box-to-box midfielder Asa signed with West Brom in 1967 and remained with the club until 1974 (214/18). A rebuilding programme after the relegation in 1972/73 saw Hartford move to Manchester City in August 1974 for £210,000, where he was to win the League Cup in 1975/76. The year prior to this had seen Asa almost moving to Leeds but a medical had discovered a hole in his heart and so the Elland Road club backed out. Asa is 26th in the all-time English league appearance list, so it never held him back.

European and international competitions

In light of the success of the European Cup there was a desire to create an additional competition (the Inter-Cities Fairs Cup was also up and running but was not under the auspices of UEFA) and so there was established a tournament for national cup winners which would run in tandem with the tournament for national champions. The European Cup Winners' Cup commenced in season 1960/61 with a semi-official pilot tournament which comprised just ten clubs including Wolverhampton Wanderers, who lost to Glasgow Rangers at the semi-final stage. Rangers would lose the two-legged final to Fiorentina of Italy.

As fate would have it, the European breakthrough for English clubs (as well as for non-Latin European sides) came about in the Cup Winners' Cup, in season **1962/63** when Bill Nicholson's Tottenham Hotspur crushed the holders Atlético Madrid 5-1 in the final at Stadion Feijenoord in Rotterdam in front of a crowd of 49,143. Spurs were 2-0 ahead at half-time through Jimmy Greaves and John White before a penalty from Spanish international Enrique Collar narrowed the gap in the 47th minute and at that point it was game on, with the 'Mattress Makers' – as Atlético were known because of their working-class roots – in the ascendancy. However, 20 minutes later fortune favoured the Spurs when Atlético keeper Edgardo Madinabeytia misjudged the flight of a miscued, looping cross by Terry

Dyson which brushed the Argentine's digits before dropping into the net, thus restoring Tottenham's two-goal advantage and totally deflating the defending holders. Apparently *casualidad* is the Spanish word closest to 'flukey', but it loses something in the translation

No matter, for Greaves and Dyson again put the icing on the cake with goals in the 80th and 85th minutes. Their delighted skipper, Northern Ireland international Danny Blanchflower, lifted the trophy – his fourth major success.

Spurs' first Euro adventure had taken place the season previous when as English champions they had reached the semi-finals of the European Cup before losing to the eventual winners, a Eusébio-inspired Benfica.

For Spurs' successful run in Europe three Anglos featured prominently – goalkeeper Bill Brown and inside-forward John White playing in all seven matches plus left-half Dave Mackay who unfortunately missed the final itself due to injured stomach muscles. Mackay netted two goals en route to the final while White netted four in total with Spurs scoring an impressive 24 goals across the seven games.

On Halloween 1962, Scot Symon's Glasgow Rangers knocked on the front door at White Hart Lane for the first round proper, said 'Trick or treat?' then got walloped 5-2 with 58,859 looking on. John White got Spurs' first goal after just four minutes with the others coming from Jimmy Greaves, Les Allen, a Bobby Shearer own goal plus one from Maurice Norman.

In the return leg at Ibrox on 5 December (which had been postponed the week previous due to fog) and in front of a crowd of 80,000 Spurs won again, 3-2 this time with Greaves netting the opening goal. Rangers then twice drew level before a last-minute goal from Bobby Smith, his second of the evening, settled matters. The London outfit progressed 8-4 on aggregate.

Incidentally, in the Rangers souvenir programme – eight pages for six pre-decimal pennies – there was a quote from the *Daily Express* (English edition) journalist Desmond 'The Man in the Brown Bowler' Hackett, 'Salute the summit soccer men of Spurs and the mighty Glasgow Rangers. We salute both sides for their skill of effort that shone with pride of club, and for conduct that brought nothing but honour to British football.'

In the quarter-finals, Spurs went behind the Iron Curtain to communist Czechoslovakia and surprisingly lost 2-0 to Slovan Bratislava. In the return leg, however, they turned it on in cruising to a 6-0 victory in front of 61,504 with Mackay and White contributing a goal apiece, plus a clean sheet from Bill Brown. The other four goals came from Greaves [2], Smith and Welsh winger Cliff Jones.

In the semis they were back to eastern Europe, to Yugoslavia to face OFK Beograd of Belgrade. Spurs won 2-1 with John White putting the visitors ahead in the 27th minute before Milorad Popov equalised from the penalty spot nine minutes before half-time. In the 75th minute Spurs got the winner from that man Dyson and please note the author's continued refusal to introduce tabloid-style puns associated with the words sweeper and vacuum cleaner. Anyway, earlier in the second half Greaves had been dismissed for alleged violent conduct, his first and only red card, involving Blagomir Krivokuća. The England hit-man (sorry) incurred just a one-match ban and thus was able to play in the final.

Back at the Lane, a crowd of 58,736 saw a Greaves-less Tottenham win 3-1. Mackay got the opener after 23 minutes with future European Golden Shoe winner Josip Skoblar equalising five minutes later. Jones then put his side in front two minutes from half-time and four minutes after the restart a goal from Smith sealed the deal. Next up was a date with destiny in Rotterdam on 15 May 1963 closely followed by a victory procession through north London complete with open-top bus, brass band, and prominent, quaintly worded placards which declared 'Salute the Spurs by name', 'Praise and Magnify them' and 'Rejoice and be Proud'. Try as we may, we couldn't spot any banners in the archives which told their rivals from N5 to 'Go forth and multiply!'

In defence of their trophy in 1963/64, Spurs lost to FA Cup holders Manchester United at the second round stage. Having won the first leg in London 2-0 with Mackay and Terry Dyson scoring, the Lilywhites then slumped to a 4-1 defeat in Manchester – a brace each from Hamilton-born David Herd and Bobby Charlton either side of a goal from Jimmy Greaves. Not to worry, no-one can take Spurs' European first away from them.

* * *

The UK's second European trophy was won by another London outfit when in **1965**, Ron Greenwood's West Ham United, in their first foray into continental competition, defeated TSV 1860 Munich in the Cup Winners' Cup Final at Wembley. The Hammers' success was an all-English affair that included their holy trinity of Martin Peters, Geoff Hurst and Bobby Moore and for the latter two it was the second part of a wonderful mid-60s Wembley hat-trick of winners' medals. Martin Peters would of course also enjoy the World Cup Final glory, though sadly Spurs' Jimmy Greaves would not.

* * *

In 1965/66 and 1966/67 Liverpool and then Leeds United lost out in the finals of the Cup Winners' Cup and Fairs Cup respectively with an aggregate total of eight Anglo-Scots having to be content with runners-up medals. However, six successive seasons from 1967/68 to 1972/73 brought an aggregate return of nine European trophies for eight English clubs.

In 1966/67 Celtic were the UK's first winners of the European Cup, achieving the feat with 11 home Scots, some of whom would eventually head to England in the early 1970s. Mercurial winger Jimmy 'Jinky' Johnstone would have a brief spell at Sheffield United and there would also be others for defender Jim Craig at Sheffield Wednesday and striker Willie Wallace at Crystal Palace. Defender (and Danny Kaye lookalike) Tommy Gemmell had a couple of seasons with Nottingham Forest while midfield playmaker Bobby Murdoch, the finest footballer to come out of the Royal Burgh of Rutherglen, played over 100 games for Middlesbrough, helping Jack Charlton's outfit win promotion to the English top flight in 1974 as well as providing sound advice to a young Graeme Souness.

It's also worth remembering that goalkeeper Ronnie Simpson and midfielder Bertie Auld were both medal winners, at Newcastle United in the 1950s and Birmingham City in the early 1960s respectively, prior to their European Cup exploits back in their home city of Glasgow.

* * *

In **1968** Matt Busby's Manchester United brought home the big one – the European Cup – via another final at Wembley, overcoming Benfica 4-1 after extra time. Gorbals-born Pat Crerand played in all nine matches in the Euro run, versus Hibernians of Malta in the first round (4-0 at home, 0-0 away), Sarajevo in the second round (0-0 in Yugoslavia, 2-1 at Old Trafford), Górnik Zabrze in the quarter-finals (2-0 in Manchester, a 1-0 defeat in Poland) and Real Madrid in the semi-finals (1-0 at home, 3-3 at the Bernabéu) as well as the final itself. There were no away wins en route but there was a first victory over Real Madrid for the Old Trafford outfit with a stadium-entry and a seat ticket for the game in Madrid fetching £1,100 at auction in February 2024. By comparison, injuries restricted Denis Law's appearances in the competition to just three matches – home and away versus Hibernians in the first round, netting a brace at Old Trafford, and at home to Real Madrid in the first leg of the semi-final.

Pat Crerand spent six trophy-less years at Celtic before joining United in February 1963 and picking up an FA Cup winners' medal three months later. League winners' medals followed in 1964/65 and 1966/67 for the 'case-hardened, Scottish tough-nut' whose accuracy at passing ensured that plenty of goalscoring opportunities came the way of Messrs Law, Charlton and Best. Crerand made around 400 appearances for the Red Devils before retiring in 1971. He then had a spell as assistant manager to Tommy Docherty at Old Trafford between 1972 and 1976. He also won 16 Scotland caps although only five of them came while he was at Manchester United.

While Crerand was the only Scot to play in the 1968 final, another four of his countrymen in addition to Law played supporting roles in getting United to Wembley – Francis Burns (seven Euro appearances at left-back before losing out to Irishman Shay Brennan for the semi-final second leg), John Fitzpatrick (two appearances – away to Sarajevo and Górnik), Jimmy Ryan (one appearance, at home to Górnik) and prolific striker David Herd in his final season at Old Trafford (one appearance, away to Górnik).

Manchester United was the first senior club for Glenboig-born Francis Burns, joining them in 1965 and leaving in 1972 having made over 150 appearances. Burns's playing career continued at Southampton, Preston North End and Shamrock Rovers. He made one appearance for his country, in a World Cup qualifier away to Austria in 1969.

Wing-half John Fitzpatrick was another Aberdeen-born footballer whose first senior club was Manchester United, making over 100 appearances between 1965 and 1972 before retiring on medical advice. In the first leg of the 1968/69 European Cup semi-final versus AC Milan at the San Siro, Fitzpatrick was sent off, following which he had to have a police escort to the changing room as United lost 2-0 in defence of their trophy. In the return leg a goal from Bobby Charlton gave the home side, which featured Crerand, Burns, Law and Willie Morgan, a 1-0 victory, which of course was not enough.

Stirling-born Jimmy Ryan played in the 1967/68 home leg against Górnik but in his seven years at Old Trafford, the striker only managed

John White, a double winner with Spurs in 1960/61 before going on to win the FA Cup in 1962 and the European Cup Winners' Cup in 1963

around 30 first-team appearances before continuing his playing career at Luton Town then Dallas Tornado and Major Indoor Soccer League club Wichita Wings. Ryan also enjoyed a couple of spells as Alex Ferguson's assistant manager at United.

For manager Matt Busby, the former Lanarkshire coal miner and player with Liverpool and Manchester City, the 1968 European Cup was his last major trophy at Old Trafford and he was given a knighthood shortly thereafter. Busby managed the club from 1945 to 1969, winning the First Division on five occasions to move United from ninth to joint first on the all-time winners list (in the 1970s and 1980s Arsenal, Everton and Liverpool in particular would all surge ahead before Alex Ferguson put United out in front again). Busby would also steer United to two FA Cup victories and overall would contribute significantly to the Manchester club becoming a global giant on and off the field. In the 'Mount Rushmore' of great Scottish/British football managers Busby is there along with Jock Stein, Bill Shankly and Sir Alex.

* * *

It was season 1968/69 before Leeds United won the **1967/68** European Fairs Cup in that the two legs of the final against Ferencváros of Hungary didn't take place until 7 August, winning 1-0 at Elland Road with England international Mick Jones netting and 25,268 watching on, and 11 September, drawing 0-0 at the Népstadion in Budapest in front of a crowd of 76,000, and it was the first English victory in the competition having lost out in four previous finals – London XI v Barcelona in 1958, Birmingham City v Barcelona in 1960 and Roma in 1961, and Leeds v Dynamo Zagreb in 1967.

Furthermore, Leeds were unbeaten across all 12 matches played in the competition, winning seven and drawing five, scoring 26 goals and conceding four. Dundee-born Peter Lorimer was their top European marksman with eight goals. Over at the Leeds City Varieties Music Hall, Leonard Sachs, the chairman of long-running TV show *The Good Old Days*, was noted for his elaborate, sesquipedalian introductions of performers, and we can't help but wonder how he would have described Don Revie's troupe of entertainers.

Four Anglo-Scots contributed to Leeds' success with Lorimer leading the way with 12 appearances, closely followed by skipper Billy Bremner on 11 including both legs of the final. Winger Eddie Gray started the first leg of the final as well as seven other Euro matches. Future Scotland goalkeeper David Harvey also got the nod ahead of Welsh international Gary Sprake on four occasions including the second leg of the semi-final. Other regular non-Scottish 'entertainers' included Terry Cooper, Paul Reaney and Norman 'Bite Yer Legs' Hunter.

The successful campaign began 11 months earlier in October 1967 when CA Spora Luxembourg were thrashed 16-0 on aggregate: 9-0 at the Stade Josy Barthel with Scots contributing five of the goals – four from Peter Lorimer and one from Billy Bremner – and 7-0 in Leeds with Lorimer scoring just the one this time. In the second round it was off to Yugoslavia and a 2-1 win in Belgrade against FK Partizan with Lorimer giving the visitors an early lead. Back in Yorkshire, a 1-1 draw ensued and yet again it was Lorimer who put Leeds in front.

Somewhat ironically, Super Leeds progressed through the next three rounds at the expense of Scottish opposition – Hibernian, Rangers and Dundee respectively. In the third round first leg, played just five days before Christmas, and refereed by Northern Ireland's Jack Russell, it was the Yorkshire Terriers who triumphed 1-0, the goal coming from Glaswegian Eddie Gray in the fourth minute in front of an Elland Road crowd of 31,522. In the return leg in Edinburgh it was Hibs' Colin Stein who scored in the fourth minute to get the crowd of 40,503 all over-excited before Jack Charlton netted in the 87th minute to eliminate the Easter Road club.

In the first leg of the quarter-finals, United travelled to Ibrox Park and played out a goalless draw with Rangers in front of an incredible attendance of 85,000. There were 50,498 at the second leg which Leeds won 2-0 thanks to first-half goals from Irishman Johnny Giles and that man Lorimer again.

Both legs of the semi-final were played in May and in the first match, at Dens Park, it was honours even at 1-1. Paul Madeley gave the visitors the lead in the 26th minute with Bobby Wilson equalising for Dundee ten minutes later in front of 30,000. A smaller crowd of 23,830 witnessed United win the return leg 1-0, Eddie Gray scoring ten minutes from time to send Leeds into the final – and then everyone went off on their summer holidays with the final commencing three months later although it had been under threat of not taking place at all due to growing east-west tensions following the Warsaw Pact invasion of Czechoslovakia in late August. Just seven days after lifting the Fairs Cup in Budapest,

Leeds would begin the defence of their trophy against Standard Liège of Belgium.

* * *

Newcastle United won the **1968/69** Fairs Cup having qualified for the competition by finishing tenth in the league the season previous. Spurs and Arsenal had finished in seventh and ninth respectively but the one city, one club rule meant that London's representatives were Chelsea, who finished in sixth place. Similarly, Everton (fifth) also lost out to Liverpool (third) for a place in Europe. Conversely, with second-placed Manchester United winning the European Cup and Manchester City the First Division, the two Manchester clubs qualified for Europe's premier competition. Meanwhile, eighth-placed West Bromwich Albion also helped Newcastle's cause by winning the 1968 FA Cup Final and thus qualified for the Cup Winners' Cup. Oh yes, and fourth-placed Leeds winning the 1968 Fairs Cup meant an additional place was available to English clubs in the Fairs Cup. Hopefully that makes sense.

Five Scots made varying but significant contributions throughout Newcastle's successful run, and like the previous season, the 1969 Fairs Cup had a bit of a late finish with the two legs of the final taking place on 29 May and 11 June. A month later the USA put two men on the moon just to add to the celebrations. The Magpies had landed. Sort of.

Newcastle had started their campaign with a magnificent 4-0 win in the home leg of the first round over Feyenoord on 11 September 1968 – the same day Leeds clinched the previous season's competition in Budapest. Falkirk-born Jimmy Scott put his side ahead after six minutes in front of a Geordie crowd of 46,348. United lost the second leg in Rotterdam 2-0 but progressed 4-2 on aggregate, while the following season Feyenoord would give the Netherlands its first Euro success when they defeated Celtic in the final of the European Cup in Milan. Incidentally, Perth-born skipper Bobby Moncur missed the first-round tie through injury but in his absence, the defence was well marshalled by Coatbridge man John McNamee.

Opposition in the next three rounds all came from the Iberian peninsula. In the second round, United overcame Sporting Lisbon 2-1 on aggregate, drawing 1-1 in Portugal with Jimmy Scott netting again in a game that was almost abandoned due to a storm and torrential rain, before winning 1-0 on Tyneside with Sunderland-born Bryan Stanley Robson 'popping-up' in the tenth minute to net the winner.

For the third round it was off to north-east Spain for a narrow 3-2 defeat against Real Zaragoza before a 2-1 win in north-east England put United through on the away goals rule, West Lothian's Tommy Gibb adding to Robson's earlier strike.

In the quarter-finals it was Portuguese opposition again in the shape of Vitória de Setúbal but at a snowy St James' Park, United comfortably won 5-1 with Tommy Gibb netting the final goal of the game in the 89th minute. The venue for the second leg was switched to Sporting Lisbon's Estádio José Alvalade due to a lack of floodlights and ongoing maintenance work at Vitória's ground but a goal from Welsh international Wyn 'the Leap' Davies made sure the visitors went in at the break level. After 66 minutes, however, United were 3-1 down and things got a bit hairy as they battled to close the door and go through 6-4 on aggregate.

Rangers stood in the way of Newcastle and a place in the final but in the first leg in Glasgow a crowd of 75,580 saw the visitors' Northern Ireland goalkeeper Willie McFaul save Andy Penman's penalty as the two sides fought out a goalless draw. In the return leg, second-half goals from two Scotsmen – Jimmy Scott and Fife winger Jackie Sinclair – saw Newcastle through.

In the final, Newcastle faced Újpesti Dózsa of Hungary, who had eliminated holders Leeds at the quarter-final stage. A crowd of 60,000 packed into St James' Park for the first leg and saw a goalless first half. In the second 45 Bobby Moncur led the way with a brace of goals before Jim Scott completed the tartan treble to make it 3-0. In truth it was largely a triumph for British football as the 12 players used on the night consisted of four Scots, three Englishmen, two from Northern Ireland, two from Wales and one Dane – plus English manager Joe Harvey.

It was the same 'Determined Dozen' who played in the second leg in Budapest. At half-time however United were 2-0 down but again the skipper showed the way in the second half when Moncur scored one minute after the restart to be followed by goals from Preben Arentoft and Alan Foggon to give the visitors a 3-2 victory on the night and a 6-2 aggregate win overall. A delighted Moncur received the trophy from FIFA president Sir Stanley Rous.

A highly impressive victory for the Magpies in their maiden season in European competition but of course little did we realise that this would be

Newcastle's last major success for more than half a century, if you discount the Texaco Cup wins of 1974 (in which Bobby Moncur netted the extra-time winner against Burnley) and 1975.

Newcastle's five Euro tartan specials were skipper Bobby Moncur, John McNamee, Tommy Gibb, Jimmy Scott and Jackie Sinclair with only McNamee not appearing in the final itself

For Moncur, Newcastle were his first senior club, joining in 1962. The defender made over 300 appearances for the Magpies but is credited with having scored only three league goals – the same tally he netted across the two legs of the Inter-Cities Fairs Cup Final. He captained Newcastle in their losing 1974 FA Cup Final against Liverpool and shortly after signed for local rivals Sunderland who had surprisingly won the FA Cup Final the season previous. At Wearside he helped the Black Cats win the Second Division championship before ending his playing career at Carlisle United. Moncur also made 16 appearances for his country, skippering them on seven occasions.

Coatbridge man McNamee played for Celtic and Jock Stein's Hibernian before joining Newcastle in 1966 where he often formed a fine central defensive partnership with Moncur. McNamee made over 100 appearances for United before leaving for Blackburn Rovers in 1971. He also had stints at Hartlepool United, Lancaster City and Workington.

Bathgate boy Tommy Gibb spent five seasons at Partick Thistle before joining Newcastle in 1968 where the midfielder made over 200 appearances including the aforementioned 1974 FA Cup Final. He joined Sunderland in 1975 and ended his playing career at Hartlepool.

Jimmy Scott spent eight seasons at Hibernian before joining Newcastle in 1967 where he enjoyed two good seasons before heading for Crystal Palace in 1969. The outside-right played for Scotland in a friendly against the Netherlands in 1966, and his elder brother Alex was also an international whose playing career included a successful spell at Everton, as well as time with Rangers. Their father played for Falkirk and Burnley.

Jackie Sinclair was a winger who played for Dunfermline Athletic then Leicester City before heading to Newcastle in January 1968 and later leaving for Sheffield Wednesday in December 1969. Sinclair played against Eusébio's Portugal at Hampden Park in 1966 as the visitors prepared for that summer's World Cup finals in England.

* * *

The 1960s were a lean time for Arsenal domestically speaking (two losing League Cup finals in 1968 and 1969 was about as 'good' as it got), but in **1969/70** they triumphed in Europe for the first time, winning the Fairs Cup by defeating Anderlecht in the final 4-3 on aggregate – losing 3-1 in Brussels before winning 3-0 at Highbury in front of a crowd of 51,612. The Belgians had edged out holders Newcastle in the quarter-finals on the away goals rule. At the final whistle jubilant Arsenal fans ran on to the pitch to celebrate the end of the famine, while for skipper Frank McLintock it was his first success after picking up four runners-up medals – two with Leicester and two with the Gunners.

The north London club had qualified for the Fairs Cup after finishing fourth in the First Division and then went on to win their first major trophy since their league championship title of 1952/53. They did so with the regular assistance of four Scots – goalkeeper Bob Wilson, Frank McLintock and midfield men Eddie Kelly and George Graham – all of whom played in the final alongside some damn fine English players in Peter Storey, Jon Sammels, John Radford and Charlie George with the latter three netting 14 Euro goals between them.

Overall, George Graham appeared in ten of the 12 Fairs Cup matches that season, Bob Wilson made nine appearances, Frank McLintock seven and Eddie Kelly seven. In terms of goals, Graham hit five including braces against Glentoran and Sporting Lisbon while Kelly netted the opener in the second leg of the final in London.

A fifth Scot, 20-year-old Peter Marinello, the club's £100,000 record signing from Hibernian in January 1970, played a supporting role with four Euro appearances, at home to Rouen of France in the second leg of the third round, Dinamo Bacău of Romania in the quarter-final, and in the first leg of the semi-final against Ajax. Ajax, who included Ruud Krol, Piet Keizer, Johan Cruyff and Wim Suurbier, could only win the second leg 1-0 having been beaten 3-0 at Highbury in the first match. Marinello was dubbed 'the next George Best' by the UK press, however a 'celebrity party lifestyle' and a knee injury restricted the number of appearances the striker made while at Arsenal to around 50. Indeed, twice as many appearances were subsequently made at the likes of both Portsmouth and Motherwell.

A sixth Scot, ex-St Mirren and Spurs winger Jimmy Robertson, also did his bit on the Euro run before the arrival of Marinello, playing in the first five games versus Glentoran in the first round (3-0 at home and 1-0 away), Sporting Lisbon in the second round (0-0 away and 3-0 at home) and Rouen in the third round (0-0 away and 1-0 at home).

When Jimmy Robertson left St Mirren in 1964, the first leg of his tour of England took him to Tottenham Hotspur and while at White Hart Lane he scored the first goal in Spurs' 1967 FA Cup Final win against Chelsea. The associated match programme notes read, 'Tricky, fast, goal conscious. Plays on either wing.' He made over 180 appearances for Arsenal's north London rivals before joining the Gunners in 1968. After he left Highbury in 1970 he added Ipswich Town, Stoke City, Walsall and Crewe Alexandra to his collection. Robertson made one full appearance for Scotland – versus Wales in Cardiff in October 1964.

For Arsenal, their 1970 European success would prove to be a springboard for a majestic 1970/71 double-winning domestic season, while in defence of the Fairs Cup they were a tad unfortunate to lose out in the quarter-finals to 1.FC Köln on the away goals rule.

* * *

Like West Ham, Manchester City's **1970** Cup Winners' Cup-winning line-up (which this time included a substitute) was a full English special, with some of the players very special indeed – Tony Book, Alan Oakes, Colin Bell and Francis Lee for example. On 29 April, 24 hours after Arsenal won the Fairs Cup, City defeated Górnik Zabrze of Poland 2-1 in a rain-soaked Praterstadion in Vienna in front of a crowd of only 7,968 which was due in part to local apathy and Soviet bloc travel restrictions. In early 2024 a match ticket from the final was sold at auction for £360.

The achievement should not be understated however, for in winning the Cup Winners' Cup Manchester City also became the first English club to win a domestic competition, having already claimed the League Cup, and a European trophy in the same season (if you accept that in 1967/68 Leeds' Fairs Cup addition to their League Cup triumph actually came about a month into the following season). Incidentally, City's victory in Vienna was not televised live in the UK as it clashed with the FA Cup Final replay/foul fest between Chelsea and Leeds at Old Trafford.

There was however an Anglo-Scottish cameo role for Falkirk-born Arthur Mann, whose European appearances were apparently restricted by his fear of flying. Mann did however appear in both legs of the quarter-final against Académica de Coimbra of Portugal with Joe Mercer's side drawing 0-0 away before winning the return leg 1-0 after extra time.

* * *

At international level, Ian McColl's Scotland were outright British champions in both 1961/62 and 1962/63 while in 1966/67 the British title was accompanied with a cheeky 'Unofficial World Champions' claim following Bobby Brown's first game in charge – a victory over Alf Ramsey's 'wingless wonders' at Wembley which ended England's run of 19 games without defeat.

The 1961/62 clean sweep began with a 6-1 thrashing of a Northern Ireland team that included Manchester United's Harry Gregg, Terry Neill of Arsenal and Danny Blanchflower of Spurs at Windsor Park in Belfast in October 1961 in front of 41,000. Home Scots still continued to dominate the line-ups with just three Anglos on the field of play – Spurs' Bill Brown in goal with club-mate John White plus Anfield hero Ian St John in attack. The following month, Wales were dispatched 2-0 at Hampden with 74,329 looking on – a brace from St John who again had Anglo-Scottish company in the shape of Brown and White. Against England at Hampden in April 1962 there was another 2-0 victory for the home side with the aforementioned southern trio supplemented by Torino's Denis Law. An incredible crowd of 132,431 saw Scotland defeat their nearest and dearest on home soil for the first time since 1937.

The following season, Scotland kicked off with a 3-2 win at Cardiff's Ninian Park in October with no real change in respect of Anglo-Scot representation – Brown, White, St John and Law who had left Italy in the summer to sign for Manchester United. It was Law who netted Scotland's second goal against the Welsh. In November there was another convincing win over Northern Ireland at Hampden – 5-1 with Law getting four of them. Law's Anglo colleagues were the usual suspects of Brown, White and St John plus outside-left George Mulhall of Sunderland who was winning the second of his three caps, all of which were against Northern Ireland. The 'auld enemy' were then beaten 2-1 at Wembley and this time Spurs provided three players – Brown, White and Dave Mackay. Just for consistency their two main forwards were Law and St John although it would be Rangers midfield maestro Jim Baxter who netted both the Scots' goals. For most of the match Scotland played with ten men when skipper Eric Caldow of Rangers sustained a broken leg in the fifth minute. In 1963/64 a surprise defeat in Belfast would cost Scotland a third consecutive British title.

And so to season 1966/67 when the British Championship (which included the reigning world champions) doubled as a qualifying group for the 1968 European Championship along with the 1967/68 home internationals.

Arguably, Scotland's game against Wales in Cardiff on 22 October 1966 should have been postponed, coming as it did just one day after the Aberfan disaster. It went ahead however and a goal from Southampton's Ron Davies in the 76th minute put the Welsh in front before Law equalised for the visitors four minutes from time. Yet again there were a mere three Anglos in the Scotland line-up – the aforementioned Law plus Billy Bremner of Leeds who was winning his eighth cap plus Jim Baxter who was now with Sunderland. Conversely, and as was often the case, Wales comprised 11 Anglos including goalkeeper Gary Sprake of Leeds, centre-half and skipper Mike England of Spurs, and Bolton Wanderers striker Wyn Davies.

At Hampden Park on 16 November, against a Northern Ireland side whose line-up comprised ten players from the English leagues plus striker Sammy Wilson of Dundee, Scotland came from behind to win 2-1. The home team played but one Anglo-Scot that evening – Leeds' Billy Bremner – plus six from Celtic, three from Rangers and Kilmarnock goalie Bobby Ferguson who would sign for West Ham the following year and spend 13 years at the east London club.

At Wembley on 15 April 1967 there were five Anglo-Scots in the side which humbled the team that had the Jules Rimet Trophy in their display cabinet at the time, winning 3-2. The fab five were defender Eddie McCreadie of Chelsea, two Yorkshire-based midfielders in debutant Jim McCalliog of Sheffield Wednesday and Billy Bremner, Denis Law and Jim Baxter. England were 'subdued, tormented and outclassed' with an abiding memory being Baxter playing keepie-uppie with the ball at one stage in the second half. In 1967/68 Scotland would draw 1-1 with England at Hampden but despite taking three points from a possible four from the world champions, Scotland were out of the Euros, undone earlier by George Best's Northern Ireland in Belfast.

Moving further afield, the closest Scotland got to actually appearing at the finals of a major tournament in the 1960s was losing to Czechoslovakia in a play-off for the 1962 World Cup finals which were held in Chile.

In a three-nation qualifying group, Scotland defeated the Republic of Ireland 4-1 at home with sole Anglo David Herd of Arsenal netting a brace, and 3-0 away with another brace from the lone Anglo – this time Alex Young of Everton. Scotland then crashed 4-0 to Czechoslovakia in Bratislava with Herd winning his fifth and final cap. For the return match at Hampden in September 1961 back came Bill Brown and John White plus Ian St John and Denis Law and a 3-2 victory was secured with a double from Law and a goal from St John.

And so to a play-off match at the Heysel Stadium in Brussels on 29 November 1961, played in front of a crowd of just 7,000. Twice St John put Scotland in front but twice the opposition equalised, the second coming eight minutes from time. In extra time White hit the bar but then the Scots faded and went down 4-2. In South America, Czechoslovakia went all the way to the final itself where they took the lead against Brazil before eventually losing 3-1. Sigh.

3

Seaside Celebrities

By Robert Marshall

Scots have always enjoyed visiting English seaside resorts to savour the sights – be it the 2.16km-long Southend Pier dating from 1889, the 158m-tall Blackpool Tower which dates from 1894, or Bournemouth's Ted MacDougall hitting nine goals at Margate in an FA Cup first round tie dating from November 1971.

As an aside, the Margate goalkeeper that day was another Scot, Duntocher-born Chic Brodie, who made over 400 appearances in the Football League for Gillingham, Aldershot, Wolverhampton Wanderers, Northampton Town and Brentford but whose professional career came to an end as a result of being seriously injured when a dog ran on to the field of play in a game at Colchester and impacted Brodie's leg, damaging ligaments in his knee. Brodie represented Scotland at Junior and Schoolboy level in the 1950s.

Blackpool

Three Victorian Pleasure Piers. Ballroom dancing. The Comedy Carpet. Little and Large. Cannon and Ball. The 1940s outside-left George Dick, and the robust early 21st-century central midfielder Charlie Adam, not to be confused with his Glaswegian namesake who played for Leicester City from 1938 to 1952.

Within the match programme for the 1948 FA Cup Final it is revealed how George Dick, Blackpool's number ten that day, had worked as a waiter in the seaside resort when he asked the club for a trial – which begs the question, was Dick the real inspiration behind the Human League's 1981 smash hit 'Don't You Want Me'? Dick, who was born in Torpichen, West Lothian, in 1921, left the British Army on the Rhine (where he had been a cruiserweight boxing champion) in 1946 and headed for the Lancashire coast. There he got his trial with the Seasiders, and within ten minutes was signed on by manager Joe Smith.

George made his debut in October 1946 against Arsenal at Bloomfield Road and scored the second goal – Stan Mortensen got the first – in a 2-1 win over the Gunners in what was the first full season since before the war and Blackpool would finish in fifth place. As well as Mortensen, team-mates included George Eastham Senior and Jock Wallace Senior. Dick would enjoy two seasons with Blackpool, playing over 50 matches, culminating in the 1948 FA Cup Final which was lost 4-2 to Manchester United after twice leading. Dick had two fellow Scots for company in the Blackpool XI – left-half Hugh Kelly and inside-right Alex Munro – and as well as playing in all six FA Cup ties that season he also scored one of the goals in the 4-0 victory over Leeds United in the third round. The 'Waiter on the Wing' would also play for several other English clubs before taking up coaching posts in Belgium, Denmark and Turkey.

Incidentally, during the 1947 close season, George could have visited Blackpool's Palace Theatre which was the venue for a week-long run by the world's greatest-ever comedy double act, Laurel and Hardy. However, by the time Morecambe and Wise first rolled into town in April 1949, Dick was at West Ham.

A quick shout out for Stuart McCall's father Andy, from Lanarkshire, who played for Blackpool between 1947 and 1951 and who supplemented his low wage by working on the Pleasure Beach during the summer months.

'Kiss-me-Quick' shout-outs also for two attacking midfielders, Glasgow's Tony Green, and Tommy Hutchison of Cardenden in Fife, Blackpool Hall of Famers who helped the Seasiders to Anglo-Italian Cup glory in June 1971, beating Bologna 2-1 in the final in northern Italy.

And so to Dundonian Charlie Adam whose route to Bloomfield Road was altogether different from that of George Dick – starting off at Glasgow Rangers in 2003 while loan spells took him to Ross County and St Mirren before arriving at Championship outfit Blackpool in February 2009 by which time he had also picked up a couple of Scotland caps. He would win 26 in total, 24 of them while down south with Blackpool (ten), Liverpool (five) and Stoke City (nine).

Adam was a key player in the Blackpool side that won promotion to the Premier League at the end of 2009/10. Indeed, he skippered the club to glory, scoring a match-winning penalty against Nottingham Forest in the play-off semi-final first leg, while in the final he netted from a free kick as the Seasiders beat Cardiff City 3-2 at Wembley. Adam's fine form continued in the Premier League and he received a nomination for the PFA Player of the Year award. Alas, he could not prevent Blackpool from being relegated at the end of the season and in July 2011 he transferred to Liverpool for £6.75m. Adam made 98 appearances for the Bloomfield Road side, scoring 34 goals, contributing 22 assists and picking up 30 yellow cards. I never said he was perfect.

I ventured down to Blackpool in September 2010 to take in the Seasiders v Blackburn Rovers in a Premier League match. Bloomfield Road had been transformed since my previous visit 31 years earlier; indeed it was still being transformed. Gone were the terraces, rickety old grandstands and floodlight pylons to be replaced with three modern stands complete with executive boxes. Back in 1979 I was able to pay at the gate but now I had a nice souvenir ticket stub (complete with an image of the Wembley play-off celebrations in the background) to remind me that I had paid £34 for a restricted view seat in the temporary East Stand. Nice vista of the Blackpool Tower though.

On the pitch I ironically witnessed an own goal from Charlie boy give the visitors a first-half lead before 'future Scot' Matt Phillips equalised on his debut for Blackpool five minutes from time. Seasider hopes were dashed however when Australian Brett Emerton scored the winner for Blackburn three minutes into stoppage time. Post-match, we headed off towards the North Pier to see what Thwaites beer and 'entertainers' such as Joey Blower and Angel Delight could do to raise our spirits – but that is another story.

Plymouth

The Hoe. The 17th Century Royal Citadel. Smeaton's Tower. The Plymouth Gin Distillery. A football club with a Scottish-sounding suffix (they may have been named after the Argyll and Sutherland Highlanders regiment). Managers Paul Sturrock and Derek Adams.

Sturrock, who was born in Ellon, Aberdeenshire, enjoyed a successful playing career as a striker with Dundee United between 1974 and 1989, winning medals and Scotland caps in the process. He also managed United and later St Johnstone before taking over the reins at Plymouth – for the first of two stints – in October 2000.

Super Ted MacDougall, although he played for Manchester United, West Ham and Norwich, he is best remembered for his goalscoring exploits with Bournemouth.

At that time, the Pilgrims were struggling in the Third Division, however the following season he guided them to the title, breaking records in the process including a club and league points total of 102. In March 2004 Sturrock left Home Park with Plymouth top of the Second Division table to take over at Premier League Southampton. Plymouth would finish the season as champions and move up to the First Division. A subsequent poll by BBC Devon named Sturrock as the manager of Argyle's 'Team of the Century'. The same poll included Motherwell-born Sammy Black, who made almost 500 appearances for Plymouth at outside-left, netting 182 goals between 1924 and 1938.

In November 2007, Sturrock returned to Home Park, that English football outpost as some soccer scribes like to describe it, and at the end of 2007/08 the Pilgrims finished tenth in the Championship, their highest league position in 20 years. In 2008/09 however the team struggled and finished one place outside the relegation zone. Things got worse in 2009/10 when, in December, the club chairman moved Sturrock into a 'business support' role, though eventually the former Scotland international said something along the lines of 'Bugger this for a game of soldiers' and left to pursue managerial opportunities elsewhere. Not long after, it emerged that the board had mis-managed the finances of the Devonshire outfit and Plymouth Argyle entered administration.

Within a few weeks of Sturrock being removed as manager, there was a major meteorological event known as 'The Big Freeze' which brought severe snowy weather to the UK and even balmy Devon was brought to a standstill as the county disappeared under a blanket of the white stuff. Now I have no hard evidence to suggest the two events are linked but I do think it's something to ponder.

From 1992 to 2009, Derek Adams played his club football in Scotland at outfits such as Motherwell and Ross County with the latter also providing the Glaswegian with his first managerial role. In June 2015, however, Adams was appointed as Plymouth's manager and in his first season he guided the Pilgrims to the League Two play-off final at Wembley – which they lost to AFC Wimbledon. In 2016/17 a second-placed finish ensured promotion to League One.

In the 2017/18 Plymouth narrowly missed out on a play-off place as they finished seventh in League One. Following a difficult end to 2018/19, though, Adams was relieved of his duties in April – when, no doubt, it was deemed well nigh impossible for the 'angry snows' to be summoned again.

Adams subsequently had two spells at another seaside club, Morecambe, whom he led to promotion to the third tier via the play-offs at the end of season 2020/21. He can therefore be credited with bringing sunshine to a town that still suffers from the aftershock of 'Blobbygate'.

Torquay

The English Riviera. Agatha Christie. Basil Fawlty. E for evening kick-off at 7.30pm. Jim McNichol. Matt Elliott.

Jim McNichol was a Glasgow-born central defender who was capped seven times for Scotland at under-21 level but who played all his club football in England. His clubs included Luton Town, Brentford and Exeter City but it was at Torquay United in the late 1980s that he made the headlines.

On 9 May 1987 the Plainmoor outfit were 45 minutes from departing the Football League, trailing 2-0 to Crewe Alexandra at half-time in the last game of the season with future England hero David Platt one of the scorers. United needed two goals to ensure survival. Soon after the restart McNichol pulled one back from a deflected free kick, then in the dying moments he ran to the corner flag to whip in a cross, not realising his run would confuse a nearby police dog, a German Shepherd called Bryn, into thinking the Scotsman was about to attack his handler. The 'teutonic towser' bit McNichol on the leg and the player had to be treated and during the minutes added on due to the injury, Torquay scored and Lincoln City were the club to lose their league status on goal difference.

McNichol was subsequently appointed club captain and led the Gulls to the final of the 1989 Associate Members' Cup, at the time the Sherpa Van Trophy and now the EFL Trophy, at Wembley. Alas, Torquay, who were managed by former Spurs hero Cyril Knowles, would lose to Bolton Wanderers, who were managed by former Liverpool hero Phil Neal. The Torquay starting XI included two other Scots – Tom Kelly, a former youth squad player at Partick Thistle and Matt Elliott.

Elliott was born in Wandsworth, sarf London, but qualified to play for Scotland due to a Scottish grandmother and he would win 18 caps and net one goal between 1997 and 2001 while with Leicester. Between 1989 and 1992, however, he played over 100 games for Torquay.

He obviously made an impression in sarf Devon because in 2023 a Torquay fan group known as Retro Gulls included the commanding centre-back in their all-time greatest XI. Also selected were former Wales international goalkeeper Neville Southall and former West Ham full-back John Bond.

Coincidentally, during Matt's (and McNichol's) time in Torquay, another London Scot, comedian Jim Davidson, was regularly pulling them in at the town's Princess Theatre. For all Mr Davidson's perceived shortcomings, at least he never got red-carded for violent conduct in a Euro 2000 qualifier against the Faroe Islands which, embarrassingly, finished 1-1.

To be fair to Mr Elliott, his commitment to Scotland's cause was total, often forming a formidable defensive partnership with Colin Hendry.

Bournemouth

Overcrowded beaches. Mary Shelley's grave. Robert Louis Stevenson's clifftop pad. Chines and Cherries. Ted MacDougall and Warren Cummings.

Edward John 'Ted' MacDougall was born in Inverness (a mere 600 miles from Bournemouth), moved to Widnes in Lancashire when he was 12 and joined Liverpool as an apprentice in 1964. Things didn't work out at Anfield but at Fourth Division York City, 'SuperMac' started to bang the goals in. Ted then joined Bournemouth and Boscombe Athletic as they were known in the summer of 1969, and a purple patch ensued until his departure in September 1972 by which time the Cherries were called AFC Bournemouth.

Despite MacDougall contributing 21 goals, B&BA were relegated to the Fourth Division in 1970. In 1970/71 however the Cherries finished runners-up to Jimmy Sirrel's Notts County to win promotion back to the Third Division with MacDougall contributing an incredible 42 league goals – plus six past Oxford City in an FA Cup tie.

In 1971/72 AFCB narrowly missed out on a second successive promotion, finishing third at a time when only two clubs went up. In November 1971 there were also those nine goals by Ted in the 11-0 FA Cup thrashing of Margate as some of the top-tier clubs began to take an interest in him. Incidentally, that cup thrashing was probably some sort of revenge for non-league Margate's 3-0, FA Cup first round victory over B&BA at Dean Court in November 1961 when the Cherries, who included Edinburgh-born striker Alex Bain, were top of the Third Division at the time.

Anyway, after 126 goals in 165 appearances for the (then) Hampshire outfit, Ted moved for £200,000 to Frank O'Farrell's Manchester United who would soon thereafter become Tommy Docherty's Red Devils. I understand that Manchester's thriving nightclub scene can be attractive to many, but in the early 1970s Bournemouth's Winter Gardens theatre could offer up the likes of Pink Floyd, T. Rex, David Bowie, Elton John – and *The Dick Emery Show*! Also, apparently it always rains in Manchester.

Following stints at Manchester United (only 18 league appearances before the Doc 'signed him off'), West Ham United (a dressing-room punch-up with Billy Bonds didn't help matters), Norwich City (seven Scotland caps, three goals and a Wembley cup final appearance) and Southampton (European football and promotion to the top tier at the end of 1977/78), MacDougall rejoined Bournemouth in November 1978 for a two-year spell but was not as prolific as before and in February 1980 he left to try his luck at coaching. In 2013 the redeveloped south stand at Bournemouth's Dean Court stadium was named after Ted MacDougall in recognition of his service at the club.

Fast-forward to 2000 when Warren Cummings, an Aberdonian Chelsea loanee, first arrived in Bournemouth. Cummings was also loaned out to West Bromwich Albion, Dundee United and Bournemouth again before signing a permanent deal with the Cherries in 2003. The defender remained in Dorset (isn't local government re-organisation marvellous?) until 2012, playing over 250 games. For his services to the club, Cummings received a testimonial match against AC Milan on 3 September 2016; it marked the club debut for England international Jack Wilshire. The Italian version of the Red and Blacks won 2-1.

Cummings' time at Bournemouth was not without incident, however – a double leg break versus Swindon Town in 2005, a broken arm against Northampton in 2007 and relegation to League Two at the end of 2007/08 following a points deduction for the club entering into administration. On the plus side though, at the end of season 2009/10 promotion back to League One was achieved under manager Eddie Howe.

Brighton and Hove

The labyrinthian Lanes. The Indo-Saracenic style Royal Pavilion. Cheeky Chappie Max Miller. Fictional gangster Pinkie Brown. Mods and Rockers exchanging pleasantries on the pebbly beach. ABBA winning the 1974 Eurovision song contest at the Brighton Dome. Gordon Smith missing a great goalscoring opportunity in the 1983 FA Cup Final. Billy Gilmour. Two very different midfielders from Ayrshire.

'And Smith must score!' – so bellowed BBC Radio commentator Peter Jones in the final minute of extra time with the scores tied at 2-2, but he didn't, instead Manchester United goalie Gary Bailey pulled off an excellent save and United won the replay 4-0. D'oh!

To be fair to Smith, he did indeed score – the opening goal in the 14th minute to put Brighton & Hove Albion in front in the Seagulls' first major cup final. Unfortunately for the Goldstone outfit, Frank Stapleton equalised in the 55th minute before Ray 'Butch' Wilkins put United in front after 72 minutes. Three minutes from time however a Gary Stevens equaliser meant another 30 minutes of play, but there were no more goals and no penalty shoot-out decider in those times. In the replay five days later, United romped home.

It's worth remembering the Seagulls' impressive route to the final – eliminating Newcastle United away, Manchester City 4-0 at home, Liverpool away during a season in which the Reds went on to win the League Cup and First Division, Norwich City at home and Sheffield Wednesday in the semi-final at Highbury. It's probably best to forget that as well as the cup final agony, the Seagulls also lost their top-flight status at the end of 1982/83.

Gordon Smith, having enjoyed collecting winners' medals in three years at Rangers, joined Brighton for a record transfer fee of £440,000 in the summer of 1980, a time when the middle-distance running rivalry between local hero Steve Ovett and Seb Coe was at its height. Smith would then enjoy three seasons in the First Division with the Sussex club, playing in over 100 league games before joining Manchester City in March 1984. He then had a short spell at Oldham Athletic before playing in Austria and Switzerland, finishing his playing career with Stirling Albion. Gordon's subsequent career involved the media, as a football agent and as chief executive of the SFA. The erudite Mr Smith made a positive impact in all of them.

In the late 1980s and early 1990s, Seagulls fans with a supreme sense of irony produced a fanzine entitled *And Smith Must Score!*. Of course, no player should be defined by one perceived error – I personally have long since forgiven Manchester City's Willie Donachie for his last-minute pass-back/own goal against Wales in the 1978 British Championship, Liverpool's Steve Nicol for his glorious opportunity squandered against

Uruguay at the 1986 World Cup, and Wolves' Chris Iwelumo for his absolute sitter missed against Norway in a 2008 World Cup qualifier. I just can't *forget*, that's the problem!

After the near-miss of the 1983 final, Brighton would have to wait another 40 years before successfully qualifying for Europe, in the shape of the 2023/24 UEFA Europa League, when a certain Billy Gilmour was a member of a multi-national squad that played attractive, attacking football.

Brighton departed the Goldstone Ground in 1997, ground-shared with Gillingham for two seasons, nearly went out of business completely, started to turn things around by leasing the Withdean Athletics Stadium (Steve Ovett's home track) before completing the 'regeneration process' at the Falmer Stadium (known as the AMEX for sponsorship reasons) from the start of 2011/12. The club won promotion in 2016/17, returning to the top flight for the first time since 1983.

Billy Gilmour was born in Irvine, North Ayrshire, in 2001, the same year the unitary authority of Brighton and Hove was formally granted city status by Queen Elizabeth II. Gilmour started out with the Rangers youth team before moving to the Stamford Bridge equivalent and then making his Chelsea senior debut in season 2019/20 under manager Frank Lampard but in both that season and 2020/21 his first-team appearances were restricted, although he did gain some Champions League experience under Lampard and his successor Thomas Tuchel. He was also an unused substitute for the 2021 FA Cup and Champions League finals. In July 2021, Gilmour joined fellow Premier League side Norwich City on a season-long loan. He appeared 28 times for the Carrow Road club, however the Canaries finished bottom of the table and were relegated. Valuable experience?

In September 2022, Gilmour transferred to Brighton on a four-year deal and in 2022/23 he helped his new club to a sixth-placed Premier League finish, their highest in the top flight. In his second season at the AMEX Gilmour's appearances noticeably increased having rubbed shoulders with the likes of Argentina's 2022 World Cup winner Alexis Mac Allister, Germany's Pascal Groß and England's Danny Welbeck. More European experience was gained via eight matches in the Europa League – reaching the last 16 before falling to Roma.

In June 2024, Gilmour celebrated his 23rd birthday as part of Scotland's squad at the Euro finals, having already appeared at the delayed

Euro 2020 finals; indeed the midfield maestro now has over 30 Scotland caps to his name. Somewhat surprisingly though, season 2024/25 saw Gilmour strut his stuff at another seaside location, Naples, although unfortunately I don't think Italy's third-largest city does end-of-the-pier shows. Hopefully continued improvement and an increased number of first-team appearances await for the defensive midfielder. For all his talent and progress so far, I can't help but wonder if Billy Gilmour ever gets all 'Quadrophenia-like' and yells, 'Can you see the real me? Can ya? Can ya?' I think we've all still to see the best of oor Billy, wherever it may be.

Scarborough

Two beautiful bays separated by a high rocky promontory on top of which lies the ruins of an 11th-century castle. The Japanese-themed Peasholm Park. The legendary Spa Orchestra. The also-legendary Steve Richards and Tommy Graham – two of (Neil) Warnock's Warriors from Dundee and Glasgow respectively.

Scarborough FC were founded in 1879 but spent most of their existence playing non-league football until their manager Neil Warnock guided his side to the 1986/87 Conference title and in so doing became the first club to be automatically promoted to the Football League via this route instead of the long-standing re-election system.

Warnock stayed as manager of Scarborough until he left for Notts County in November 1988 and Scarborough remained in the fourth tier until 1999 – twice losing out in the promotion play-off semi-finals, to Leyton Orient in 1989 and Torquay United in 1998. The early 21st century however brought Conference football then administration followed by liquidation with debts of around £2.5m. In 2007 a new supporter-owned phoenix club called Scarborough Athletic FC was created.

Tommy Graham and Steve Richards were part of the late 1980s halcyon years, joining Scarborough in 1986 and 1987 respectively and departing in 1990 and 1991.

Graham's football odyssey began with Junior outfit Arthurlie, from Barrhead near Glasgow. He crossed the border in 1978 and moved around Yorkshire clubs Barnsley, Halifax Town and Doncaster Rovers before spells with the steel town clubs of Motherwell and Scunthorpe United. While at Scunthorpe he helped the Iron win promotion to the Third Division at the end of 1982/83, most noticeably by scoring two goals in a 2-1 away win at Chester on the last day of the season.

At Scarborough, Graham played over 150 matches including a memorable League Cup second round tie versus top-flight Chelsea. In the first leg, a highly commendable 1-1 draw was achieved at Stamford Bridge, but in the return match at the McCain Stadium (known locally as 'The Theatre of Chips') the Blues led 2-0, and 3-1 on aggregate with 24 minutes remaining. Quite incredibly though Scarborough netted three times – the first goal coming from the head of Graham – to eliminate Chelsea, who included future England internationals Dave Beasant and Tony Dorigo plus Super Stevie Clarke, 4-3 on aggregate.

After leaving the seaside outfit, Graham had one last tango with Halifax before becoming a chiropodist in Barnsley. Tyker feet? Sorry.

Steve Richards' senior career path began at Hull City before stops at York City, Lincoln City and Cambridge United took him to Scarborough where he made over 170 appearances. Richards also appeared in both of the aforementioned games against Chelsea, and he is also remembered for an exquisite own goal, an inch-perfect lob from outside the penalty box over his own keeper in front of deliriously happy visiting Carlisle United fans in 1988. Yet another one from the YouTube classic cock-ups collection to be savoured in the comfort of your own home.

So here's to players like Tommy Graham and Steve Richards who helped bring to one seaside resort probably as much entertainment and excitement, one way or another, as did regular visitors and legendary Rotherham outfit – the Chuckle Brothers. To me, to you!

4

1970/71–1979/80

Overview

There is a tendency to view the 1970s as a period of crisis and discontent with skyrocketing inflation and unemployment, a wide range of strikes, power cuts and states of emergency. Thank goodness then for football and popular culture, from the skilful and highly entertaining Queens Park Rangers who featured Frank McLintock, Don Masson and Stan Bowles, to *The Benny Hill Show*, *Morecambe and Wise* and *Are You Being Served?*. And there's more.

Yesterday's Hero (1979) was a tacky/clichéd/predictable/thoroughly enjoyable football movie starring Ian McShane, Adam Faith and Paul Nicholas which echoed the life of George Best, but which was not biographical, and includes footage from the 1979 Nottingham Forest-Southampton League Cup Final. The screenplay was written by novelist Jackie Collins whose books *The Stud* and *The Bitch* provided the inspiration for two other 'classic' movies of the 70s, both starring her big sister Joan Collins.

Musically speaking, the 70s gave us the glorious trinity of glam rock, disco and punk. However, mid-decade Scotland inflicted the tartan-clad Bay City Rollers on England and beyond and so on behalf of the Scottish nation, the two authors would like to take this opportunity to offer their sincere apologies. It's possible to laugh off the antics of Wembley 1977 but 'Shang-a-Lang' not so much. That said, England would retaliate via Black Lace and 'Agadoo' etc.

TV football continued to advance as new technology allowed match action to be shown in slow-motion. Arguably, the biggest transfer of 1973 was when Jimmy Hill joined *Match of the Day* from London Weekend Television's *The Big Match*. Another major signing by the BBC was former Arsenal and Scotland keeper Bob Wilson to front *Football Focus* in 1974.

In the commentary boxes, John Motson and Barry Davies were as effective for the BBC as John Toshack and Kevin Keegan were on the pitch for Liverpool.

The 1970s saw a rapid increase in the value of transfer fees with Keegan leaving Liverpool for Hamburg in 1977 for £500,000 while in February 1979, Trevor Francis became Britain's first £1m player when he moved from Birmingham City to Nottingham Forest. Come September 1979, Aston Villa and Scotland striker Andy Gray transferred to Wolverhampton Wanderers for £1.49m.

In 1979, Liverpool struck a deal with Hitachi, the Japanese electronics giant, to become the first English top-flight side to have a commercial logo on their jerseys. Such sponsorship deals in the 1970s and early 1980s were often thwarted though; BBC and ITV initially refused to show highlights of any team who wore sponsored shirts. By the end of the 1980s however the lucrative sponsorship genie was well and truly out of the bottle.

Liverpool were easily the most successful English club of the 1970s, although Brian Clough's Nottingham Forest also achieved an impressive trophy haul. No one club was successful in winning all three domestic trophies across these ten seasons. The decade provided a poor return for Manchester United who also suffered the ignominy of relegation from the top flight at the end of 1973/74. Equally surprising was Spurs' relegation to the Second Division at the conclusion of 1976/77, although both clubs bounced back after just one season below.

The squads for nine of the ten championship-winning clubs contained at least two Scots – Liverpool in 1976/77 were the exception. Leeds United's successful squad of 1973/74 saw no fewer than nine Scots make some sort of appearance – from half a game (Stirling-born Gary Liddell) to all 42 matches (Stirling-born Billy Bremner). In the FA Cup, 17 of the 20 finalists contained Scots with the 1973 final, Sunderland v Leeds, having an aggregate total of eight Anglos on the Wembley turf. In the League Cup, Scots made it into the starting line-up of 18 of the finalists with the 1979/80 final, Wolverhampton Wanderers v Nottingham Forest, seeing six Scots across the two picks.

This was a vintage decade for English clubs in Europe with no fewer than nine successes – four European Cup, one Cup Winners' Cup and four combined in the Fairs Cup and UEFA Cup – spread across Chelsea, Leeds, Liverpool, Nottingham Forest and Spurs. Anglo-Scots appeared in seven of those winning line-ups, the exceptions being Liverpool's 1976 UEFA Cup and 1977 European Cup triumphs.

Trophy winners 1970/71 to 1979/80

Successful clubs	League	FA Cup	League Cup	European	Total
Liverpool	5	1	-	4	10
Nottingham Forest	1	-	2	2	5
Leeds United	1	1	-	1	3
Arsenal	1	2	-	-	3
Tottenham Hotspur	-	-	2	1	3
Derby County	2	-	-	-	2
West Ham United	-	2	-	-	2
Aston Villa	-	-	2	-	2
Wolverhampton Wanderers	-	-	2	-	2
Chelsea	-	-	-	1	1
Ipswich Town	-	1	-	-	1
Manchester United	-	1	-	-	1
Southampton	-	1	-	-	1
Sunderland	-	1	-	-	1
Manchester City	-	-	1	-	1
Stoke City	-	-	1	-	1
TOTALS	**10**	**10**	**10**	**9**	**39**

The 1970s also gave birth to some short-lived though memorable competitions such as the Watney Cup, the Anglo-Italian Cup, the Texaco Cup, and its successor, the Anglo-Scottish Cup.

A quick mention then for Bellshill-born Ian Hector McKechnie, and his 'trailblazing exploits' as a goalkeeper for Hull City in the semi-final of the inaugural Watney Cup in August 1970 against Manchester United at Boothferry Park. With the score tied at 1-1, McKechnie became the first goalkeeper ever to save a penalty in a competitive penalty shoot-out, from Denis Law, as well as to concede a penalty, from George Best. McKechnie subsequently took the deciding kick to take the shoot-out to a further five penalties from each team, but his effort went over the bar and so Hull went out. The former Arsenal and Southend United number one was therefore also the first goalkeeper to take a penalty in a shoot-out, and the first player to miss the decider. United would subsequently lose 4-1 to Derby County in the final with Scots Dave Mackay, John McGovern and John O'Hare all picking up winners' medals.

* * *

On the international front, Scotland were outright British champions in 1976 and 1977, achievements which were bookended by appearing at the 1974 and 1978 World Cup finals as the UK's sole representative. Absolutely marvellous.

* * *

Domestic competitions

1970/71

Arsenal achieved the double, winning the league on the last day with victory over Tottenham (Leeds were second, a point behind the Gunners on 64 points), and the FA Cup with victory over Liverpool in the final.

Captain Frank McLintock played in all 42 league games, scoring five goals. It was to be the apex of his Gunners career (314/26), and he left in 1973 for QPR. He remained with the Loftus Road club until retiring in 1977 (127/5). Frank also had spells managing Leicester City and Brentford.

Bob Wilson also played in all 42 games with George Graham playing in 37, scoring 11 goals. Graham moved to Manchester United in 1972 (43/2) for £120,000 where he would soon be reunited with Tommy Docherty before moving to Portsmouth (61/5) then Crystal Palace (44/2). He ended his playing career in the NASL with California Surf, subsequently moving into management where his stock would rise considerably.

Midfielder Eddie Kelly joined Arsenal as a youth in 1966, making his debut in 1969. He played in 23 games in 1970/71, netting four goals. Eddie was to captain Arsenal before leaving in 1976 (175/13). He joined QPR for a season (28/1) before heading to Leicester with McLintock for three years, winning the Second Division title with the Foxes after Frank left (85/3). He ran down his career with spells at Notts County (27/1), Bournemouth (13/0), Leicester again (34/0), Kettering Town (1/0) and finally Torquay 1984 to 86 (35/1).

Arsenal paid £100,000 for Peter Marinello from Hibernian (45/3) in 1970 but his career never reached the heights it was hoped for, playing in just three league games that season and only 37 altogether, scoring three goals. Among his other clubs were Portsmouth (95/7), Motherwell (89/12), Fulham (27/11), Hearts (27/1) and Partick Thistle (6/0).

Topping the scoring charts in the Fourth Division with an incredible total of 42 goals was Ted MacDougall of Bournemouth. Ted had already hit the headlines that season for his nine goals v Margate in the FA Cup. He failed to make the grade as a youth at Anfield and moved to York City in 1967 (84/34), before his first spell at Bournemouth. Two moves in quick succession from 1972 to Manchester United (18/5) and West Ham (24/5) were followed by a longer term at Norwich City.

Arsenal won the FA Cup, beating Liverpool 2-1 after extra time with Wilson, McLintock, Graham and Kelly all playing. Substitute Kelly is sometimes credited with the first Arsenal goal but more often it is given as George Graham's. So, at last McLintock overcame his Wembley hoodoo although he returned a fortnight later and was part of the Scotland side that lost 3-1 to England in the British Championship.

In Shankly's Liverpool side the only Scot was industrious midfielder Brian Hall. Born in Glasgow, Brian was raised in Lancashire and made his debut for Liverpool in 1969. Never a standout among the players around him, Brian was still a vital part of the Liverpool side in the early 70s.

Tottenham won the League Cup, beating Aston Villa 2-0 thanks to two Martin Chivers goals. Alan Gilzean was the only Scot in the Spurs team.

Charlie Aitken, who had played in the 1962/63 League Cup Final loss against Birmingham City, was one of five Scots in the Villa side. In their midfield were Pat McMahon and Bruce Rioch.

McMahon had won the Scottish Junior Cup with Kilsyth Rangers in 1967 and was soon on the books at Celtic (3/2). Signing at Villa in 1969, Pat spent six years with the club (130/25) before heading across the Atlantic to play in Portland, Colorado and Atlanta.

Born in Aldershot to Scottish parents, Bruce Rioch moved to Villa in 1969 for £100,000 after five years with Luton Town (149/47), winning the Fourth Division title with the Hatters in 1967/68. After five years (154/34) Bruce moved to Derby County in February 1974 where he was to win the First Division in 1974/75 and earn his first Scotland caps.

Bustling striker Andy Lochhead was adored by the Villa fans after his move from Leicester just six months or so after losing the 1969 FA Cup Final with the Filbert Street outfit. Andy was to hit 19 goals as they were promoted out of the Third Division. Leaving Villa in 1973 (131/34) for Oldham (45/10), Andy spent the summer of 1974 in the US with Denver Dynamos before retiring in 1975.

Former Leicester forward Dave Gibson, who played in the Foxes' FA Cup Final defeats of 1963 and 1969 as well as the League Cup win of 1964 and loss of 1965, was an unused sub for Villa.

1971/72

Derby County won the league for the first time in their history, led by the redoubtable Brian Clough. They finished on 58 points, one clear of Liverpool, Leeds and Manchester City. Playing in 40 games each were John McGovern, John O'Hare, and Archie Gemmill.

Montrose-born McGovern was raised in Hartlepool, and it was there that he began his football career and where he first played under Clough, making his debut aged 16 in May 1966. It was over a year after Clough and Peter Taylor left for Derby that John transferred for £7,500 in September 1968 (72/5). Derby's final game of the season saw them play title rivals Liverpool and John scored the only goal, one of his four that season. John would leave the Baseball Ground in August 1974 (190/16) for Leeds but would find success with Clough at Nottingham Forest.

John O'Hare, from Renton, was bought by Clough from Sunderland (51/14) for £20,000 in August 1967. Although he was never a prolific scorer in his first four seasons with Derby, he hit double figures in goals in each (248/65). He contributed 13 in the title-winning season. Like McGovern, he would follow Clough to Leeds and then Forest.

Paisley-born Archie Gemmill started out at his hometown club St Mirren (65/19) in 1964, moving south to Preston North End in June 1967 for £13,000. After three years at Deepdale (99/13) Clough convinced him to sign for Derby for £60,000 in September 1970. Gemmill was to win two titles with the Rams and would eventually join Clough at Forest. In this championship season Archie scored three goals.

Elsewhere, Ted MacDougall once again bagged a lot of goals for Bournemouth, hitting 35 to top the goalscoring list for the Third Division this time.

Leeds won the FA Cup for the first time, beating Arsenal 1-0 in the final with Allan Clarke scoring. Keeper David Harvey, Billy Bremner, Peter Lorimer and Eddie Gray all took part. On the Arsenal side Frank McLintock lost again at Wembley as did George Graham. This was the second instance of both finalists being captained by Scots this century, the first being in 1965, while the third and last time was only a year away.

BILLY
BREMNER
Leeds United
and Scotland

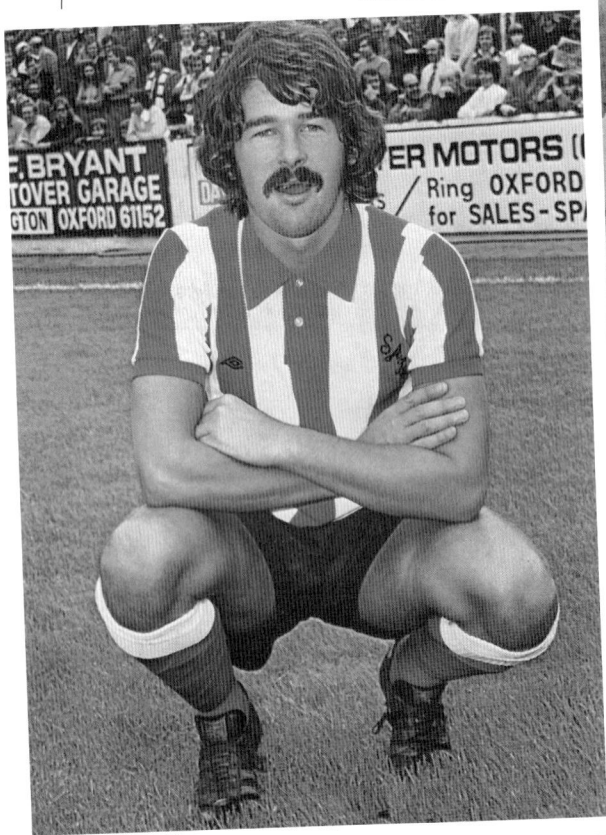

Billy Bremner and Bobby Kerr who captained their sides in the 1973 FA Cup Final.

The League Cup was won by Stoke City, although there were no Scots in their side as they beat Chelsea 2-1. For the Blues, Charlie Cooke, an FA Cup winner in 1970, was the only Scot on duty.

1972/73

Liverpool came out on top with 60 points and Arsenal were second, three points adrift. Brian Hall continued to play his part, competing in 21 games and scoring two goals.

Joining Brian in the midfield was Peter Cormack. Peter had started out at Hibernian in 1962 (182/75), when former Leicester manager Matt Gillies, now at Nottingham Forest, paid £80,000 for him. Things didn't work for Gillies or indeed Cormack as Forest were relegated in 1972 (74/15). Bill Shankly signed Cormack and was often quoted as saying that Peter was the 'final piece of the jigsaw' in pushing Liverpool to greater heights. So it proved. Peter was bought for £110,000 and in his first season he played 30 games, scoring eight goals. He went on to win the UEFA Cup, FA Cup and two titles with the Reds.

The FA Cup was won by the unfancied Sunderland, who beat Leeds 1-0. Second Division Sunderland had already beaten Manchester City and Arsenal on the way to the final, but Leeds were expected to dispatch them readily.

David Harvey, Billy Bremner, Peter Lorimer and Eddie Gray were all part of the full-strength Leeds team. As for Sunderland, they had four Scots in their side, led by their captain, the redoubtable Bobby Kerr.

Slightly smaller than Billy Bremner, Alexandria-born Kerr matched him as a combative, tough midfielder. Despite the setback of two broken legs early in his Sunderland career, after making his debut in 1966 Bobby played 368 games for the Rokerites, scoring 56 goals. Later he was to play for Blackpool (22/2) and finished his career with Hartlepool (49/2).

At right-back was former Ayr United player Dick Malone. Born in Carfin, North Lanarkshire, Malone had started out at Junior club Shotts Bon Accord before joining Ayr (163/2). He moved to Sunderland for a seven-year spell in 1970 (236/2). He spent a season at Hartlepool (36/2) before joining Kerr at Blackpool under FA Cup-winning manager Bob Stokoe (49/1). He ended his career with a 43-game run at Queen of the South and a stint with Gateshead.

Ian Porterfield was to score the winning goal in the final. Ian had started out at Raith Rovers (117/17) before moving to Sunderland for a reported £45,000 in 1967. He remained with Sunderland for ten years (230/17), before spending two years with Sheffield Wednesday (106/3). Ian then went into management with Rotherham and Reading before a spell at Aberdeen as the first in a long line of Dons managers to try and live up to Sir Alex Ferguson's legacy. Ian also had a period at Chelsea and managed several international sides too.

Billy Hughes was the younger brother of Celtic legend John Hughes. He joined Sunderland as a youth in 1966, making his debut aged 18. Billy spent 11 years at Roker Park and amassed 287 appearances, netting 74 times. After Sunderland he played for Derby (19/8), Leicester City (37/5) and a five-game loan spell at Carlisle.

Overall, these four Scots played a combined total of 1,121 league games for Sunderland, contributing 149 goals.

Tottenham won the League Cup, beating Norwich 1-0 through a goal from 'Combover King' Ralph Coates. Alan Gilzean was the only Scot in their side, picking up his second League Cup winners' medal.

Norwich, managed by Ron Saunders, were captained by Duncan Forbes, who came from Edinburgh and was a double club Hall of Fame member with Colchester United and Norwich for his service to both teams. Centre-half Duncan joined Colchester in 1961 from Musselburgh Athletic and stayed with the Layer Road club for seven years (270/3) when Norwich paid £10,000 for him. He spent 13 years at Carrow Road (295/10), leading them to the top flight in 1971/72. Duncan ended his days playing in non-league football. Following his death in 2019 a permanent mural depicting Forbes was unveiled at the club. It is inscribed with the classic chant of 'Six foot two eyes of blue, Duncan Forbes is after you'. Like Jim Holton, the other Scot synonymous with that song, Forbes didn't quite stand at 6ft 2in but like Jim he was a fierce competitor.

Playing up front for Norwich was Jim Blair, who was to have a relatively short career with the Canaries. Born in Calderbank, North Lanarkshire, Jim started out at Shotts Bon Accord and moved on to St Mirren in 1967. He left Paisley (84/40) for Edinburgh and Hibs (18/5) for season 1970/71 before returning to Love Street for a couple of years (50/20). He then headed Norwich way (6/0) after which he played for Mechelen in Belgium (93/14), where he was to finish his career and set up home until he passed in 2011.

1973/74

Leeds United won the league, five points clear of Liverpool with an unbeaten run of 29 games clinching it for them. Billy Bremner played in all 42 games, contributing ten goals. Peter Lorimer made 37 appearances, scoring 12 goals. Eddie Gray was out for most of the season with injury, only playing in eight games and scoring once. David Harvey was the first-choice keeper and appeared 39 times.

These four were supplemented by some younger Scots players in the squad. Keeper Davie Stewart had arrived from Ayr United (193/0) in October 1973 and played three games that season. Following a car crash in early 1975, Harvey was sidelined and Stewart took over in the European Cup Final in May of that year. He left Leeds in 1979 (55/0), moving on to West Brom for 18 months without playing before joining Swansea (57/0) and then finishing his playing career in Hong Kong.

Eddie Gray's younger brother, left-back Frank, had begun to break into the first team at Elland Road, making six appearances and netting once in the title year. Frank would also take part in the European Cup Final of 1975 as well as the 1980 final with Nottingham Forest. He joined Forest in August 1979 for £500,000, ending his first stint at Elland Road (193/17).

Joe Jordan joined Leeds from Greenock Morton after a handful of games (6/1) on the recommendation of former player Bobby Collins for £15,000 in 1971. With Allan Clarke and Mick Jones up front, it was hard for Jordan to break through but an injury to Jones saw Joe progress, playing 33 games and netting seven in 1973/74. He left Leeds (170/35) in January 1978 for Manchester United, fetching a price of £350,000.

Gordon McQueen followed Joe a month later to Old Trafford for £500,000. McQueen had joined Leeds from St Mirren (57/5) for £30,000 in 1972 and with the retirement of Jack Charlton he became the first-choice centre-half. Gordon competed in 36 games in the title win and 141 overall, netting 15 goals.

Don Revie would soon depart Elland Road for the England job, and his side began to decline. September 1976 would see Billy Bremner leave the club after 16 years (587/97) for Hull City (61/6). He then moved into management with Doncaster for several years, playing in a handful of games. A return to Leeds started off brightly in October 1985 but after three years Billy was sacked and soon headed back to Doncaster before quitting the game altogether in 1991.

Peter Lorimer remained with Leeds until 1979 (450/191) and enjoyed some time in Canada with Vancouver Whitecaps and Toronto Blizzard over the next few years. Domestically he had a season with York City in 1979/80 (29/8) before returning to Leeds for a final couple of years in 1983 (76/17).

Eddie Gray played on until 1983 (452/52), becoming player-manager in 1982 until he was sacked in 1985 to make way for Bremner. Gray has since served the club in a coaching capacity over the years.

David Harvey, like Lorimer, also played for Vancouver in two different spells, eventually leaving Leeds in 1985 (349/0). Afterwards, he played one game with Partick Thistle, six with Bradford City and three for Morton before moving into non-league football.

The FA Cup Final was won by Liverpool who convincingly beat Newcastle United 3-0. Shortly after the final Bill Shankly announced his retirement although his legacy continues to imprint itself on the club. Bill won three First Division titles, one Second Division, two FA Cups and the UEFA Cup.

Brian Hall and Peter Cormack both played in the final. Hall remained at Liverpool until 1976 and was an unused sub in both legs of the 1976 UEFA Cup Final win (154/14). Brian had a season at Plymouth (51/16) before moving to Burnley for 43 games, netting four and retiring from football in 1979.

Cormack left Anfield shortly after Hall in October 1976 (125/21), signing for Bristol City (67/15) where manager Alan Dicks had a colony of Scots in situ, including keeper John Shaw, Don Gillies, Gerry Sweeney and Gerry Gow among others. In 1980 Cormack went on to play 20 more games for Hibernian before moving into management with Partick Thistle.

Bobby Moncur and Tommy Gibb had both played and scored in the Fairs Cup Final with Newcastle in 1969 and appeared at Wembley that day in 1974. Perth-born Moncur, who captained the side in both finals, was with the Magpies from 1962 to 1974 (296/3). He joined local rivals Sunderland for a two-year period (86/2) before moving into management with Carlisle where he played 11 matches. Bobby then took charge of Hearts, Plymouth and Hartlepool before retiring from the game in 1989.

Midfielder Gibb had started out at Partick Thistle (111/18), joining Newcastle in 1968 (199/12), and like Moncur moved briefly to Sunderland

(10/1) in 1975. He finished his career with Hartlepool (40/4) in 1977/78 before retiring.

Gibb came on in the 75th minute to replace maverick winger Jimmy Smith. Smith had joined the Magpies from Aberdeen (103/21) in July 1969 for a fee of £80,000. At Pittodrie he was known as 'Jinky' for his mazy dribbling skills and on Tyneside he was beloved by the fans too. Recurring knee injuries were to see his career end prematurely aged 29 (129/13).

The League Cup was won by Wolves, beating Manchester City 2-1 at Wembley with goals from Kenny Hibbitt and John Richards; Colin Bell scored for City.

The only Scot on the Wolves side was Frank Munro. Born in Broughty Ferry, Frank's career started at Tannadice with Dundee United (50/14) in 1964, moving to Aberdeen (43/8) in 1966 for £10,000. Initially midfielder Frank caught the eye of the then Wolves boss Ronnie Allen during the summer of 1967 when the Dons became the Washington Whips and Wolves the Los Angeles Wolves as part of an experiment in US soccer. Frank and the Whips lost 6-5 to Allen's Wolves in the championship play-off final with Munro hitting a hat-trick.

Moving to Molineux in October 1968 for £80,000 and stepping back into the heart of the defence, Frank remained at Wolves for nine years (296/14), winning the League Cup and Texaco Cup. A short spell with Celtic in 1977/78 (15/0) followed before he finished his career in Australia.

In between the sticks for City was Glasgow-born Keith MacRae. Keith had started out at Motherwell (119/1) where he was occasionally played outfield by the club. He joined City in October 1973 for a fee of £110,000. Initially he claimed the number one spot, but Joe Corrigan was able to re-insert himself into the team and at one point MacRae went five years without playing a league game. He spent the summer of 1978 with Philadelphia Fury but left City in 1980 after only 56 appearances to play for Portland Timbers. He did sign on at Leeds in 1982 but made no appearances and left the game after this.

Left-back Willie Donachie was a mainstay of the City side throughout the 70s. Willie was already part of the youth setup at the club when he signed professional terms in 1968, making his debut in February 1970. He remained with the club until the decade's end and was part of the team that won the League Cup in 1976.

Denis Law played up front for City that day, having joined at the start of the 1973/74 season after being let go by Tommy Docherty at United. Denis retired after the start of the following season (24/9).

1974/75

Dave Mackay joined Derby County (122/5) as a player from Spurs in 1968. After winning the Second Division title with the club in 1968/69 he moved on to Swindon (26/1) as player-manager. Retiring as a player, he moved full-time into management and was soon with Nottingham Forest but with the sacking of Brian Clough he took over the reins at Derby in October 1973.

Derby won the league with 53 points, two clear of Bob Paisley's Liverpool and Bobby Robson's Ipswich. Captaining the side was Archie Gemmill, who played in 41 of the 42 matches. Joining him in midfield was Bruce Rioch, who had signed for Derby in February 1974 from Aston Villa for £200,000. Bruce was Derby's top league scorer in the title run with 15 goals, playing in all 42 games.

Bruce left Derby in late 1976 (106/34) for Everton, although his time at Goodison was less than a year (30/3) before new manager Tommy Docherty brought him back to the Baseball Ground. His second period at Derby was not as successful and, like many a player before him he caught the ire of the Doc and was frozen out of the side (41/4). Short loan spells followed at Birmingham City (3/0) and Sheffield United (8/1) before he spent the 1980/81 season with Seattle Sounders. He ended his playing days at Torquay (71/6) where he began coaching. It was there he first took on a management role. He then went on to manage at Bolton, Millwall and Middlesbrough with his stock high enough to take over at Arsenal in 1995/96.

The FA Cup Final was won with West Ham defeating Fulham 2-0, although neither side had any Scots on display.

The League Cup Final was won by Aston Villa against Norwich with Bristolian Ray Graydon scoring the only goal. For stalwart Charlie Aitken, following the League Cup Final defeats in 1962/63 and 1970/71, it was a case of third time lucky.

Also in the Villa side was Ian Ross who was brought up in Milton, Glasgow, and joined Liverpool as a youth in 1963 then made his debut for the first team in January 1967. Ian never fully established himself in the side (48/2) and moved to Villa in February 1972 for £60,000. He captained Villa in 1974/75 as they won the promotion out of the Second Division and lifted the League Cup (175/3). By 1976 however Ian was loaned out for short periods at Notts County (4/1) and Northampton (2/0) before joining Peterborough United for a three-year period (112/1). He moved into coaching, first with Wolves from 1979 to 1982 and then Hereford where he also played 15 games. Ian had success when managing Valur to two championships in Iceland in 1985 and 1987. He also took charge of Huddersfield Town in 1992/93 and Berwick Rangers in 1996.

Although primarily a left-back, Bobby McDonald played in the midfield for Villa that day. Aberdeen-born McDonald joined Villa in 1971 (39/3), turning professional a year later. He moved to Coventry City in 1976 for £60,000. Bobby played at Highfield Road for four years with all his games being consecutive (161/14) and was touted for a Scotland place but to no avail. He joined Manchester City in 1980 for £270,000 and appeared in the 1981 FA Cup Final defeat to Spurs.

Duncan Forbes once more captained Norwich as he had in the 1972/73 final. Up front for the Canaries was former Bournemouth goalscoring machine Ted MacDougall. After disappointing periods at Manchester United and West Ham, Ted joined Norwich in December 1973 teaming up with former Bournemouth manager John Bond and strike partner Phil Boyer.

The unused sub on the Norwich bench was Kirkmuirhill-born Billy Steele. Billy joined the Canaries in 1973 but much of his career was hampered by injuries, retiring early in 1980 (68/3). Billy had a brief loan spell with Bournemouth in 1975/76 (7/2) and ventured out to Canada after leaving Carrow Road.

1975/76

Liverpool edged out an excellent QPR team by one point to take the First Division title with 60 points. Tommy Docherty's Manchester United, having won the Second Division the season before, came third with 56 points.

Peter Cormack and Brian Hall, in their last full season with the Reds, played 17 and 13 games respectively in the championship win. Hall contributed two goals and Cormack one.

Top scorer in the league that season was Ted MacDougall, helping newly promoted Norwich to tenth place with 23 goals. However, Ted soon joined Southampton, helping them win promotion from the Second Division in 1976/77 with another batch of 23 goals.

By 1978 Ted had swapped the Dell (86/42) for a return to Dean Court and Bournemouth (52/16). He had a short stint at Blackpool (13/0), and also played abroad in the US and Australia before stints in non-league football. Other than Hughie Gallacher, Ted is the only Scot in the top 40 of the list of all-time English league goalscorers with 256 goals in 535 games.

The FA Cup was won by Second Division underdogs Southampton against the much-fancied Manchester United. At the centre of the Southampton defence in a man of the match-worthy performance was Jim Steele, from Edinburgh.

Jim had started his professional career at Dundee as a teenager in 1967 (75/5). In January 1972, Southampton splashed out £80,000 for him, and he remained at the Dell until 1977 (161/2). Although Steele had a five-game loan spell at Ibrox with Rangers before eventually leaving Southampton, Jim spent the rest of his football career in the States with the likes of Washington Diplomats and Pittsburgh Spirit among others.

Former Scotland international Jim McCalliog provided the assist for Bobby Stokes to score the only goal of the final. Jim had been part of the Sheffield Wednesday side that lost the 1966 FA Cup Final to Everton. Jim had left Wednesday in 1969 for Wolves (163/34) before heading to Tommy Docherty's Manchester United in March 1974 (31/4). This was his second spell with Docherty having played under him with Chelsea in the 60s. However, by February 1975 he was on his way to Southampton and cup glory. Jim spent a couple of seasons with Southampton (72/8) before heading to Chicago Sting in 1977 and brief coaching spells in Norway and with Lincoln City.

The unused sub that day was midfielder Hugh Fisher, from Pollok, Glasgow. Hugh joined Blackpool in 1962 (55/1) and moved to the Dell in 1967 for £35,000. Fisher spent ten years with the club (302/7) and his last-minute equaliser against Villa had kept them in the cup on their way to the final. However, injury saw him benched for the semi-final and final. Like so many of this era, Hugh had played in the States, on loan with Denver Dynamos in the summer of 1975. He wound down his career as player-manager at Southport (60/0).

United were of course led by Tommy Docherty who had joined the club in December 1972. Since leaving Chelsea in 1967, Docherty had an unsuccessful and nomadic managerial career with short spells at Rotherham, QPR, Villa and Porto. However, his time in charge of Scotland had seen his management stock rise and so he took over the reins at Old Trafford. His first full season, 1973/74, saw the Reds relegated but they bounced straight back with a clutch of young stars such as Steve Coppell, Stuart Pearson and Sammy McIlroy. There was a plethora of Scots among his side too.

Alex Forsyth had been bought from Partick Thistle (56/4) in Docherty's first month at United for £100,000. The emergence of Jimmy Nicholl at right-back saw Forsyth lose his place in the side (101/4) and he left for Rangers in 1978, initially on loan but then on permanent transfer in August 1979. His spell at Ibrox saw him play 16 games and score four goals in his loan spell and then only play four times as a fully fledged Rangers player. Moves to Motherwell (19/0), Hamilton (63/9) and Queen of the South (2/0) followed before finishing his career at Junior side Blantyre Victoria.

Dunoon-born left-back Stewart Houston started his youth career at Chelsea with Docherty in charge, signing professionally a couple of months before the manager's departure in August 1967. He spent five years at Stamford Bridge (9/0), heading to Brentford in 1972, initially on loan (15/2) before joining permanently (62/7). Docherty brought him to United in December 1973 for £55,000. Houston spent seven years at Old Trafford (205/13), leaving for Sheffield United in July 1980. After three years (94/1) he left for Colchester United, finishing his playing career there in 1986 (107/5).

Martin Buchan captained the side, but he and Lou Macari were to have a better day of it in the final one year later.

Manchester City won the League Cup, beating Newcastle 2-1 at Wembley. Willie Donachie was still there from the losing side of 1973/74. Leaving the club in 1979, he joined Portland Timbers in the States. He did return to the UK to play for Norwich (11/0) in 1981/82 before moving to Burnley (60/3) and finishing up at Oldham Athletic (169/3). Willie has been involved in a variety of coaching jobs over the years.

Asa Hartford had been on the losing side when Manchester City beat West Brom in the 1970 League Cup Final. He finally left the Hawthorns in 1974, joining City for the first time, for £210,000. After five years (185/22), Brian Clough's Nottingham Forest laid out £500,000 for Hartford in July 1979. Deciding he was the completely wrong fit for his side, Clough hocked him to Everton (81/6) for £400,000 after just three games for Forest, a month later. By October 1981 he was back at City at a cost of £375,000 (75/7). With City being relegated at the end of 1982/83 Hartford left for Fort Lauderdale Sun but in 1984 returned to join Norwich briefly and help them win the League Cup.

On the losing side for Newcastle was Tommy Craig. Tommy had started out at Aberdeen (45/8) and moved to Sheffield Wednesday in May 1969 for £100,000, a British record for a teenager at the time. The midfielder spent six years at Hillsborough (214/38) before moving to Tyneside. After three years with Newcastle (124/22) he joined Aston Villa in January 1978 (27/2). By July he was on the move to the Vetch Field and Swansea (52/9), finishing his playing career with Carlisle (98/10) then Hibs (11/0). Tommy has had a variety of coaching posts over the years, mainly in Scotland, and had a short spell at St Mirren as manager in 2014 having previously coached there.

1976/77

Liverpool won the league with 57 points, one ahead of Manchester City. Peter Cormack, the only Scot at Anfield, was a Liverpool player at the start of the season but by November he had not taken part in any matches and found himself on his way to Bristol City.

The FA Cup was won by Tommy Docherty's Manchester United, beating Liverpool 2-1 with goals from Stuart Pearson and Jimmy Greenhoff. For Docherty it was to be the pinnacle of his managerial career. For all his bluster and self-promotion, the Doc only ever won that one FA Cup, a League Cup with Chelsea, and a Second Division title with United. Within months of the victory, he was sacked after it was revealed he was having an extramarital affair with the wife of the United physio.

Captaining the Red Devils and heading into the record books was centre-half Martin Buchan, still the only player to captain victorious Scottish Cup and FA Cup teams. Buchan started out at his hometown club Aberdeen (133/9) where he won the 1970 Scottish Cup against Celtic. Joining United for a fee of £120,000 in February 1972, he was to spend 11 years at Old Trafford (376/4) before finishing his playing career at Oldham (28/0). Martin managed Burnley briefly in 1985.

At left-back was Arthur Albiston. Edinburgh-born Arthur joined the club in July 1972 as an apprentice, graduating to the first team by 1974/75. Seen as a more steady, reliable player rather than a star, nonetheless Arthur went on to make just under 500 appearances for the club and picked up three FA Cup winners' medals in 1977, 1983 and 1985.

Lou Macari was one of a group of young Celtic players who broke through into Jock Stein's side in the late 1960s and early 70s. They were known as the 'Quality Street Kids' and included the likes of David Hay, Kenny Dalglish and Danny McGrain. Docherty had capped Macari for Scotland during his tenure as Scotland boss and it was no surprise when United splashed out £200,000 for Lou in January 1973 (58/26). A midfielder with an eye for goal, Lou was a very popular player at Old Trafford. He would also be part of the side that would lose the FA Cup Final to Arsenal in 1979.

The League Cup was contested between Aston Villa and Everton, and it was Villa who triumphed in the second replay at Old Trafford. Two Scots graced the Villa side in the first match: Alex Cropley and Andy Gray.

Cropley was born in Aldershot as his father Jack was playing for the Hampshire club at the time (162/3), but he grew up in Edinburgh and joined Hibs in 1968. As part of the 'Turnbull Tornadoes' side from the early 70s, midfielder Cropley is still idolised by many a Hibernian fan. He moved south to Arsenal in December 1974 for £150,000 (118/27). However, by the January he suffered the first of two broken legs and although he was to return to the Arsenal team in the following season, he was unable to retain his place (30/5). By September 1976 Alex was with Villa but in December 1977, he suffered another leg break. His time at Villa (67/7) also saw a three-game loan spell at Newcastle before he headed to Canada to play with Toronto Blizzard (15/0). On his return he signed on at Portsmouth before retiring due to persistent injury issues. It has often been said that the slighty built Cropley was as hard as nails, not unlike the man playing centre-forward for Villa that day.

Andy Gray began his career at Dundee United (62/36) under Jim McLean in 1973 and in season 1974/75 he was equal-top league scorer with Motherwell's Willie Pettigrew in Scotland with 20 goals. Villa bought the 19-year-old for £110,000 in October 1975. In his first full season, 1976/77, Andy hit 29 goals, topping the league scoring list with Malcom Macdonald of Arsenal with 20. Not only would that campaign see him win the League Cup, he also received the PFA Player of the Year and Young Player of the Year awards, becoming the first player to achieve this. Andy was to win the League Cup again in 1980 but as a Wolves player having left Villa (113/54) in September 1979 for £1.49m.

Gray missed the second replay of the League Cup Final and Cropley the first replay. Gordon Smith, from Partick, was involved in the third and final encounter, coming on as a sub in extra time for John Gidman. His cross was diverted into the path of Brian Little to score the winner in the 119th minute. Full-back Smith, not to be confused with the Gordon Smith who would play for Rangers and Brighton, had started out at St Johnstone in 1972 (112/8). He moved to Villa in 1976, spending three years there (79/8). A three-year period at Tottenham followed (38/1) before moving to Wolves in 1982 (38/3). In 1985, after a season spent with Pittsburgh Spirit, he ran down his career at Barnet (22/0).

In the Everton side at centre-back was Ken McNaught. Ken's father Willie had been at Raith Rovers for 16 years from 1946 to 1962 (657/1), gaining five Scotland caps. Ken joined Everton in 1974 and spent three years with the club (66/3) before heading to Villa where he was to win the league and European Cup, although he never emulated Willie in gaining international recognition.

Falkirk-born Jim Pearson, a former St Johnstone team-mate of Gordon Smith, appeared as a sub in the first replay and also played in the second replay for the Toffees. Midfielder Jim joined Willie Ormond's Saints in 1970 and enjoyed four years at Muirton Park (105/40). He then moved to Goodison for four years (93/15) before a brief stay at Newcastle (11/3) where injury ended his career.

1977/78

Brian Clough's Nottingham Forest had scraped into the top flight by the skin of their teeth the previous season and were not expected to flourish in the First Division. However, with a few canny buys including Kenny Burns, Peter Shilton and Archie Gemmill, Clough's team emerged as champions, seven points clear of Liverpool.

When Clough undertook the Forest job in 1975 one of his first tasks was to rescue John McGovern and John O'Hare from Leeds United having signed them in his 44-day reign. With Clough's departure from Elland Road, McGovern and O'Hare were ostracised, playing only four and six games respectively with the latter scoring once.

Club captain McGovern played in 31 of the 42 league games in Forest's title win, scoring four goals. McGovern would also captain the side to two European Cup wins and the Super Cup as well as two League Cups, all without getting a sniff at a Scotland cap.

O'Hare played in only ten of the matches without scoring and would be used sparingly over the next few years, but he was on the bench for both European Cup successes and played in the second game.

Already in situ at Forest was the unlikeliest of footballers, in mercurial winger John Robertson – a scruffy, overweight smoker, but give him an inch or rather a yard and he'd be past you and pinpointing the ball on to a forward's head. John had been with Forest since 1970 but was on the transfer list when Clough arrived. However, in the following years his league appearances were 39, 41, 42, 42 and 42. Often seen as Forest's all-time greatest player, in 1977/78 John was the club's top league scorer with 12 goals alongside Peter Withe, and was to hit the winning goal in the League Cup Final that year too.

Kenny Burns was bought from Birmingham City (170/45) for £150,000, where he had been converted from a centre-half to a centre-forward. Clough reversed this situation, and it worked a treat with Burns playing in 41 matches, netting four times with Forest only losing three times in the league. Burns was also to pick up the Football Writers' Association Footballer of the Year trophy too.

Brought from Derby County for £25,000 and a player, keeper John Middleton, to work once more with Clough and Peter Taylor was two-time title winner Archie Gemmill. Archie played in 32 matches, scoring three goals.

Top scorer in the Third Division was Dundee-born Alex Bruce with 27 goals for Preston North End. This was during Bruce's second spell with the club. He had joined them as a teenager in 1971, spending three years at Deepdale (62/22) before a move to Newcastle in January 1974 beckoned. On Tyneside he was unable to command a regular starting place (20/3) so by August 1975 he was back at Preston. This eight-year spell saw him hit 135 goals in 301 matches and he stands second on the all-time scoring list for the club behind the great Tom Finney. He ended his career prematurely at Wigan (43/7) due to a knee injury aged 33 in 1985.

The FA Cup Final was won 1-0 by Bobby Robson's high-flying Ipswich Town against Arsenal with George Burley and John Wark in their line-up.

Ayrshire-born Burley joined Ipswich as a 16-year-old in 1972, making his debut a year later. The full-back spent 12 years with the club (394/6).

John Wark who had three spells with Ipswich, making 679 appearances and netting 179 goals.

He then played at Sunderland (54/0) and Gillingham (46/2) before heading back to Scotland, starting at Motherwell in 1989 (54/0) before becoming player-coach at Ayr United for two years (67/0). For all intents and purposes Burley's playing career was over from then as he moved into management fully with some modicum of success at Ipswich and Hearts among others before a stab at the Scotland job, which he lasted in for only 14 games.

John Wark is one of Ipswich's most beloved players but he's also a bit of a cult figure among Liverpool and Scotland fans and indeed lovers of the film *Escape to Victory*. Of course, some of it is to do with his goalscoring exploits but mainly it's the moustache. John joined Town in 1975 and in his first period with the club he played 266 games, scoring 94 goals. He left in 1984 for Liverpool where he was to win two league titles.

On the losing side for the Gunners was Willie Young. Central defender Willie had started out at Aberdeen (133/10) in 1967, moving to Spurs in 1975 (54/3). Playing for two seasons under Terry Neill, he moved with the manager to Arsenal. He had several seasons with the Gunners (170/11) and played in three FA Cup finals before moving to Nottingham Forest (59/5) in 1981. Injuries meant that his final club spells at Norwich, Brighton and Darlington saw him compete in only a handful of games for each, calling time on his career in 1984.

As stated, Forest also won the League Cup that season with McGovern, Burns, Robertson and O'Hare all taking part (Gemmill was cup-tied). It took two games to overcome Liverpool with a penalty from John Robertson deciding the tie. McGovern was injured during the first match with O'Hare taking his place as sub and for the full second game.

In the Liverpool team, the only Scot was Kenny Dalglish. The irrepressible Kevin Keegan had left Anfield in the summer of 1977 for Hamburg and the big conundrum for Bob Paisley was how to replace him. For a fee of £440,000, £60,000 less than Keegan was sold for, Dalglish surpassed all expectations and in the coming years was at the forefront of the successes to come to the club. His first season had seen him hit 20 league goals and 31 overall including the European Cup Final winner.

Kenny had been with Celtic since 1969 (204/111), winning four titles and four Scottish Cups. However, it was consistent that he would lose his first League Cup Final in England having lost five out of six Scottish League Cup finals. Over the next decade Kenny and Liverpool would put that to rights though.

1978/79

Liverpool won the title, eight points clear of Nottingham Forest on 68 points. Kenny Dalglish led the charge, playing in all 42 games and scoring 21 league goals, which would be his highest in any season with the Reds. Meanwhile, two more Scots had also become fixtures in the side.

In the heart of the defence was Alan Hansen, signed from Partick Thistle (86/6) in May 1977 for £100,000, and often cited by Bob Paisley as his best transfer. Hansen made his debut in September 1977 and made a total of 18 league appearances in 1977/78, also playing in the 1978 European Cup Final. In 1978/79 he played in 34 matches, scoring once.

Signed in January 1978 for £352,000 was the uncompromising Graeme Souness, known for his tough tackling, but possessing some sublime skill too. Graeme had started at Spurs but moved to Middlesbrough for £30,000 in 1972 without making any competitive domestic appearances for the White Hart Lane club. At Ayresome Park, Souness blossomed alongside Lisbon Lion Bobby Murdoch and had won a handful of Scottish caps. In six years at Boro he played 176 matches, scoring 22 goals. He had played in 15 games for Liverpool in 1977/78, netting twice, and, in 1978/79, 41 games, scoring eight goals.

The FA Cup Final was won by Arsenal in a crazy last five minutes, with Manchester United scoring two goals to draw level from 2-0 down before Alan Sunderland won it for the Gunners in the 89th minute. Still in the defence for Arsenal was Willie Young as the lone Scot.

Martin Buchan and Arthur Albiston were still playing in defence for United, as was Lou Macari in attack. For Buchan it was to be his last final appearance for the club although he wouldn't leave until 1983. They had been joined by two 1973/74 Leeds title winners in Gordon McQueen and Joe Jordan. McQueen had started the comeback with a goal in the 86th minute and was to appear in two more finals for the club.

Jordan was the first of the Scots to depart Old Trafford (109/37), leaving for AC Milan in 1981. He spent two seasons with the Italian giants (52/12), moving to Hellas Verona for the 1983/84 season (12/1). On his return to England he joined Southampton for three years (48/12) before finishing his playing career and latterly beginning his managerial one with Bristol City (57/8).

The League Cup was won once more by Brian Clough's Nottingham Forest, defeating Southampton 3-2. Garry Birtles hit a brace and Tony Woodcock the other with David Peach and Nick Holmes netting for the Saints. John McGovern, Archie Gemmill and John Robertson all participated in the match but for all it was to be their last domestic trophies as players.

Disgruntled at missing out on the 1979 European Cup Final, Gemmill left Forest (58/4) and headed to Birmingham City in August 1979. Remaining at St Andrew's for three seasons (97/12), Archie then spent some time in the States with Jacksonville Tea Men (32/2) before a spell at Wigan (11/0) and ending his playing career once more at Derby from 1982 to 1984 (63/8). Archie moved into coaching initially at Derby but also returned to work under Clough at Forest before managing Rotherham for two years alongside John McGovern.

As to Lawrie McMenemy's Southampton, they had no Scots on show although the future Dundee United manager, the Yugoslav right-back Ivan Golac, was picked.

1979/80

Liverpool retained the title with 60 points, two ahead of Dave Sexton's Manchester United. Again Hansen, Souness and Dalglish all played their part with 38, 41 and 42 appearances respectively and goal counts of four, one and 16. Fellow Scot Frank McGarvey had joined the club from St Mirren (132/52) in May 1979 for £270,000 and returned north to Celtic for the same amount in March 1980 without playing a first-team game.

West Ham won their third FA Cup but for the first time in a final they fielded a Scotsman in Perthshire-born Ray Stewart. Right-back Stewart joined the Hammers from Dundee United (44/5) at the start of the season for £430,000, and scored his first goal from the spot a month later. 'Tonka', as he was christened by the club's supporters, would eventually take 86 penalties overall for the east London outfit, missing only ten. Stewart would score from the spot in the 1980/81 League Cup Final against Liverpool.

Nottingham Forest were going for their third League Cup win in a row but were undone by a goal from Andy Gray, who had joined Wolves in September 1979 from Aston Villa and his winning goal in the final went some way to repaying the club for their outlay. Gray saw Wolves through relegation and promotion (133/38) before heading to Everton and further success in November 1983.

Also in the Wolves side that day was fellow Scot Willie Carr. Midfielder Willie had come to prominence in the Coventry City team of the late 60s, joining the club in 1967 just after they had gained promotion to the top flight for the first time in their history under the guidance of Jimmy Hill. Willie left the Sky Blues in 1975 (252/33) for Wolves. He was a popular player at Molineux as he was at Highfield Road and spent seven years there (237/21). In 1982/83 he had an eight-game stint at Millwall before moving into non-league football.

Starting the game for Forest were John McGovern, John Robertson and Kenny Burns. The 1980/81 season was to be Kenny's last at Forest (137/13) before moving to Leeds for £400,000. Three seasons spent at Elland Road (56/2) were followed with spells at Derby (39/2), Notts County on loan (2/0) and Barnsley (21/0) before heading briefly to IF Elfsborg in Sweden. By 1986 Kenny moved to non-league football and finally quit the game by 1993.

McGovern left the City Ground at the end of the 1981/82 season (253/6) to take over as the player-manager at Bolton (16/0), a position he held for a few years. Other than the Rotherham post he worked in non-league football.

Robertson quit Forest (386/61) for Derby (72/3) in the summer of 1983 for an injury-hampered couple of seasons. He returned to the City Ground for a final 11 games before moving into non-league football. Robertson has since worked in a coaching capacity with former Forest team-mate Martin O'Neill at Wycombe, Norwich, Leicester, Celtic and Villa.

Playing at left-back for Forest was Frank Gray who signed from Leeds in 1979 for £500,000. Gray took part in the 1980 European Cup success but left in 1981 for a return to Leeds under former team-mate Allan Clarke for £300,000 (81/5). With the sacking of Clarke shortly afterwards, Gray found himself under the management of his brother Eddie for four years. He left Leeds (139/10) for Sunderland in 1985 (146/8) before taking a player-coach position at Darlington (85/8). He has had several managerial positions in the non-league game over the years.

On the bench for Forest was unused sub John O'Hare, who was to retire from the game in 1981 (101/14).

* * *

European and international competitions

In **1971** Chelsea ensured that the European Cup Winners' Cup remained in England when their classy side, which included Peter 'the Cat' Bonetti, John Hollins, Alan Hudson and Peter Osgood as well as the Scottish duo of defender John Boyle and winger Charlie Cooke, defeated Real Madrid 2-1 in the replayed final in Athens after the first match finished 1-1. They were also the third London club to lift the trophy; Arsenal would become the fourth in 1994.

Coincidentally, the Blues' glory run began in Greece, away to Aris Thessalonika (named after Ares, the ancient Olympian god of war, just in case you wondered). Like Chelsea, Aris had won their national cup competition for the first time the season previous. In the Macedonia region to the north-east of the country, Chelsea came from behind to earn a 1-1 draw before overwhelming their guests 5-1 at Stamford Bridge.

In the second round, Chelsea headed east again, behind the Iron Curtain, to Bulgaria to take on and defeat CSKA 1-0 in Sofia. The Pensioners, as they were sometimes known, did the same at home to go through 2-0 on aggregate.

The third Scottish stalwart, defender Eddie McCreadie, had his appearances in a Chelsea strip in 1970/71 severely restricted due to injuries but these outings included the two quarter-final matches against Club Brugge. In Belgium the visitors went down 2-0 but back at the Bridge (not *De Brug*) Chelsea turned it on to win 4-0 and go through 4-2 on aggregate.

In the last four Chelsea were drawn against the holders Manchester City, who now had Glasgow lad Willie Donachie bolstering their defence. Unfortunately for City, Donachie couldn't prevent Chelsea from winning the first leg 1-0 in London courtesy of a goal from South African striker Derek Smethurst. Regular City keeper Joe Corrigan missed the second leg at Maine Road through injury and unfortunately for the home side, a calamitous own goal by his replacement, Ron Healey, two minutes from half-time effectively killed the tie.

For all their European achievements including 15 European Cups and two UEFA Cups, Real Madrid never managed to win the Cup Winners' Cup – losing in two finals to British opposition, Dave Sexton's Chelsea in 1971 and Alex Ferguson's Aberdeen in 1983.

Greece had to wait until 1971 until it welcomed its first European final and then it hosted a second one just two days later. On 19 May, a crowd of 45,000 in the Karaiskakis Stadium – named after Georgios Karaiskakis, a military hero from the 1820s Greek War of Independence – saw Peter Osgood give Chelsea the lead after 56 minutes only for Ignacio Zoco, a 1964 European Championship winner with Spain, to equalise in the 90th minute. There were no more goals in extra time and there were no penalties to settle matters so the game went to a replay at the same venue in front of a much lower attendance of 19,917. Incidentally, the first match was not shown live on UK television, thus 'inspiring' several Blues fans to nip across the channel to Belgium where they could watch it on French/Flemish-speaking goggleboxes.

By 21 May the majority of both clubs' supporters had now returned home having booked return tickets on the assumption that only one game would be required, but several hardy Chelsea fans stayed on, apparently sleeping in 'improvised accommodation' around Athens. Their loyalty was rewarded when first-half goals from John Dempsey and Peter Osgood and a solitary second-half reply from Sebastián Fleitas meant that the cup headed down Kings Road and not around the neoclassical Fountain of Cybele. It was Real's first trophy-less season since 1952/53 while Chelsea would not win another major piece of silverware until the 1997 FA Cup Final. Oh yes, and for many people Charlie Cooke was the man of the (second) match.

In defence of the trophy, Chelsea lost to Swedish side Åtvidabergs in the second round on the away goals rule, having earlier eliminated Luxembourg's Jeunesse Hautcharage 21-0 on aggregate.

* * *

Five days after Chelsea's Cup Winners' Cup triumph over two games, Leeds United played the first of three matches necessary to conclude and win the **1971** Inter-Cities Fairs Cup Final. It was their second victory in the competition; the Elland Road side thus became the first British club to achieve more than one success in Europe. They would also lose the 1973 Cup Winners' Cup and 1975 European Cup finals in controversial circumstances.

The successful campaign began with a goal from Peter Lorimer resulting in a 1-0 away win in Sarpsborg, Norway – the birthplace of Harald Dahl, father of the famous Cardiff-born writer, Roald. Back in Yorkshire, Leeds were comfortable 5-0 winners, which included a brace for Billy Bremner plus another goal for Lorimer.

In the second round, Leeds received a visit from Dynamo Dresden, the club affiliated with the East German police, and a Lorimer penalty gave the home side a 1-0 victory. Behind the Iron Curtain, Leeds suffered their only reverse of the campaign, losing 2-1 but going through on the away goals rule.

Round three saw a second visit from a club from the Soviet bloc – Sparta Prague of Czechoslovakia, who were dismantled 6-0 at Elland Road, which this time included a brace from Eddie Gray and one from Bremner. At the Letna Stadium in Prague, Leeds were 3-0 ahead at half-time with Gray netting the first before the home side got two second-half goals to give their defeat a look of respectability.

At the quarter-final stage, Vitória de Setúbal came to Leeds for the first leg and promptly took the lead in the second minute. Lorimer equalised in the 19th minute while a second-half penalty from Irish midfielder Johnny Giles gave United a 2-1 win to take to Portugal. In the port city of Setúbal, a goal from Lorimer in the 17th minute gave Leeds the advantage which they held until the 84th minute when the home side equalised, but a 1-1 draw was enough to take United through to the semi-finals.

Leeds then had to face a trip to Anfield to take on Bill Shankly's Liverpool and in front of a crowd of 52,577 they came away with a 1-0 win courtesy of a Bremner goal in the 67th minute. A crowd of 40,462 were at Elland Road for the second leg which was refereed by Scottish legend Tom 'Tiny' Wharton. The 6ft 4in official oversaw a goalless draw as Leeds progressed to the final, their third in the Fairs Cup in five seasons.

They faced Italian giants Juventus, who were backed by the Fiat motor company, and who in both legs fielded ten Italian players including Fabio Capello, Pietro Anastasi, Roberto Bettega and Franco Causio, plus West German international Helmut Haller. Conversely, the Leeds dozen were a bit more diverse with two Scots, one Welshman, one Irishman and eight Englishmen including stalwarts Jack Charlton and Norman Hunter.

On Wednesday, 26 May the first leg at the Stadio Comunale in Turin duly kicked off but was abandoned in the 51st minute due to heavy rain and a waterlogged pitch with the score at 0-0. Unfortunately, Eddie Gray aggravated a shoulder injury during the unfinished match and so missed out on an appearance in the final.

Two days later a crowd of 58,555 at the same stadium saw Leeds, in unfamiliar red jerseys and red socks, come from behind twice to earn a 2-2 draw. Bettega and Capello netted for the home side while the equalisers came from England right-back Paul Madeley and midfielder Mick Bates – both Yorkshiremen incidentally, as was overlapping full-back Terry Cooper, along, of course, with manager Donald George Revie.

On Thursday, 3 June the second leg also finished all square, 1-1, which was enough to give 'Super Leeds', as they were sometimes called, the trophy on the away goals rule. In front of 42,483 Alan 'Sniffer' Clarke put Leeds in front, typically firing in a low shot from inside the box after 12 minutes, with Anastasi equalising eight minutes later.

Incidentally, while the game at Elland Road was reffed by East German Rudi Glöckner, who had been the man in the middle at that memorable Brazil-Italy World Cup Final 12 months previous, the 10p, 18-page match programme contained an article on 'Tiny' Wharton, who apparently impressed in the semi-final.

With skipper Billy Bremner and Peter Lorimer appearing in the final that gave them ten Euro appearances in total apiece – Bremer missing the quarter-finals, Lorimer the semis. Eddie Gray would miss more than half of season 1970/71 through injury however and his four starts in Europe came in the first and third rounds. As with Leeds' 1967/68 Fairs Cup success, Scots goalie David Harvey would make four Euro appearances including both legs of the quarter-final against Vitória Setúbal. There were also a couple of substitute appearances for a young Joe Jordan at home to Setúbal and Liverpool.

Ultimately, winning the final Fairs Cup competition would offer Leeds some consolation for missing out on the 1970/71 First Division title to Arsenal by one point – a surprise 2-1 home defeat by West Bromwich Albion in mid-April three days after triumphing 1-0 at Anfield in the Fairs Cup semi proving costly.

* * *

Rangers won the Cup Winners' Cup in **1971/72** to keep that trophy in the UK for the third successive season, and during and shortly after their successful campaign three significant members of their squad chose to try their luck down south. Outside-right Willie Henderson headed to Sheffield Wednesday, striker Colin Stein joined Coventry City and outside-left Willie Johnston signed for West Bromwich Albion.

* * *

In season **1971/72** the European Fairs Cup competition was replaced by the UEFA Cup and came under the formal jurisdiction of the European football governing body. The first final of the new competition was an all-English affair – Tottenham Hotspur versus Wolverhampton Wanderers, who had finished third and fourth respectively in the First Division the season previous, and, not surprisingly for that era, both managers were English – Bills Nicholson and McGarry. Four Anglo-Scots joined the party – Alan Gilzean of Spurs and Frank Munro, captain Jim McCalliog and Hugh Curran of Wolves – along with three from Northern Ireland including Coatbridge-born Wolves midfielder Danny Hegan, one from the Republic of Ireland and one Welshman, Mike, whose surname was England.

Spurs' route to the final consisted of them overcoming Keflavík 15-1 on aggregate, Nantes 1-0, Rapid Bucureşti 5-0, UT Arad 3-1 and AC Milan 3-2. By comparison Wolves defeated Académica de Coimbra 7-1, ADO Den Haag 7-1 with Jim McCalliog scoring in the 3-1 win in the Hague, Carl Zeiss Jena 4-0, Juventus 3-2 with McCalliog getting the equaliser in the 1-1 draw in Turin and Ferencváros 4-3, with Frank Munro netting in both legs. Neither English side lost an individual match along the way.

Alan Gilzean was the lone Scot throughout Spurs' successful campaign, save for a cameo appearance by 18-year-old Graeme Souness when he replaced Alan Mullery for the last 20 minutes of the opening game against Keflavík – Souness's only appearance for Tottenham before he headed north to Middlesbrough in 1972.

'Gillie' played in 11 of the 12 ties, missing the semi-final second leg away to AC Milan. The big, likeable striker scored six goals in the Euro run: a hat-trick away to Keflavík then a brace in the return match at White Hart Lane plus the equaliser in the 1-1 draw against UT Arad in the quarter-final second leg in north London. Spurs had won the first leg 2-0.

In the first leg of the final at Molineux, in front of a crowd of 38,362 two goals from Martin Chivers – which took his tournament tally to eight – helped Spurs to a 2-1 win, with McCalliog netting for Wolves. Back at White Hart Lane, 54,303 saw Spurs, with a line-up which included Pat Jennings in goal, Cyril Knowles in defence and Steve Perryman and Martin Peters in midfield, lift the trophy as the game ended 1-1 with skipper Alan Mullery on target and Dave Wagstaffe replying for Wolves.

The only disappointment for the Lilywhites was in respect of their wives and girlfriends who, early on in the competition, had been promised by the club an all-expenses-paid away trip to the final if Tottenham managed to reach it. So the ladies dreamed of trips to Madrid, Paris and Rome – and ultimately it proved to be Wolverhampton.

(Top) Alan Gilzean who was part of the Spurs side that won the 1972 UEFA Cup Final, beating Wolves over two legs.

(Bottom) John Robertson who won two successive European Cups with Nottingham Forest.

* * *

Liverpool are Britain's most successful club abroad, but it wasn't until **1972/73** that they won their first European competition, the recently created UEFA Cup – becoming the ninth English club to lift Euro silverware – and they did so under the management of Ayrshire's Bill Shankly with the help of midfield Anglos Peter Cormack and Brian Hall. Seven years earlier, Liverpool had suffered European heartbreak at Hampden Park of all places when they were beaten 2-1 by Borussia Dortmund in the final of the 1966 Cup Winners' Cup with four Scots – Tommy Lawrence, Ron Yeats, Willie Stevenson and Ian St John – in Shankly's starting line-up.

Liverpool's route to UEFA Cup glory involved defeating four teams from Germany – two from the East (Dynamo Berlin in the third round, 3-1 on aggregate, and Dynamo Dresden 3-0 in the quarter-finals) and two from the West (Eintracht Frankfurt in the first round, 2-0 on aggregate, and Borussia Mönchengladbach 3-2 in the final). In addition, AEK Athens were overcome 6-1 on aggregate in the second round with holders Tottenham Hotspur being eliminated at the semi-final stage on the away goals rule after the tie finished 2-2.

Peter Cormack played in ten of Liverpool's 12 matches in the UEFA Cup run – missing the home game against Dynamo Dresden and the away match in north London – while scoring in the 3-0 win over AEK Athens in Liverpool.

Four of the eight appearances Brian Hall made in the competition came as a substitute for Kevin Keegan (twice), Phil Boersma and Steve Heighway, in the first leg of the final. Hall started both quarter-final matches, netting in the 2-0 win over Dresden at Anfield, as well as the two legs against Spurs in the semis.

The first leg of the final at Anfield was abandoned after 27 minutes due to heavy rain making it impossible for the players to pass the ball to one another. The false start proved fruitful to Bill Shankly who now reckoned that defender Günter Netzer was suspect in the air and thus decided to replace Brian Hall with John Toshack in an attempt to exploit this perceived weakness.

Twenty-four hours later, on Thursday, 10 May, Liverpool won 3-0 with a brace from Keegan and one from Larry Lloyd, but in the return match on 23 May Mönchengladbach were 2-0 up after 40 minutes with Jupp Heynckes beating Ray Clemence twice. Netzer, Rainer Bonhof, Berti

Vogts, Herbert Wimmer and co. could not manage a third goal however to take the match to extra time and so skipper Tommy Smith collected the trophy in the Bökelbergstadion and duly celebrated along with team-mates such as Emlyn Hughes, Ian Callaghan and John Toshack.

Incidentally, in the 16-page, 5p match programme for the Anfield leg (which, of course, is dated Wednesday, 9 May 1973 and with UEFA Cup spelt 'EUFA Cup') there was an advert from Towns Travel Service Ltd and its 'branches throughout Merseyside' for trips to West Germany for the second leg – £26 for a one-day air tour and £36 for a two-day trip.

By the way, please don't ask the two Scotland-supporting authors of this book what they had to shell out to reach Germany for the Euro 2024 finals – at least not within earshot of their wives.

* * *

Sandwiched between the two legs of the 1973 UEFA Cup Final was the 1973 Cup Winners' Cup Final in which Leeds, featuring five Anglo-Scots but no Billy Bremner who was suspended, lost 1-0 to AC Milan in Salonika, Greece. There was much perceived bias towards Milan by the Greek referee who was later banned from officiating for life by UEFA for unrelated match-fixing.

* * *

With Liverpool also winning the 1972/73 First Division they did not defend their UEFA Cup in 1973/74. As it turned out, there were no English Euro successes in that season 1973/74 or in 1974/75 (Spurs lost to Feyenoord in the 1974 UEFA Cup Final while Leeds fans still maintain that Bayern Munich/dodgy refereeing robbed them 2-0 in Paris in the 1975 European Cup Final which featured no fewer than six Anglo-Scots including a livid Billy Bremner). Euro silverware was, however, brought back to 'Blighty' from 1975/76 to 1981/82 inclusive.

* * *

In **1975/76** Liverpool, now under the guidance of Bob Paisley, won the UEFA Cup for the second time. On this occasion the adventure started in Edinburgh at Peter Cormack's old stomping ground of Easter Road. Hibernian won the first leg 1-0 thanks to a 19th-minute goal from Joe Harper, who had returned to Scotland the year previous after a spell at Everton. With ten minutes remaining Ray Clemence kept the deficit to one by saving a John Brownlie penalty. Brownlie would subsequently play for Newcastle United, Middlesbrough and Hartlepool United. In the second leg at Anfield it was 1-1 at the interval before two second-half goals from John Toshack saw the Welsh international complete his hat-trick and help the Reds to a 3-1 victory, 3-2 on aggregate. Peter Cormack and Brian Hall appeared in both games.

In the second round Real Sociedad were trounced 9-1 on aggregate – 3-1 in Spain and 6-0 in Liverpool – while in the third round, against Śląsk Wrocław, again home and away victories were recorded, 2-1 in Poland – the match programme went for £190 at auction in 2024 – and 3-0 on Merseyside. Hall played in all four matches while Cormack got game time in the first leg against the Spanish side and in the second leg against the Poles.

Sadly Cormack's appearances in the Liverpool first team ended in December 1975 following on from a cartilage injury and he would move to Bristol City in 1976 where he would pick up an Anglo-Scottish Cup winners' medal in 1978 as Alex Ferguson's St Mirren were beaten in the two-legged final.

Brian Hall would also leave Anfield in 1976 – moving to Plymouth Argyle – but not before completing his support role in the 1975/76 UEFA Cup triumph. In the quarter-final against East Germany's Dynamo Dresden, the same opponents as in 1973, the Reds battled to a 0-0 draw behind the Iron Curtain with Hall a late substitute for David Fairclough – the striker who would be dubbed 'Super Sub' ironically – while back on Merseyside, Liverpool won 2-1.

In the semi-final against a Barcelona side that included the dynamic Dutch duo of Johan Cruyff and Johan Neeskens, Hall was a late substitute for Jimmy Case in both legs with Liverpool winning 1-0 at the Camp Nou and drawing 1-1 at home.

In the first leg of the final against Club Brugge of Belgium at Anfield, Liverpool found themselves trailing 2-0 after just 15 minutes before three second-half goals gave them a slender 3-2 advantage. In Bruges (three weeks after the first leg, and some 30 years before Colin Farrell and Ralph Fiennes did their stuff) a Kevin Keegan equaliser helped Liverpool to a 1-1 draw and the silverware, to add to their league title won that season. Brian Hall was an unused substitute in both legs of the final.

* * *

Two weeks prior to Liverpool clinching the 1976 UEFA Cup in Bruges, John Lyall's all-English West Ham United lost 4-2 in the final of the Cup Winners' Cup to a Belgian-Dutch combo with François Van der Elst and Rob Rensenbrink sharing Anderlecht's goals in Brussels.

* * *

Just like three seasons previous, Liverpool did not defend their UEFA Cup trophy but instead gave the European Cup a go and thus in **1976/77** they emulated the feat achieved by their good friends Manchester United nine years earlier, by winning the competition. Liverpool also won their tenth league title that season but missed out on a glorious treble by losing to Manchester United in the FA Cup Final.

As a sporting aside, just outside Liverpool at Aintree racecourse, Red Rum won his third Grand National in April 1977 and later that year appeared as a studio guest at the BBC Sports Personality of the Year awards ceremony – which was won by Wimbledon champion Virginia Wade. Not surprisingly, Liverpool were named the Team of the Year to emulate Tottenham Hotspur (1961), West Ham United (1965), Glasgow Celtic (1967), Manchester United (1968) and Sunderland (1973).

In the final at Rome's Stadio Olimpico, Liverpool defeated Borussia Mönchengladbach, who still boasted Berti Vogts, Rainer Bonhof, Herbert Wimmer and Jupp Heynckes plus 1977 European Footballer of the Year Allan Simonsen, 3-1 with Terry McDermott, Tommy Smith and Phil Neal netting. Bob Paisley's winning XI comprised nine Englishmen, with Emlyn Hughes now the skipper, plus Welshman Joey Jones and Ireland's Steve Heighway. The absence of a Scottish contribution would soon be rectified, however, with the signing of a tartan triumvirate like no other in the shape of defender Alan Hansen from Partick Thistle, striker Kenny Dalglish from Celtic, and midfield man Graeme Souness from Middlesbrough.

In winning their third European trophy Liverpool edged ahead of Spurs and Leeds to become England's most successful club in continental competitions, a position they would strengthen over the next 50 years or so.

* * *

The European Cup was retained by Bob Paisley's Liverpool in **1977/78** by defeating another old friend, Flanders' finest - Club Brugge, in the final [the first Belgian side to reach this stage of the competition] and this time the Scots made their presence felt.

As reigning champions, Liverpool received a bye to the 2nd Round where they met yet another old friend, Dynamo Dresden. Whilst the East Germans were brushed aside 5-1 at Anfield in the 1st leg [with Alan Hansen netting the opener], in the return leg Dresden beat Liverpool at the sixth attempt, 2-1, but losing 6-3 on aggregate.

At the last eight stage, Liverpool recorded impressive away and home wins over Benfica, 2-1 in Lisbon's Estadio da Luz with 80,000 watching on, and 4-1 back in Liverpool with Dalglish grabbing the second goal.

In the semi-finals the opposition was Borussia Monchengladbach - yes, them again! [Incidentally, Borussia is the Latin word for Prussia, a former European state that comprised of what today is Germany, Poland, Lithuania and Russia. Similarly, Albion is the ancient Greek name for Great Britain – but I don't know why I'm telling you this as it's Liverpool and not West Brom who are featured!]

Anyway, as with Dresden, this German outfit won their home leg 2-1, with the match being moved to the much larger Rheinstadion in Dusseldorf to accommodate a crowd of 62,000. At Anfield however, the usual suspects [Vogts, Wimmer, Heynckes etc] crashed to a 3-0 defeat [with Dalglish netting the second goal] to lose 2-4 on aggregate.

Wembley Stadium hosted its fourth European Cup final in 1978 but posted missing for Liverpool were Tommy Smith who had dropped a pick-axe on his foot and broken a toe whilst regular striker David Johnston was out due to strained knee ligaments.

In the 64th minute the crowd of 92,500 saw Dalglish receive the ball in the opposition penalty box from a Graeme Souness pass before chipping his shot over Danish keeper Birger Jensen and that solitary goal settled the game. Quintessential Dalglish as YouTube footage will confirm. A Scot scoring the winner at Wembley is always something special to savour, and according to the pen pics in the 40 pence, 32-page match programme Dalglish was 'Probably the best all-round forward playing in Britain'. Agreed.

Kenny Dalglish played in all seven of Liverpool's European Cup matches whilst Alan Hansen got game-time in four [the final plus the two 2nd Round matches and a substitute appearance in Lisbon] and Graeme Souness appeared in three [the final plus game-time in both semi-final matches].

* * *

It was Brian Clough's Nottingham Forest who prevented Liverpool from achieving three successive European Cups by eliminating them at the first round stage before going on to win the trophy itself in **1978/79**. Throughout the competition they utilised, to varying degrees, the services of several Scots including Kenny Burns, Archie Gemmill, John O'Hare, John Robertson and skipper John McGovern. In the first leg of the first round at the City Ground, Forest ran out 2-0 winners while in the return game at Anfield, neither of England's top two international goalkeepers, Ray Clemence and Peter Shilton, conceded and so the Tricky Trees marched on.

In the second round there was no Greek tragedy as AEK were beaten 2-1 in Athens, McGovern scoring the opener after ten minutes, and 5-1 at the City Ground with O'Hare making an appearance. In the quarter-finals Grasshoppers of Zurich were beaten 4-2 in Nottingham having led 1-0 after 11 minutes before a fightback which included goals from Robertson and Gemmill, while in Switzerland a 1-1 draw was achieved – Northern Ireland midfielder Martin O'Neill hitting a first-half equaliser.

At the semi-final stage Forest did things the hard way, drawing 3-3 in the first leg at the City Ground against 1.FC Köln, who had eliminated Glasgow Rangers in the quarter-finals, before winning 1-0 in the Müngersdorfer Stadion in front of 60,000. Indeed, in the first leg, Brian Clough's men were 2-0 down after 20 minutes before storming back to lead 3-2, John Robertson scoring the third, and then conceding a late equaliser.

In the final at the Olympiastadion in Munich, Forest's unlikely opponents were the defensive-minded Malmö of Sweden. The one moment of magic came in first-half injury time when tricky winger Robertson beat two Swedish defenders before whipping in a cross for England international Trevor Francis to head home. And that was that. The trophy was duly lifted by skipper John McGovern – a player with a sack-full of winners' medals in England yet somehow was never capped for his country.

A total of three Scots played in the final – McGovern, Burns and Robertson – with John O'Hare and Archie Gemmill as unused substitutes. While O'Hare had made only one Euro appearance, Gemmill had played in seven of the eight ties and was integral to Forest's progress in the competition. Apparently he was led to believe he would play in the final and so was not a happy (balding) bunny that evening. As the match programme said, 'Archie ist mit Sicherheit einer der besten Mittelfeldspieler in ganz Grossbritannien.' Gemmill departed Forest for Birmingham City a couple of months later but he would be replaced (sort of) by another Scot, defender Frank Gray from Leeds United.

And so Nottingham Forest joined Real Madrid, Inter Milan and Celtic as clubs to have won the European Cup the first time they competed in the competition. They also won the League Cup for the second successive season. Furthermore, Forest became the third English club to win Europe's top prize, and English football (ably supported by Scots, Irish and Welsh players – until recent times) has provided more European Cup winners, in terms of different clubs, than any other nation.

* * *

Nottingham Forest lifted a second successive European Cup in **1979/80** and to date have won more Euro titles than English top flight titles. The route to glory started with another victory over a Swedish club – Östers IF of Växjö (birthplace of tennis star Mats Wilander) – 2-0 at the City Ground followed by a 1-1 draw in Scandinavia.

In the second round Forest defeated Argeș Pitești 2-0 at home and 2-1 away. Incidentally, during the early years of the Cold War, Pitești prison was a home to communist brainwashing experimental techniques, which begs the question – six months after Margaret Thatcher's Conservative Party won the 1979 UK general election, just who was the Muntenian candidate? We digress.

In the quarter-finals it was Soviet bloc opposition again in the shape of Dynamo Berlin who visited the City Ground in the first leg and took a shock 1-0 win back to the German Democratic Republic. Not to be outdone, however, Brian Clough (aka fictional spy Harry Palmer) guided his agents to a 3-1 victory in the return leg at the Friedrich-Ludwig-Jahn-Stadion. Two goals from Trevor Francis and one from John Robertson had given Forest a 3-0 lead at half-time from which there was no way back. Funeral in Berlin for the East German champions.

The semi-final opponents were Ajax, three times winners of the competition in the early 1970s. Skipper Ruud Krol was a survivor of those 'Golden Years'. In the first leg a goal from Francis and a Robertson penalty gave Forest a 2-0 lead to take to Amsterdam's Olympisch Stadion, the venue for the 1924 summer games. Great Britain won but two athletics gold medals in that stadium and on the night Nottingham Forest lost 1-0 but that was enough to keep them on course for the big one – a showdown with Hamburg in the Santiago Bernabéu Stadium in Madrid – curiously, a major sporting city that has yet to stage the Olympic Games having made four unsuccessful bids.

Forest's starting line-up included their four Scottish regulars in skipper John McGovern, Frank Gray, Kenny Burns and John Robertson, with only Burns missing one game in all the previous rounds. John O'Hare also put in an appearance, as a 67th-minute substitute for Gary Mills. O'Hare also appeared in the away win against Argeș Pitești. Other Forest heroes were Peter Shilton, Larry Lloyd, Viv Anderson, Martin O'Neill, Ian Bowyer and Garry Birtles. Trevor Francis missed the final through injury. Hamburg started with nine German players, including Felix Magath and Manfred Kaltz, one Yugoslav in Ivan Buljan, plus Kevin Keegan.

The final produced a solitary goal – a shot from John Robertson ('the Picasso of our game' according to Clough) – which arrived in the 21st minute. This was followed by some resolute defending, during which Kenny Burns picked up his third booking of the competition. The Glaswegian, however, was much more than an aggressive defender with a 'wildman' reputation – he also possessed a shrewd footballing brain, so let's just say that two decades before Games Workshop located their HQ in Nottingham, Burns was the soccer equivalent of *Warhammer* character Roboute Gulliman, Primarch of the Ultramarines chapter – blond, bold and dangerous.

* * *

Two weeks before Forest's success in Madrid, an Arsenal side which included Edinburgh-born defender Willie Young, as well as six Irishmen from across both sides of the border, lost to Valencia on penalties in the final of the 1980 Cup Winners' Cup in Brussels. Arsenal, arguably England's great underachievers in Europe, would have to wait until 1994 to register their second continental success. In 2024, a blue and yellow Arsenal Umbro tracksuit top from the 1980 final sold for £5,000 at auction.

* * *

Such was the advantage given to European nations back in the day that ultimately 'all' Scotland had to do to qualify for the 1974 World Cup finals was win three matches out of four. In late 1972 Denmark were beaten comfortably enough, 4-1 in Copenhagen (there were seven Anglos in Tommy Docherty's starting line-up including goalscorer Jimmy Bone of Norwich City – the Carrow Road club's first Scottish international) and 2-0 at Hampden when nine Anglos got game-time including Willie Carr of Coventry City. In the crunch game against Czechoslovakia at Hampden in September 1973, the home side trailed 1-0 after 33 minutes before goals from Jim Holton of Manchester United and Joe Jordan of Leeds United sent the 100,000 crowd into raptures and Scotland to their third World Cup, their first in 16 years.

In 1974 the Scotland team that appeared in West Germany was arguably our best. Manager Willie Ormond used but 14 of his 22-man squad – nine Anglos and five home Scots as his team defeated Zaire 2-0 in Dortmund with Leeds duo Peter Lorimer and Joe Jordan getting the goals as Manchester City's Denis Law made his 55th and final appearance for his country, drew 0-0 with reigning champions Brazil in Frankfurt on the occasion of skipper Billy Bremner's 50th cap, and drew 1-1 with Yugoslavia in Frankfurt as Jordan scored Scotland's late equaliser to exit the competition as the first unbeaten side to be eliminated from a World Cup. The returning squad, which included game-time players Martin Buchan and Willie Morgan of Manchester United and Coventry's Tommy Hutchison, received a heroes' welcome at Glasgow Airport.

Sandwiched between contrasting appearances at two World Cups, Scotland also won the 1976 and 1977 British Championships. Over the course of nine days in May 1976, Scotland defeated Wales 3-1 with six Anglos in the side, Bruce Rioch of Derby and Eddie Gray of Leeds contributing a goal apiece, Northern Ireland 3-0 with Derby's Archie Gemmill and Don Masson of QPR contributing two of the goals, and England 2-1 as Masson scored the opener – all at Hampden Park.

The following season, with the ebullient Ally MacLeod now manager, Scotland drew the first match, on 28 May, 0-0 with Wales at Wrexham – with eight Anglo-Scots getting game time. On 1 June Scotland again defeated Northern Ireland 3-0 at Hampden – this time with the assistance of nine Anglos and a goal from Gordon McQueen of Leeds. Three days later came the Wembley showdown against Don Revie's England which Scotland won 2-1, the opener being a magnificent headed goal from McQueen. Nine Anglos from seven different clubs got match action. At the full-time whistle on came the Tartan Army including Rod Stewart, down came the goalposts and up came the turf as spirited but harmless football memorabilia-hunting reached an all-time peak, your honour. Let's just say it was all part of the ongoing Queen's Silver Jubilee celebrations and leave it at that.

Argentina 1978. It was the best of times, it was the bloody worst of times. Once again, Scotland had two opponents in their qualifying group – Czechoslovakia and Wales – so just like for 1974, three victories sealed the deal. Wales were beaten 1-0 at Hampden with Archie Gemmill skippering the Scots before reigning European champions Czechoslovakia were blown away 3-1 at the same venue with Joe Jordan, Asa Hartford and Kenny Dalglish netting in front of 85,000. Wales then chose to move their home tie against Scotland to Anfield where two late goals – a contentious penalty converted by skipper Don Masson and a sublime header from Dalglish on his club ground – sent Scotland to South America.

Ally MacLeod said his team *could* win the competition and somewhere along the line this became 'would win it' and thousands of us (including this book's two authors) believed it! And then it all went horribly wrong.

Poor preparations on and off the field, poor accommodation and training facilities and poor performances against Peru and Iran all combined to ensure that once again, Scotland would be home before the postcards (copyright Tommy Docherty).

In the opening match Scotland took the lead against Peru after 15 minutes thanks to a goal from Joe Jordan, now of Manchester United. Peru equalised just before the break and in the second half Don Masson had his penalty saved before Teófilo Cubillas netted a brace to give the reigning South American champions a 3-1 win.

In the second game Scotland drew 1-1 with Iran, the reigning Asian champions, but still they could qualify for the second stage – all they had to do was beat the Netherlands by three clear goals in the third group match.

And so to glorious failure. After going 1-0 down Scotland fought back to lead 3-1 with a goal from Dalglish and a brace from Gemmill, the second a 'worldie', to put the fans in dreamland. Unfortunately Johnny Rep pulled one back for the Netherlands and so the game finished 3-2 to Scotland, who were eliminated from the competition on goal difference, just like in 1974.

This time however there was no heroes' welcome home; indeed, it wasn't just the 15 Anglos in the squad who were glad that the return flight touched down at Heathrow airport first. That said, for many mostly masochistic/delusional supporters, it was fun while it lasted.

From a collector's perspective, the 1970s introduced us to the wonderful world of Panini sticker albums. Unfortunately the album and stickers for the 1974 World Cup were not readily available in the UK at the time (we blame England's failure to qualify – Jan Tomaszewski you have a lot to answer for) and as such purchasing an original, pre-owned but complete sticker album from eBay is now likely to set you back several hundred pounds.

By way of contrast, however, when we open the 1978 album at the pages containing the images of Willie Donachie, Martin Buchan, Willie Johnston and co., we can still hear the ghostly refrains of, 'We're on the march with Ally's Army, we're going to the Argentine…'.

5

1980/81–1989/90

Overview

For a lot of people in the UK, the 1980s are synonymous with 'Thatcherism' and either the pain or the prosperity that Margaret Hilda's premiership brought with it. The early years brought deep recession and high unemployment which exacerbated the north-south divide and which would sometimes manifest itself in the shape of northern football fans travelling to away games in London and being taunted by home supporters waving wads of £10 and £20 notes at them.

The prime minister was not a fan of the beautiful game and when one of the worst incidents of football hooliganism broke out at a Luton-Millwall FA Cup tie in March 1985, she overreacted. The Football Spectators Act was passed in 1989, controversially making ID cards compulsory for fans, although after the Hillsborough disaster that year, as a result of which 97 Liverpool fans ultimately died, the plan was never acted upon.

The Thatcher years also meant privatisation of nationalised industries and utilities, deregulation of bus services, the damaging legacy of the right to buy council housing stock (e.g. a shortage of new social homes) and the discriminatory poll tax. In a lighter vein, however, the decade also gave us power dressing, the launch of Channel 4 television and the music and style of the new romantics (and their successors). Adam and the Ants, Duran Duran, the Human League, Soft Cell, Spandau Ballet, Orchestral Manoeuvres in the Dark and Ultravox all offered 'antidotes' in tough times. Even 'Diamond Lights', a 1987 single by Spurs and England team-mates Glenn Hoddle and Chris Waddle which reached number 12 in the UK charts, helped distract us – and give us a good laugh.

The 1980s, arguably, gave us the greatest football movie in *Escape to Victory* (1981) starring Michael Caine and Sylvester Stallone plus a host of former and current players of the time including Bobby Moore, Pelé, Osvaldo Ardiles, Kazimierz Deyna, Paul Van Himst and Anglo-Scot John Wark – the Gene Hackman of Ipswich Town. The film is about Allied POWs who are interned in a German prison camp during the Second World War who play an exhibition football match against a German team and who, er, escape in the end.

Meanwhile, the small screen chipped in with *The Manageress* (1989–1990) starring Cherie Lunghi as the embattled first female manager of a struggling lower-division men's team. As for real TV football, in the 1980s both BBC and ITV started screening an increasing number of live games. Previously the only regular live football had been the FA Cup and European Cup finals plus the England v Scotland British Championship showdown. In 1988 Jimmy Hill ended his 15-year stint as the main presenter of *Match of the Day* and was replaced by 'Dishy' Desmond Lynam – the housewives' favourite, apparently.

Now time for another quick apology from the two Scottish authors. The 1980s. The Krankies. We're sorry. In fact, we're terribly sorry.

Back to the fitba, and 1981/82 saw the introduction of Jimmy Hill's proposal of three points for a win which was designed to encourage more attacking play, although it was 1994 before it was adopted at a World Cup finals. The first major English club competition to benefit from a sponsorship deal was the League Cup when money from the National Dairy Council in 1982 saw the tournament re-titled the Milk Cup. Subsequent sponsorships have included Littlewoods, Rumbelows, Coca-Cola, Worthington, Carling, Capital One and Carabao. It was 1993 before the new Premier League and 1994 before the FA Cup went down a similar road.

Transfer fees climbed steadily – in October 1981 Bryan Robson went from West Bromwich Albion to Manchester United for £1.5m (a league winners' medal would be achieved 12 years later) while in July 1989 Chris Waddle and his mullet moved from Spurs to French outfit Marseille for £4.25m.

The 1980s also gave us an explosion in the production of football fanzines – strictly non-official, often irreverent publications mostly produced *by* supporters of specific clubs *for* supporters of specific clubs. Campaigning, complaining, cheering and celebrating – all of that and more. Some imaginatively titled fanzines included *The Gooner* (Arsenal), *4,000 Holes* (Blackburn Rovers), *The City Gent* (Bradford City), *The*

Hanging Sheep (Leeds United) and *War of the Monster Trucks* (Sheffield Wednesday).

For the second successive decade, Liverpool were way out in front in terms of the major trophies won by English clubs. Furthermore, it was near neighbours Everton who came next in the silverware table.

Sizeable Scottish representation in the success stories also continued with nine championship-winning squads containing Anglos – Arsenal in 1988/89 were the exception to the tartan rule, managed ironically by George Graham. Conversely, Liverpool's 1985/86 title winners contained six Scots including player-manager Kenny Dalglish. And so it continued in the cup competitions – 16 of the 20 FA Cup finalists having Scots in their line-ups with the 1989 final between Liverpool and Everton being particularly notable with six getting on to the field of play at some point. Meanwhile, for the League Cup the number was 14 with the 1983 final, Liverpool v Manchester United, resulting in six Scots earning game time at Wembley.

In the early 1980s five English clubs – Aston Villa, Everton, Ipswich Town, Liverpool and Tottenham Hotspur – won six European trophies between them, totalling three European Cups, one Cup Winners' Cup and two UEFA Cups. Anglo-Scots contributed to all six successes with at least two players per final.

A dark day awaited however when 39 people were killed and hundreds injured at the Heysel Stadium in Brussels as a result of rioting before the 1985 European Cup Final. As a result, all English clubs were banned from European competitions for a period of five years. Liverpool, whose fans had largely contributed to the disaster at the final against Juventus, were banned for six years. Margaret Thatcher supported the ban, saying 'We have to get the game cleaned up from this hooliganism at home and then perhaps we shall be able to go overseas again.'

Trophy winners 1980/81 to 1989/90

Successful clubs	League	FA Cup	League Cup	European	Total
Liverpool	6	2	4	2	14
Everton	2	1	-	1	4
Tottenham Hotspur	-	2	-	1	3
Manchester United	-	3	-	-	3
Aston Villa	1	-	-	1	2
Arsenal	1	-	1	-	2

Nottingham Forest	-	-	2	-	2
Ipswich Town	-	-	-	1	1
Coventry City	-	1	-	-	1
Wimbledon	-	1	-	-	1
Luton Town	-	-	1	-	1
Norwich City	-	-	1	-	1
Oxford United	-	-	1	-	1
TOTALS	**10**	**10**	**10**	**6**	**36**

After a period of 100 years, the British Championship came to an end at the conclusion of season 1983/84 with all four nations tied on three points each but with Northern Ireland taking the trophy on goal difference.

Scotland continued to be a no-show at the Euros but appeared at the 1982, 1986 and 1990 World Cup finals – the latter making it five in a row – but on all occasions they failed to progress beyond the group stage due to a combination of bad luck, poor finishing, dreadful defending and just by being Scotland.

* * *

Domestic competitions
1980/81

Reigning champions Liverpool had a poor First Division season but were compensated by victories in the European Cup and League Cup. They languished in fifth place, nine points adrift of winners Aston Villa. Villa finished top on 60 points with Ipswich Town four points behind in second.

Three Scots featured heavily in the Villa side with two, Des Bremner and Ken McNaught, among seven players who played in all 42 games. Centre-back Allan Evans played in 39 matches, contributing seven goals. Evans had joined Villa from hometown team Dunfermline (98/14) in May 1977. He was to win, along with McNaught and Bremner, the European Cup and Super Cup with the Birmingham club and spent 12 years at Villa Park (380/51). Unlike his team-mates he was to be rewarded with four Scotland caps and played at the 1982 World Cup finals. Evans left for Leicester City in 1989 (14/0) before plying his trade in the Canadian Soccer League with Victoria Vistas, finishing his career with one league game at Darlington. Evans was later involved in coaching and managed Greenock Morton for a short period in 2000/01.

McNaught played alongside Evans in the heart of the defence. He had been part of the Everton side that lost to Villa in the 1977 League Cup

Final. Ken joined Villa around the same time as Evans but only remained with the club until 1983 (207/8). He moved across the city to West Brom for a couple of seasons (42/1) with a loan spell at Manchester City (7/0) at one point. Ken finished his career at Sheffield United (34/5), retiring early due to injury.

Fiery midfielder Des Bremner started out at Banffshire club Deveronvale before joining Hibernian in 1972 (199/18). He moved to Villa in 1979 for £275,000 and spent five years at the club (174/9) before moving to Birmingham City in 1984 (168/5). He wound down his career with spells at Fulham (16/0), Walsall (6/0), and non-league Stafford Rangers and Sutton Town, playing well into his 40s.

The FA Cup was to be won by Tottenham after a replay against Manchester City with the First Division's joint top scorer Steve Archibald being involved. Steve had a trial at East Stirling (1/0) before joining Clyde in 1974 (65/7). Aberdeen manager Billy McNeill splashed out £20,000 for Steve and he won the Premier League under Alex Ferguson in 1979/80. Always confident in his ability, Archibald left the Dons (76/29) at the end of that season, moving to Spurs for £800,000. Steve had a great first season, combining well with Garth Crooks and won the FA Cup the following year too.

The first match had finished all-square due to a goal in each half by Tommy Hutchison. Fife-born Tommy started out at Alloa Athletic in 1965 (68/4) and moved to Blackpool for £10,000 in 1968. He won promotion with the Seasiders in 1970 but left the club in 1972 (165/10) for Coventry City who paid out £140,000 plus Bill Rafferty. At Coventry, playing primarily at outside-left, Tommy was a popular player with the supporters and spent nine years with the club (314/24). Tommy also spent the summer of 1980 in the US with Seattle Sounders. He moved to Manchester City (46/4) in October 1980 for £47,000 and by the end of the season was at Wembley. He had opened the scoring with a diving header in the 30th minute but deflected a Glenn Hoddle free kick into his own net late in the game.

Season 1982/83 saw Hutchison play in Hong Kong for Bulova before joining Burnley in 1983 (92/4). He signed with Swansea aged 38 and would play his final game for the Swans when he was 43 years old (178/9). Even after that, Tommy played for non-league club Merthyr Tydfil for a further three years. Tommy sits at sixth in the all-time English league appearance list with Graham Alexander the only Scot in front of him.

Also in the Blues side were Bobby McDonald and Gerry Gow. McDonald had won the League Cup with Aston Villa in 1975. Like Hutchison he had joined City from Coventry, also in October 1980 for a higher fee of £270,000. Bobby left City (96/11) for Oxford United in 1983. There he was to win the Third and Second Division consecutively (94/14). From there Bobby went on to Leeds (18/1) and a loan spell at Wolves (6/0) before winding his career down in non-league football.

Glasgow-born Gerry Gow joined Bristol City (375/48) as a youngster in June 1969, making his debut the following year. He was one of several Scots in the side as they won promotion to the First Division in 1976. Like his countrymen Hutchison and McDonald, he joined City (26/5) in October 1980 but moved on to Rotherham in January 1982 (58/4). Gerry had a nine-game spell at Burnley before heading to Yeovil Town as player-manager for a few years.

All three players took part in the replay as did Steve Archibald for Spurs. The second meeting ended 3-2 with Argentinian Ricky Villa scoring his famous goal to clinch the cup for the north Londoners.

Liverpool won the League Cup for the first time and went on to do so in the next three seasons. However, it took a replay against West Ham United to achieve this opening victory. In the Liverpool side were Alan Hansen, Graeme Souness for the first game only, and Kenny Dalglish.

For West Ham, Ray Stewart played at right-back as he had done in the 1980 FA Cup Final. Ray was to net from the penalty spot in the 120th minute of the first match to make it 1-1, and he also played in the replay. Having joined the Hammers in 1979 he was to play for 12 years at the club (345/62) before moving back to Scotland with St Johnstone (17/3) and Stirling Albion (2/0). Ray also went on to manage Livingston, Stirling Albion and Forfar Athletic.

Paul Goddard had put the Hammers in front in the tenth minute of the replay, but Dalglish and Hansen netted in quick succession midway through the first half with the latter proving to be the winner.

1981/82

Liverpool topped the First Division despite a slow start. It was the season that three points for a win was introduced. Remarkably the Reds finished on 87 points, four ahead of Ipswich, but because both teams won 26 games each even in old money – i.e. two points for a win – Liverpool would have still been champions by four points.

Kenny Dalglish played in all 42 games that season, netting 13 goals. Alan Hansen only played in 35 matches without scoring and Souness also 35 but netting five times. In October 1981 Bob Paisley signed right-back Steve Nicol from Ayr United (70/7) for £300,000. Troon-born Steve would not feature in the first team until the following season.

The FA Cup was won once more by Tottenham, again needing a replay to overcome Queens Park Rangers this time. Glenn Hoddle would score the winner from the penalty spot in the sixth minute of the replay.

Steve Archibald was the lone Scot on parade, and although he was to win the UEFA Cup with Spurs in 1984, this was to be the last domestic honour he would land with the club. He left for Barcelona in 1984 for £1.15m and went on to win La Liga with the Catalan outfit in the 1984/85 season as well as playing in their losing 1986 European Cup Final. However, Steve fell afoul of the foreign player restrictions on the Spanish clubs at the time and saw Gary Lineker and Mark Hughes promoted ahead of him. Season 1987/88 saw him out on loan to Blackburn Rovers (20/6).

Archibald moved to Hibs in 1988 and although he only spent a couple of seasons at Easter Road he is fondly remembered by fans of the Edinburgh club (44/5). After Hibs, Steve became a bit of a 'have boots will travel' player, first heading to Espanyol (15/5), then St Mirren (16/2), and in 1992 he played a total of eight league games for Clyde, Reading, Ayr and Fulham. He then moved into a player-manager role with East Fife in 1994 (49/7) which was initially successful, but he was sacked by 1996. In 2000 he took over the running of troubled club Airdrie, but this was short-lived too.

The League Cup Final was contested between Liverpool and Tottenham with the Reds coming out on top winning 3-1. Archibald had opened the scoring in the 11th minute but a late equaliser by Ronnie Whelan took the match to extra time in which he and Ian Rush scored to win the cup. Graeme Souness, as captain, lifted the trophy. Kenny Dalglish, who had hit five goals on the run to Wembley, also played but Alan Hansen was missing due to injury.

1982/83

In what was to be Bob Paisley's last season in charge of Liverpool, they reigned supreme in the First Division, finishing 11 points clear of second-placed Watford. Dalglish once more played in all 42 matches, netting 18 goals in total. Souness played in one fewer, hitting nine goals overall. Hansen only played in 34 games, again without scoring. Steve Nicol played four times.

The FA Cup was won by Ron Atkinson's Manchester United, who overcame Brighton 4-0 in a replay after a 2-2 draw in the first match. Arthur Albiston and Gordon McQueen, who had both played in United's 1979 final loss to Arsenal, picked up winners' medals this time around. Albiston was to play in the 1985 FA Cup Final too.

As for Gordon, due to persistent knee injuries he began to see less game time and left at the end of the 1984/85 season (184/20). He played a further season with Seiko in Hong Kong before retiring from the game. Gordon tried his hand at management at Airdrie from 1987 to 1989 and had some coaching posts before moving into punditry with Sky Sports. Sadly, Gordon passed away in 2023 due to complications from vascular dementia attributed to heading the ball persistently throughout his career.

The most famous contribution to the first match was ex-Rangers player Gordon Smith who, it is often forgotten, opened the scoring in the 11th minute for the Seagulls. Sadly, he is remembered more for his miss late in the game (for more on Smith see the Seaside Celebrities chapter).

Liverpool gained a hat-trick of consecutive victories in the League Cup with a 2-1 win over Manchester United in the final. Irishman Ronnie Whelan scored once more in extra time to give Liverpool the trophy. Dalglish, Hansen and Souness, the latter still as captain, all took part.

As for United, Albiston and McQueen played with the former finishing the match up front due to an injury sustained after the allocated substitute had been used. That sub was Lou Macari, replacing the other centre-back Kevin Moran. Lou by this time was becoming a bit-part player in the side and after 12 seasons at Old Trafford (329/78) he moved on to Swindon Town in 1984, initially as player-manager (36/3) and finishing as a player in 1986. He took the Wiltshire club from the fourth tier to the second and followed this with spells at West Ham and Birmingham City, two stints at Stoke City, plus periods with Celtic and Huddersfield.

Nowadays Lou is well known for his charity work with the homeless following on from personal tragedy.

1983/84

Liverpool won the First Division for the third season in a row and the League Cup for the fourth consecutive time. Dalglish played in 33 matches, contributing seven goals. Alan Hansen competed in all 42 games and managed to score a goal this time round. As for Souness, he played in 37, scoring seven goals. Steve Nicol began to make an impact, playing in 23 games and hitting five goals.

Two other Scots appeared on newly installed manager Joe Fagan's roster: John Wark and Gary Gillespie. Free-scoring midfielder Wark was bought from Ipswich in March 1984 for £450,000. He had won the FA Cup with the East Anglian club in 1978. Only playing in nine games, John scored two goals in the title run-in.

As for Gillespie, like Nicol before him he had to bide his time to make his mark in the Liverpool team. Centre-half Gillespie had started out at Falkirk (22/0), captaining the side aged 17, and moved to Coventry for £40,000 plus a £30,000 appearance add-on (172/6). Liverpool laid out £325,000 for Gary at the start of the season but he would not make his league debut until the following season.

The FA Cup was won by Merseyside rivals Everton, beating Watford 2-0 at Wembley. Both sides had a front two of Scots: Graeme Sharp and Andy Gray for Everton and George Reilly and Mo Johnston for Watford.

Gray had already won the League Cup twice, with Aston Villa in 1977 and Wolves three years later, and had moved to Goodison Park in November 1983 from Wolves for £250,000. As for Glasgow-born Sharp, he had been bought from Dumbarton (40/17) for £120,000 and would develop into one of the most important players for Everton in this period.

Sharp opened the scoring in the 38th minute and it was Gray who added to it in the 51st minute, almost appearing to head the ball from Steve Sherwood's hands as the keeper collected a cross.

Watford's double act of Reilly and Johnston didn't reach the heights they had that season previously. Bellshill-born Reilly had started out at Northampton in 1976 (127/46), joining from his then hometown club, Corby Town. Cambridge United paid £140,000 for George's services in November 1979 (138/36) but a fall-out with the club over wages saw him move to Graham Taylor's Watford in October 1983 at a cost of £90,000.

Arriving at Vicarage Road a month later was Mo Johnston from Partick Thistle (85/41) for £210,000. In their second game together, Watford, who were struggling in the bottom half of the table, beat Wolves 5-0 with Mo hitting a hat-trick and George the other two. George and Mo became a formidable pairing on the field and off. The 'gallus' Mo loved to party alongside the likes of Charlie Nicholas and George often tagged along.

However, the partnership was broken up by Mo wanting to head back to Glasgow and Celtic in October 1984 for £500,000. Although a great goalscorer (38/23), Graham Taylor was probably happy to see him go. Mo did like a drink and the high life, but always trained hard and gave his all on matchdays. He left Celtic in July 1987 (99/52) for Nantes (66/22) in France. Almost two years later and with his contract expiring, Mo talked about heading back to Celtic. Things didn't quite go to plan as Rangers swooped in and offered him a better deal, making him to this day one of the most reviled characters in Old Firm history. He also became the first Catholic to sign for the Ibrox club. His time at Rangers came to an end in 1991 (76/31) as he moved to Everton (34/10) for £1.5m. However, he was soon on the move again on a free transfer to Hearts (35/5) and then Falkirk (41/6). Mo ended his career in the US with Kansas City Wizards in 1996 (149/31), playing for five years before going on to manage at New York Red Bulls and Toronto FC.

As for George, he too soon left Watford for Newcastle (31/10). He only remained with the Magpies for a year before moving on to West Brom for three seasons (43/9). George finished his career back at Cambridge United (20/7) before heading back to Corby and resuming his trade as a bricklayer. Years later George was attacked by a Plymouth Argyle supporter and had part of his ear bitten off. Apparently, it was 'vengeance' for Reilly having scored the winner in the FA Cup semi-final against the Pilgrims back in 1984.

The League Cup was once again won by Liverpool although it would take over ten years for them to lift it again. It took two matches to overcome city rivals Everton with Graeme Souness scoring the only goal in the contest, in the replay at Maine Road.

This was to be Graeme's last season with the club as a player (247/38). Winning the First Division, European Cup and scoring the winner in the League Cup Final was a fitting way to depart. Souness left for Sampdoria (56/8) of Italy in the summer of 1984 for £650,000.

His next role shook the foundations of Scottish and British football as he took on the player-manager role at Rangers (50/3) and scooped up many an England international too. Souness's five years at the club also included the signing of Mo Johnston, before he headed back to Liverpool as manager. Things didn't work out too well at Anfield and Souness would then go on to manage Galatasaray, Southampton, Torino, Benfica, Blackburn Rovers and Newcastle.

Hansen and Dalglish played in both matches of the League Cup Final. For the Toffees, Graeme Sharp played up front but winger Alan Irvine was in the line-up too. Glaswegian Irvine started out at Queen's Park in 1977 (88/9) before moving to Everton in 1981. He had played in every round of the FA Cup run that year but was left out of the final. He departed Everton in 1984 (60/4) for Crystal Palace (109/12). After three years Irvine headed to Dundee United (24/3) and ended his playing career at Blackburn (58/3). In his last season at Ewood Park, Blackburn won promotion to the new Premier League under the guidance of Kenny Dalglish.

Alan went into coaching with Everton and went on to be academy director at Blackburn and Newcastle and has been manager at Preston, Sheffield Wednesday and West Brom. Latterly he was assistant coach to Alex Neil at Norwich, as well as having a caretaker manager stint at Carrow Road, and Davie Moyes at West Ham. He also became part of the Scotland coaching setup under Stevie Clarke.

1984/85

Everton won the league for the first time in 15 years and lifted the European Cup Winners' Cup but lost the FA Cup Final to Manchester United. Liverpool were First Division runners-up with 77 points, a full 13 behind their dominant rivals.

Graeme Sharp played in 36 matches of the title run, scoring 21 goals. Andy Gray competed in 26, netting five times, but unlike Sharp he would not be around for the championship in 1986/87. With the signing of Gary Lineker, Andy became surplus to requirements and left Everton in the summer of 1985 (49/14) for £150,000. His two seasons at Villa were not as successful as before (54/5) and included a goalless four-game loan at Notts County. This was followed by spells at West Brom (35/10), Rangers (14/5) and non-league Cheltenham Town.

Topping the scoring charts in the Fourth Division with 31 goals was Elgin-born John Clayton. John joined Derby County in 1978 aged 17 and spent four years there (24/4). Season 1982/83 was spent in Hong Kong with Bulova (26/14) before returning to the UK and Chesterfield (33/5). The 1984/85 season saw him at Tranmere (47/35) where he hit his 31 goals. Plymouth Argyle of the Third Division paid out £24,000 for his services (77/21). However, by 1988 John moved to the Netherlands and Fortuna Sittard for £65,000. He spent four years in the Dutch leagues – two with Fortuna (47/16) and then with FC Volendam (61/18). His last hurrah in English football was with Burnley (3/1) before retiring early due to back problems. John has since been involved in coaching, mainly with Bristol City.

As stated, the FA Cup was won by Manchester United, beating Everton 1-0 thanks to a goal in extra time by Norman Whiteside. Arthur Albiston was to win his third and final FA Cup with the club after successes in 1976/77 and 1982/83. He would straddle the Tommy Docherty, Ron Atkinson and the beginning of the Alex Ferguson eras at Old Trafford before leaving in 1988 after 14 years (379/6). Albiston joined old boss Atkinson at West Brom (43/2) and after all those years with the Red Devils he became quite nomadic with spells at Dundee (10/0), Chesterfield (3/1), Chester City (68/0), Molde of Norway (24/3) and finally one game for Ayr United and finished his days playing non-league football.

Also in the United line-up was the wily, ginger-nutted Gordon Strachan. The Edinburgh-born midfielder had started out at Dundee as a youth, progressing to the first team in 1974. Following relegation for the club (69/13) Strachan was on his way to Aberdeen in November 1977. Billy McNeill was in charge at the time, laying out £50,000 for Gordon. It was all change in the summer of 1978 as McNeill moved to Celtic and Alex Ferguson took over the Dons. Over the next six years Strachan was to win two titles, three Scottish Cups, the Cup Winners' Cup and the European Super Cup.

In the summer of 1984 Ron Atkinson splashed out £500,000 for Strachan but the FA Cup win was their only success. By November 1986 Atkinson was out and Ferguson was in. Strachan and Fergie didn't always see eye-to-eye and by March 1989 Gordon would leave Old Trafford (160/33) for Leeds United and greater success. Playing for the Toffees in the final were striking duo Graeme Sharp and Andy Gray.

The League Cup was won by Norwich City, beating Sunderland. Remarkably both teams were to be relegated that season too. Lining up for Norwich in midfield was the evergreen Asa Hartford who had won the competition previously with Manchester City in 1976

After a summer of playing at Fort Lauderdale Sun in 1984, Asa returned to the UK and signed on at Norwich for a season (28/2) and it was to be his shot that was deflected into the net by Sunderland's Gordon

Chisholm. Following on came playing and coaching at Bolton (81/8) and player-manager roles at Stockport County (45/0) and Shrewsbury Town (25/0) where he hung up his boots in 1991. In between the latter two was a playing stint at Oldham (7/0).

Glasgow-born central defender Gordon Chisholm joined Sunderland aged 18 in 1978 and spent seven years at the club (197/10). He moved on to Hibs in September 1985 for £65,000, making a goalscoring debut v Rangers in the Scottish League Cup semi-final. However, Hibs were to lose to Aberdeen in the final. After two years at Easter Road (59/4) Chisholm moved to Dundee (155/15) and finished his playing days with Partick Thistle in 1992 (9/0).

Moving into coaching and management, Chisholm took charge at Dundee United at one point. The high point, though, was as manager of Queen of the South when he took the Dumfries side to the Scottish Cup Final, narrowly losing 3-2 to Rangers in 2008. Chisholm's team gained entry to the UEFA Cup but lost out to Danish club FC Nordsjælland in the qualifying round. Chisholm also went on to manage Dundee.

Up front for Sunderland was striker Ian Wallace. Glasgow-born Ian started out at Junior side Yoker Athletic before signing with Dumbarton in 1974 (34/11). Coventry paid out £70,000 for Wallace in August 1976. In three of his four seasons at Highfield Road (130/58) he emerged as the club's top scorer. A similar pattern was to follow at Nottingham Forest after his £1.5m move there in July 1980 although his goal return was not as high (134/36).

A season at Brest in France followed (16/3) before heading to Sunderland for a short stint (34/6). The 1986/87 season was spent at Marítimo in Portugal (9/0) before finishing that year with Melbourne Croatia in Australia (24/6). Latterly, Ian took charge of Dumbarton for a few seasons from 1996 to 1999.

1985/86

Kenny Dalglish took over as Liverpool's player-manager after the departure of Joe Fagan over the summer of 1985 following the Heysel Stadium disaster. In his first season Liverpool achieved the First Division and FA Cup double for the only time in their history. Kenny himself only played in 21 league games, scoring three goals. Alan Hansen played in 41 without netting. Gary Gillespie 14, hitting three goals. Stevie Nicol played 34 times with four goals.

Andy Gray, a title winner with Everton where he also won the FA Cup and the European Cup Winners' Cup.

John Wark had enjoyed a great second season at Liverpool, finishing top scorer with 27 goals in all competitions. However, injuries saw him only play in nine games in the league-winning campaign, scoring three goals.

Kevin MacDonald had joined the ranks of Scots at the club having been signed by Joe Fagan in November 1984 for £400,000 from Leicester. Kevin started out at hometown club Inverness Caledonian, joining Leicester at the age of 16 (138/8). He spent five years at Anfield but could never command a regular spot in the team (40/1) and had been loaned out twice to Leicester (3/0) and Rangers (3/0). Kevin moved to Coventry in 1989 for two years (31/0) which included a loan spell at Cardiff (8/0) before winding his career down at Walsall from 1991 to 1993 (53/7). Kevin moved into coaching and has been taken on as a caretaker manager at Leicester, and three spells at Aston Villa. He was also assistant coach of the Republic of Ireland during Steve Staunton's tenure and had a short-term period in charge of Swindon Town.

Liverpool beat Everton 3-1 in the FA Cup Final with Ian Rush hitting a brace and South African Craig Johnston also netting. Gary Lineker had opened the scoring for the Toffees. Dalglish, Hansen and MacDonald all played as did Sharp for Everton.

The League Cup was won by Oxford United, beating Queens Park Rangers 3-0. Scoring one of the three goals was Ray Houghton. Born in Glasgow, Houghton had made his first international appearance in March 1986, the month before the final. He had been selected for Scotland's youth sides, but a full cap was not forthcoming, and he took the opportunity to play for the Republic of Ireland under Jack Charlton. Ray had moved to London aged ten and was a youth player with West Ham but couldn't break into the first team, making only one appearance. He signed on at Fulham in 1982 and spent three years there (129/16) before Oxford bought him for £147,000 in September 1985. Ray was to move to Liverpool in 1987.

No other Scots took part in the final.

1986/87

Everton won the league once more on 86 points, nine clear of second-placed Liverpool. Graeme Sharp only played in 27 games, contributing five goals. He was among several Everton players to miss matches due to injuries, but the resilience of Howard Kendall's side shone through. Sharp was to have a better season in 1987/88, netting 13 times in 32 games and being chosen in the PFA Team of the Year. He also played in the 1989 FA Cup Final.

Coventry City were to win the FA Cup for the first and so far only time, beating Spurs 3-2 after extra time. After years of a smattering of Scots at Highfield Road there were none in this side, although the scorer of the second goal, Keith Houchen, did later have a spell with Hibs from 1989 to 1991.

Captaining Tottenham in his only full season with the club was Richard Gough. Born in Stockholm to his Swedish mother, Gough was brought up in South Africa but qualified for Scotland through his Glaswegian father. Charlie Gough had a brief football career with Charlton (4/0) before moving to play in South Africa with Highland Park.

Richard started out at Jim McLean's Dundee United (165/23) as a right-back and won the Scottish Premier Division in 1982/83 then reached the semi-finals of the European Cup before moving to Tottenham for £750,000 in 1986 (49/2). Rangers paid out £1m at the start of the 1987/88 season and Gough went on to captain them to nine consecutive titles and numerous other domestic trophies (294/25). He played alongside Mo Johnston at Kansas City Wizards in 1997 (17/0) before a short return to Rangers (24/1). The 1998/99 season saw him in the US again with San Jose Clash (19/2) followed by a loan spell at Nottingham Forest (7/0) before finishing his playing career at Everton (38/1). Gough did take charge at Livingston for a short period in 2004/05.

The League Cup was won by George Graham's Arsenal, beating Liverpool 2-1 with two goals from 'Champagne' Charlie Nicholas. Graham, a 1971 Arsenal double winner, began his management career at Millwall, with whom he won promotion to the second tier in 1984/85. Installed as manager at Highbury in May 1986, he quickly began to develop his style built on a solid defence and during his second title win with the club in 1990/91 his side only conceded 18 goals in 38 matches. Graham was to lead Arsenal to two championships, the FA Cup, two League Cups and the Cup Winners' Cup.

Charlie Nicholas arrived at Arsenal for £750,000 in June 1983. Starting out at Celtic (74/48), he played two matches in the 1979/80 season, netting twice, before hitting 16 goals in 29 games the following campaign. Some loss of form and a broken leg curtailed his third year, but he bounced back to score 48 goals in 53 games overall for the Glasgow club the following term.

There were plenty of clubs competing for his signature, in particular Liverpool, but Charlie opted for Arsenal and the bright lights of London. It is true that perhaps the Gunners didn't get the best out of Charlie and maybe his style might have suited Liverpool better, but he is still idolised by many fans of that era. As supporters we often want consistency from players but it's moments of magic we crave and recall most. Ironically the two goals in this match were probably the scrappiest of his career but they gave Arsenal their first trophy since the 1979 FA Cup. With George Graham looking at a more disciplined structured team, the writing was soon on the wall for Charlie, and he was to leave Highbury in 1988 (151/34).

Charlie headed north to Aberdeen where he played for two seasons (77/30), winning both the Scottish Cup and League Cup. However, he chose to return to Celtic where he played for five years without gaining further honours (112/37) and finished his career at Clyde in 1995/96 (31/5).

On the losing Liverpool side were Gary Gillespie, captain Alan Hansen, and used substitutes Kenny Dalglish and John Wark.

1987/88

Liverpool regained the title with 90 points, nine clear of second-placed Manchester United. Captain Alan Hansen made 39 appearances, scoring once. Steve Nicol played 40, netting six with Gary Gillespie on four from 35 appearances. As for player-manager Dalglish, he competed in two games all season without scoring. Kevin MacDonald and John Wark played a game apiece without netting.

Leaving in January 1988 (70/28), Wark returned to Portman Road and Ipswich for £100,000. Ipswich were a second-tier club at the time and John remained for three seasons (89/23) before moving to Middlesbrough in 1990/91 (32/2). A final return to Ipswich (154/18) occurred the following year and John played his last match for the club in November 1996 aged 39.

Ray Houghton had been bought by Liverpool for £825,000 from Oxford United, with whom he won the 1986 League Cup, in October 1987. Ray played in 28 games, bagging five goals.

The FA Cup was won by underdogs Wimbledon beating Liverpool 1-0 thanks to a Lawrie Sanchez goal. The 'Crazy Gang' as they were dubbed had no Scots on display. They were managed by former striker Bobby Gould who is best remembered for his spells with Coventry, Wolves, Arsenal and West Ham. His son Jonathan would go on to be capped for Scotland as his grandparents originally hailed from Blantyre in Lanarkshire.

Kenny Dalglish fielded Nicol, Gillespie, Hansen and Houghton in his starting line-up at Wembley.

The League Cup was also won by an unfancied team in Luton Town, who beat George Graham's Arsenal 3-2. No Scots were in either team although two of the losing Arsenal side did play in Scottish football in the 90s. Forward Martin Hayes, who scored the Gunners' opener, joined Celtic for £650,000 in September 1990. Defender Gus Caesar turned up at Broomfield, home of Airdrie, in 1992 (57/1) and appeared in the 1992 Scottish Cup Final defeat to Rangers. Later, he played one match as a trialist for Partick Thistle in 1997.

1988/89

George Graham's Arsenal won the title for the first time since 1970/71, featuring no Scots. The Gunners, needing to defeat challengers Liverpool in their final match by two clear goals at Anfield, did just that thanks to a late second goal by Michael Thomas.

The spectacle of the FA Cup was diminished by the tragedy of the Hillsborough disaster at the semi-final as Liverpool took on Nottingham Forest. It was perhaps fitting that the final took place between Liverpool and Everton with the entire Merseyside city united in grief.

Liverpool won the trophy 3-2 after extra time. John Aldridge had given them an early lead in the fourth minute but a goal with the last kick of the 90 minutes from Stuart McCall put the game into extra time. Ian Rush put the Reds in front only for McCall to equalise again. Rush netted the winner a couple of minutes later and so the cup went back to Anfield for the fourth time.

Alan Hansen, Steve Nicol and Ray Houghton were the Scots in Dalglish's Liverpool line-up.

Graeme Sharp was still leading the line for the Toffees. He was to leave the club in 1991 after 11 years (322/111) and is one of the most beloved players of this era for Everton. He joined Oldham Athletic where he spent six years, latterly as player-manager (107/30), after which a short spell at Bangor City followed.

On the right wing for Everton was Pat Nevin, a creative player with the deftest of touches. Pat had started at Clyde having been rejected by Celtic for being too small. He spent two years with the Bully Wee (73/17) when Chelsea paid out £95,000 for his services in July 1983. Chelsea were promoted as champions of the Second Division with Pat playing in 38 of the 42 matches, contributing 14 goals and no doubt numerous assists to strikers Kerry Dixon and David Speedie. He left Chelsea (193/36) after they were relegated at the end of the 1987/88 season. Everton swooped for Nevin, capturing him for a fee of £925,000 (109/16).

Pat had scored the only goal of the semi-final against Norwich City. However, by 1992 Pat did not see eye-to-eye with newly installed manager Howard Kendall. He took the ferry over the Mersey to Prenton Park for £300,000 and enjoyed several years with Tranmere Rovers (193/30).

Nevin then headed to Kilmarnock (34/6) in 1997 and finished his playing career at Motherwell (58/2) where he also took on the role of CEO. Pat is still involved in football through the media.

Both subs fielded by Everton were Scots. Stuart McCall was to make his impact on the game, scoring both of their goals. His father, Hamilton-born Andy, had played professionally in England for Blackpool, West Brom, Leeds and Halifax Town.

As to Leeds-born Stuart, he joined Bradford City in 1980, although it took a few years to break into the side, and he was an integral part of the team that won the Third Division in 1985. He left Bradford (238/37) in the summer of 1988 for Everton at a fee of £850,000.

It was three years later that Rangers offered £1.2m for the bustling midfielder and so his time at Goodison came to an end without lifting any silverware (103/6). At Rangers he won five league titles, three Scottish Cups and two League Cups (194/14) before being allowed to return to Bradford for free in 1998. City managed to gain promotion to the Premier League in his first season back. Despite relegation two years later, Stuart remained with the Bantams (157/8) until a move to Sheffield United in 2002. He spent three playing years at Bramall Lane (71/2) and another two as assistant manager to Neil Warnock when the opportunity to manage Bradford came about. Stuart has had three periods in charge at Valley Parade and has also managed at Motherwell, Rangers and Scunthorpe.

The other sub in the FA Cup Final was Aberdonian Ian Wilson. Ian had been a youth player at Aberdeen and Dundee without making the grade, so moved to Elgin City. Leicester City paid £20,000 for Ian in 1979, a record fee for a Highland League player at the time.

He spent eight years at Filbert Street and captained the side during his days there (285/17). He moved to Everton for £300,000 in September 1987. Although he played in the FA Cup Final, Wilson was not getting a regular place in the team (34/1) and in the following year he moved on to Beşiktaş in Turkey (20/1). There he won the league and cup double. Following on from this Ian played at Derby (11/0), Bury (24/0) and Wigan (5/0). He finished his playing career at Peterhead and has also managed the Blue Toon on a few occasions.

The League Cup was won by a resurgent Nottingham Forest, still managed by Brian Clough, beating Luton Town 3-1.

At centre-back alongside Des Walker was Terry Wilson. Born in Broxburn in West Lothian, Wilson joined Forest as a youth and made his first-team debut in May 1987. He was on the bench for the League Cup win the following season too.

Unused sub Lee Glover, although born in Kettering, opted to play for Scotland and was to win three Scotland under-21 caps. He missed out on the 1990 League Cup Final but was involved in the 1991 FA Cup Final.

On the losing Luton side was Dave Beaumont, a product of Dundee United's youth setup. The Dunfermline-born defender joined United in 1978 aged 15 and made his breakthrough in his early 20s. However, he was deputising for the likes of the central pairing of David Narey and Paul Hegarty as well as full-backs Richard Gough and Maurice Malpas. Beaumont was a substitute in the first leg of the 1987 UEFA Cup Final and had played in the majority of matches that season, but he left United in 1989 (87/3) for Luton. He only had a couple of seasons at Kenilworth Road (76/0) before moving back to Scotland and Hibs. There he was an unused sub in the 1991/92 League Cup victory over hometown team Dunfermline, but injury was to see him retire early from the game in 1994 (70/2).

1989/90

Liverpool won the title for the 18th time; however, their 19th would not come until 2020. They gained 79 points, nine clear of Aston Villa in second place.

Kenny Dalglish, with the championship secure, played his one and only game that season at Anfield on 1 May 1990. This was to be Kenny's

355th and final appearance for Liverpool having netted 118 times. He is one the few players to have scored over 100 league goals in both Scotland and England. Kenny was to resign his post as Liverpool manager in February 1991 with the club at the top of the table and still in the FA Cup. At the time, he put his resignation down to the stress of everyday managing a team like Liverpool. Having taken over the day after the Heysel disaster and led the club through the trauma of Hillsborough with such grace and dignity, he had more than deserved what was to be an eight-month sabbatical from football. In his time at Liverpool Dalglish won eight titles, three European Cups, two FA Cups and four League Cups. His next championship win would come as Blackburn manager in the 1994/95 Premier League season.

Playing alongside and under Kenny in all those wins was Alan Hansen, with the exception of one League Cup. The 1989/90 title was to be his final honour too. Alan played in 31 games that season, but these were to be his last for the club as injuries prevented him from playing the following season and he announced his retirement a month after Kenny's departure (434/8). Alan, of course, went on to have a long career in television on the BBC's *Match of the Day* programme.

For Gary Gillespie it was also to be his last trophy. Gary played in only 13 games that season, netting four goals. Although he took part in 31 games in 1990/91, with new manager Graeme Souness firmly in place he was seen as surplus to requirements and moved to Celtic for £925,000 in August 1991. In three years at Celtic, due to recurring injuries, Gillespie only played in 69 games for the club, scoring twice, and he did not win any silverware. Gary finished his career back at Coventry where he could only manage three appearances and eventually quit the game in 1997.

Steve Nicol played in 23 matches and scored six goals in the title win. Ray Houghton played 19, netting just the once. Both were to win the FA Cup in 1992 with Liverpool.

The 1990 FA Cup success was pivotal in Alex Ferguson's Manchester United career. After three years in charge at Old Trafford, the former Aberdeen manager was without a trophy with fans and the press alike clamouring for his dismissal. It would take a replay to overcome a Crystal Palace side with the likes of Mark Bright, John Salako and Ian Wright in their ranks. Two Scots were on show, both playing for United.

In goals was a former Aberdeen man who had served Fergie so well at Pittodrie – Jim Leighton. Johnstone-born Leighton joined the Dons in

1977, being loaned out to Deveronvale of the Highland League shortly after. At Aberdeen (301/0) he was to win two titles, four Scottish Cups, one League Cup as well as the Cup Winners' Cup and European Super Cup. Fergie signed Leighton for United in 1986 for £750,000 and initially things went well but in the first match of the final Jim was blamed by his manager for the loss of a couple of the goals in the 3-3 draw and he was sensationally replaced by Les Sealey for the replay. After this Leighton was only to play for United on one more occasion (73/0). Loan spells to Arsenal (0/0) and Reading (8/0) followed before finally leaving Old Trafford for Dundee (21/0) in 1992. Jim's career was fully resurrected during his time at Hibs from 1993 to 1997 (151/0), also returning to the Scotland team. Jim ended his career at Aberdeen (82/0), retiring in 2000.

Up front for United was Brian McClair. Bellshill-born Brian had started out at Aston Villa but failed to make the grade and returned to Scotland, signing for Motherwell in 1981 (40/15). A move to Celtic followed where he was to win the Scottish Cup and Premier Division (145/99). United paid out £850,000 for McClair in July 1987 and Brian was to spend 11 years at Old Trafford, taking part in many of their accomplishments in the 1990s.

United won the replay with full-back Lee Martin scoring the only goal and so the Fergie era was allowed to continue and blossom.

As to the League Cup Final, once more Nottingham Forest were to contest it, defeating Oldham Athletic 1-0 thanks to a Nigel Jemson goal. Terry Wilson was an unused substitute. However, despite twice being a PFA Young Player of the Year nominee, Wilson began to fall out of favour at Forest. He had loan spells at Hønefoss BK in Norway and then a two-game spell at Newcastle in 1992. A knee injury saw his time at Forest come to an end in 1993 and he moved into non-league football with Rushden & Diamonds and later won the Scottish Junior Cup with Whitburn.

* * *

European and international competitions

For the third successive season, England was represented in the European Cup by Liverpool and Nottingham Forest. However in **1980/81** it was the holders Forest who were eliminated in the first round, by CSKA Sofia, while the Anfield outfit went on to win the competition for the third time and in so doing became part of Europe's super elite along with the likes of other three-times winners Ajax and Bayern Munich and six-times champions Real Madrid.

In the first round Liverpool overwhelmed Finnish side Oulun Palloseura 11-2 on aggregate, although that included a 1-1 draw in the first leg in the resort town of Oulu in the Gulf of Bothnia. The 10-1 hammering at Anfield included a hat-trick for Graeme Souness as well as a treble for Terry McDermott.

The second round pitted the Reds of Anfield against the Reds of Aberdeen. Alex Ferguson's Scottish champions were beaten home and away, 1-0 at Pittodrie and 4-0 in Liverpool with Kenny Dalglish and Alan Hansen netting the third and fourth goals.

In the quarter-finals, Liverpool beat CSKA Sofia home and away – 5-1 at Anfield with Souness grabbing another hat-trick, and 1-0 in Bulgaria. In the semi-finals, it was a clash of the titans as Liverpool squared-up to Bayern Munich and two drawn matches were fought out, 0-0 on Merseyside then 1-1 in Bavaria, with the English champions just shading it on the away goals rule. Ray Kennedy had given the visitors to the Olympiastadion the lead after 83 minutes with Karl-Heinz Rummenigge equalising two minutes from time. Apparently Liverpool were given an added incentive when prior to kick-off it was discovered that pamphlets were being distributed to home supporters advising on travel arrangements for the final.

And so to the Parc des Princes in Paris on 27 May where Liverpool defeated Real Madrid whose starting XI featured former Borussia Mönchengladbach midfielder Uli Stielike and ex-West Bromwich Albion winger Laurie Cunningham. Kenny Dalglish and Alan Kennedy had recently returned from injury while the latter scored the only goal of the game eight minutes from time and Bob Paisley, the English manager with the Scottish surname, became the first boss to win the European Cup three times.

Dalglish and Hansen played in all nine of Liverpool's ties with Souness missing the first leg of the semi-final through injury. Souness's tally of six goals made him the tournament's joint top goalscorer that season alongside team-mate Terry McDermott and Bayern's Rummenigge. Skipper Phil Thompson collected the trophy, as he had done with the League Cup the month previous, however early in the following season the captaincy would be given to Souness.

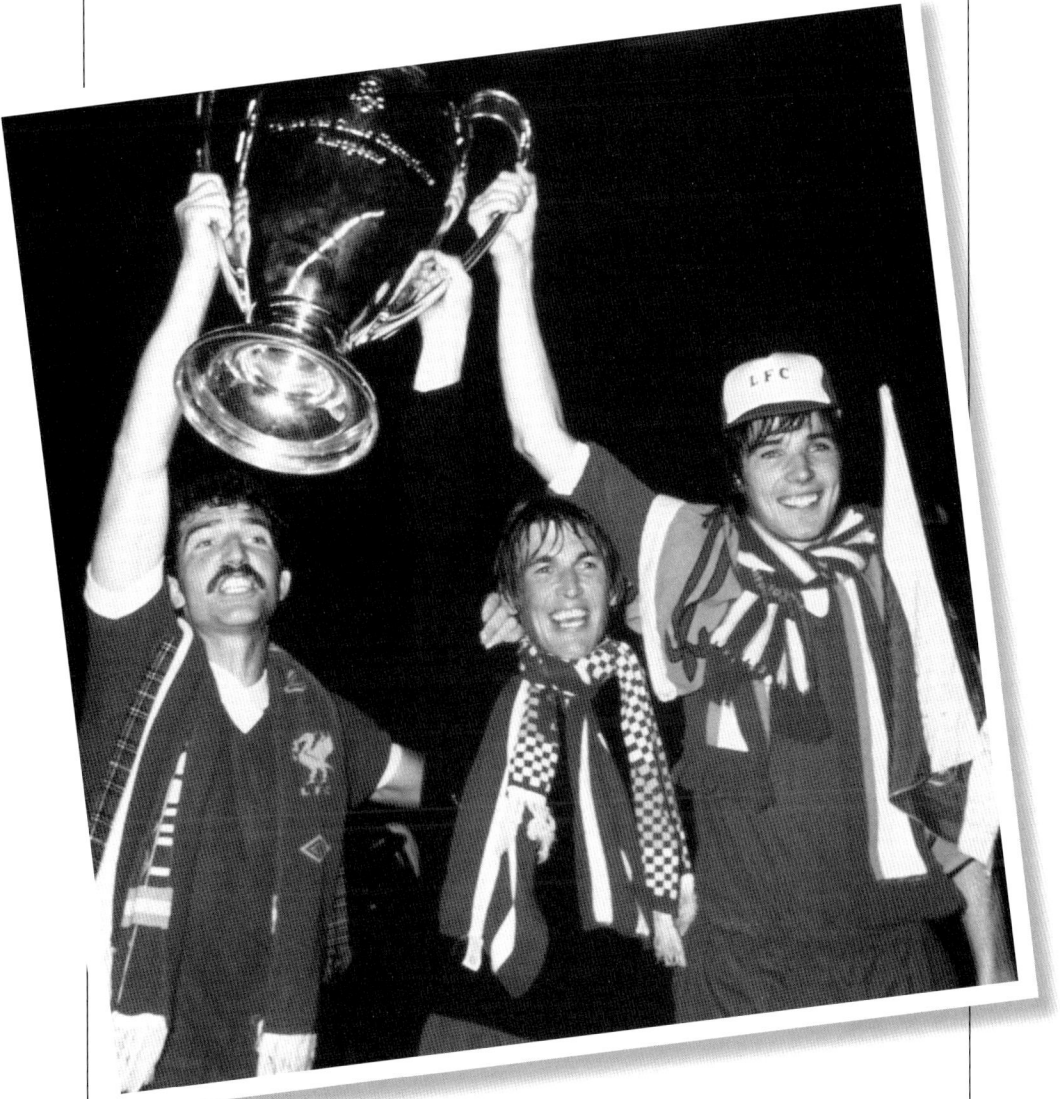

Souness, Dalglish and Hansen celebrate victory over Real Madrid in the 1981 European Cup Final.

* * *

Ipswich Town have competed in the UEFA Cup on ten occasions and in their sixth attempt, in **1980/81,** they won it. No, they did not scythe their way to glory – they did it with some style, scoring 28 goals in the process. Just for good measure, the East Anglian outfit also participated in the European Cup in 1962/63 and the Cup Winners' Cup in 1978/79 and to date have yet to lose a home match in European competitions.

After finishing third in the First Division the season previous, Ipswich duly ebbed and flowed past Aris of Greece, Bohemians Prague of Czechoslovakia, Widzew Łódź of Poland, Saint-Étienne of France, 1.FC Köln of West Germany and AZ Alkmaar of the Netherlands to become the sixth different English club to lift the Fairs Cup or UEFA Cup.

In winning what was only the third major competition in their history (four, if you include the 1972/73 Texaco Cup triumph over local rivals Norwich City), Bobby Robson's Ipswich had the assistance of their own Tartan triumvirate: midfielder John Wark and striker Alan Brazil, who both played in all 12 Euro matches, plus defender George Burley who made five appearances in the opening three rounds before injury intervened.

In the first leg of the first round, midfield maestro John Wark scored four goals as Aris were hammered 5-1 at Portman Road with centre-forward Paul Mariner also getting on the scoresheet. In Greece, however, the 'Agricultural Aristocrats' (a preferable moniker to the 'Tractor Boys') made life awkward for themselves by going 3-0 down after 65 minutes before Eric Lazenby Gates steadied the nerves with a goal ten minutes later. It finished 3-1 with Ipswich going through 6-4 on aggregate.

In the second round against Bohemians, there was another Jekyll and Hyde performance from the 'Suffolk Sophisticates' – 3-0 winners at home with a brace from Mr Wark and a wonderful free kick from former England centre-half Kevin Beattie, followed by a 2-0 defeat in Czechoslovakia with the legendary Antonín Panenka grabbing the second with fully 39 minutes remaining. In round three against Widzew, who were skippered by future UEFA vice-president Zbigniew Boniek and who had earlier eliminated Manchester United and Juventus, the 'Portman Road Professors' again won at home but with a much greater safety margin of 5-0, featuring a hat-trick from Wark and one from Brazil, before losing 1-0 in Poland.

In the quarter-finals the opposition were the much-fancied Saint-Étienne who included future UEFA president Michel Platini. By way of a pleasant change, the 'Cobbold Connoisseurs' won 4-1 away from home – Dutch legend Johnny Rep gave the *Massif-Central Saints* the lead after 16 minutes but Scottish legend John Wark netted the fourth for Ipswich – and 3-1 back in the flatlands where this time Wark's goal came from the penalty spot.

'Orwell's Originals' also managed home and away victories in the semi-final against a Köln side that included former Forest striker Tony Woodcock, who would net the final goal in British Championship history. Both of Ipswich's victories over 'the Billy Goats' – that's Köln's nickname – were 1-0, Wark the scorer in East Anglia, England international Terry Butcher netting in West Germany.

And so to the two-legged final where a crowd of 27,532 at Portman Road saw 'Robson's Real Deals' take an impressive 3-0 lead against the 'Cheese-Farmers' of Alkmaar into the second leg. In Amsterdam's Olympisch Stadion, 40km from Alkmaar, and in front of a crowd of 22,291, the visitors fielded two Dutch internationals – Arnold Muhren and Frans Thijssen – with the latter giving Ipswich the lead after four minutes. AZ hit back to go 2-1 in front before that man Wark made it 2-2 after 32 minutes. However, just to make things interesting, Ipswich conceded two more goals in the 40th and 73rd minutes before deciding enough is enough and shutting up shop to win 5-4 on aggregate. Significantly, goalkeeper Paul Cooper was named the man of the match.

England international (and Stanley Baker lookalike) Mick Mills received the trophy, but Alkmaar would have the consolation of winning their first Dutch championship in 1980/81 whereas Ipswich would be runners-up in the First Division that season as well as in 1981/82.

John Wark set a competition record by scoring 14 goals, which was later exceeded by Jürgen Klinsmann of Bayern Munich who scored 15 in the 1995/96 tournament. A big shout-out though for England striker Paul Mariner who also contributed six goals in Ipswich's glory run.

As befitting the achievement, a civic reception was held on Sunday, 24 May 1981 where around 50,000 supporters were present at Ipswich Town Hall to see the team and the trophy. As a (big) aside, the Town Hall is a Grade II-listed building from the Victorian era built in the Italianate style with a figure head of King John decorating the front wall. We like to think that is a nod towards Mr Wark of Glasgow. And as for the good people of Norwich, we guess it's a case of you Wensum, you lose some. Sorry.

* * *

In attempting to defend their 1981 Euro crown, Liverpool would lose out to CSKA Sofia in the quarter-finals of the European Cup while Ipswich would be eliminated by Alex Ferguson's Aberdeen in the first round of the UEFA Cup. Not to worry, however, for Aston Villa would win the **1981/82** European Cup to make it six in a row for English clubs. Villa were the fourth team from England to lift the big one and their previous Euro experience consisted of just two appearances in the UEFA Cup – a first-round exit in 1975/76 and defeat in the quarter-finals of 1977/78.

Villa's glory run would take them to Iceland, East Germany, the USSR and Belgium before a final in the Netherlands. Four Scots helping them out along the way were defenders Ken McNaught and Allan Evans plus midfielders Des Bremner and Andy Blair.

Bremner appeared in all nine Euro matches, Evans in eight and McNaught five, having come in at the quarter-final stage. Blair appeared in three matches. The only Scot to hit the net was Ken McNaught who got the second goal against Dynamo Kiev in the last eight at Villa Park. Tony Morley was the main Villa hitman with four goals, while fellow England internationals Gary Shaw and Peter Withe netted three apiece.

In the first round, Icelandic club Valur were beaten 5-0 at Villa Park and 2-0 in Reykjavík. The second round, however, was less straightforward, for after the Villans won 2-1 away to Dynamo Berlin, the Stasi Socceratti came to Birmingham and won 1-0 – Frank Terletzki, a 1980 Olympic Games football silver medal winner with the DDR, giving the visitors the lead after 15 minutes. Apparently, Villa were rampant but were kept at bay by a stunning performance from Dynamo keeper Bodo Rudwaleit, another silver medal winner from 1980. And so Ron Saunders' men progressed to the quarter-finals on the away goals rule.

In the quarter-finals, Villa – now led by Tony Barton after Saunders' mid-season departure – came up against the Soviet Union's most successful club side, who were not Russian, but were Dynamo Kiev of Ukraine. Somewhat surprisingly only two Kiev players, Volodymyr Bezsonov and Sergei Baltacha, featured in the USSR squad which won the bronze football medal at the 1980 Olympics – hosted by Moscow with Kiev, Leningrad and Minsk in support.

Dynamo's pitch in early March 1982 was ruled out due to a severe winter, so the first leg was played at the Lokomotiv Stadium in Simferopol, Crimea – 1,000km to the south. The game ended 0-0 with the hosts, including local hero Oleg Blokhin, hitting the woodwork and having a goal disallowed. Back in the tropical Midlands, Villa won 2-0 with both goals coming in the first half.

At the last-four stage, Birmingham's finest faced their Brussels counterparts in the shape of Anderlecht, Belgium's most successful club domestically and in Europe Villa kept another two clean sheets and thanks to a goal from Morley in the 28th minute in the first leg at home, they marched on to the final at Stadion Feijenoord – aka De Kuip.

Villa's opponents in the final were Bayern Munich, who at that point had a perfect record of four previous Euro finals [three European Cup and one Cup Winners' Cup] and four victories. Bayern's starting line-up consisted of 11 Germans, seven of whom had represented their country at one level or another, with skipper Paul Breitner a World Cup winner from 1974 and Karl-Heinz Rummenigge a European Championship winner in 1980, plus Dieter Hoeneß, the tournament's top scorer with seven. By comparison, Villa's starting 11 comprised eight Englishmen plus a trio of Scots in McNaught, Evans and Bremner, and Blair on the substitutes' bench.

Goalkeeper Jimmy Rimmer, who had been a Euro ever-present, had to be subbed after ten minutes due to a recurring shoulder injury and was replaced by Nigel Spink, who, in only his second first-team appearance for the club played remarkably well; he would become Villa's first-choice keeper over the next decade. Peter Withe's 67th-minute ricochet goal would ensure that the trophy went to Birmingham and not Bavaria.

In defence of their crown the following season, Aston Villa would reach the quarter-finals before bowing out to Juventus.

* * *

In **1982/83**, Alex Ferguson's Aberdeen won the European Cup Winners' Cup, beating the mighty Real Madrid in the final. Several of the 'Dandy Dons' went on to make a name for themselves down south – none more so than midfielder Gordon Strachan who would have a stellar career with Manchester United, Leeds United and Coventry City. Goalkeeper Jim Leighton would have mixed fortunes at Manchester United while winger Peter Weir had a short spell with Leicester City. Striker Mark McGhee tried his luck at Newcastle United and Reading, midfielder Neale Cooper played for Aston Villa and Reading, while hard-man defender Doug Rougvie made his marks at Chelsea, Brighton & Hove Albion, Shrewsbury Town and Fulham.

(Top): Steve Archibald who won the UEFA Cup with Spurs in 1984.
(Bottom): Graeme Sharp holds aloft the European Cup Winners' Cup after
victory over Rapid Vienna in Rotterdam.

* * *

In **1983/84** Liverpool, now managed by Liverpudlian Joe Fagan, won the European Cup for the fourth time and along the way they had the assistance of four Scots – old hands Kenny Dalglish, Alan Hansen and Graeme Souness plus 1983/84 season regular Steve Nicol. Dalglish, Hansen and Souness all played in all nine Euro matches while Nicol got game time in three of them. Stirling-born defender Gary Gillespie was an unused substitute in the final.

Liverpool's fairytale fourth title began, appropriately enough, in the Danish city of Odense, the birthplace of Hans Christian Andersen where OB were beaten 1-0, the goal coming from Dalglish. Back at Anfield, OB were beaten 5-0 and this time Dalglish grabbed a brace.

In the first leg of the second round, Athletic Club of Bilbao came a-calling and held the 'Pool to a goalless draw. However, over in the Basque Country a goal from Welshman Ian Rush in the 66th minute was enough to see the visitors through.

The Iberian peninsula also provided Liverpool with their quarter-final opponents – Benfica – who were beaten 1-0 on Merseyside and then 4-1 in Lisbon. The semi-finals also produced home and away wins, defeating Dinamo Bucureşti 1-0 at Anfield and then 2-1 in Romania.

The final was against Roma, who had 'robbed' Dundee United in the semi-final, in their own backyard – the Stadio Olimpico. The 'home' side's starting XI featured nine Italians, including 1982 World Cup winner Bruno Conti, plus Toninho Cerezo and Falcão of Brazil – arguably the best team at Espana 82 and tormentors of Scotland in Seville.

The extremely hostile atmosphere inside the stadium was reminiscent of the 'good old days' at the Colosseum but nevertheless, a funny thing happened 8km north-west of the Forum – defender Phil Neal gave Liverpool the lead after 13 minutes. Two minutes later a volleyed goal from Souness was disallowed for offside. Three minutes from half-time, however, a glancing header from Roberto Pruzzo made it 1-1.

The best chance of the second half came five minutes from time when Steve Nicol, who replaced midfielder Craig Johnston in the 72nd minute, received a pass from Dalglish in the Roma penalty box but had his shot saved by Franco Tancredi. Extra time didn't produce any goals either but unlike with the 1974 final stalemate there would be no replay – instead it was the first European Cup Final to be decided on penalties. Steve Nicol took the first one – and missed. Fortunately, four of his team-mates, including Graeme Souness, successfully converted their shots from 12 yards and with goalkeeper Bruce Grobbelaar wobbling his legs between the sticks and two Roma penalties sailing over the bar, Joe Fagan's Liverpool won the European Cup 4-2 on penalties and into the trophy cabinet it went to sit between the league championship trophy and the League Cup.

So Messrs Dalglish, Hansen and Souness all collected their third European Cup winners' medal – to equal the achievements of the likes of Ferenc Puskás, Johan Cruyff and Franz Beckenbauer – with Souness becoming only the third Scot to captain a winning side following on from Billy McNeill with Celtic in 1967, and John McGovern with Nottingham Forest in 1979 and 1980.

* * *

In **1983/84** there was further English success when Tottenham lifted the UEFA Cup for the second time, their third European trophy overall. As Chas & Dave had sung two years previous – 'Tottenham, Tottenham, no one can stop 'em' – and so it proved as Drogheda United, Feyenoord, Bayern Munich, Austria Vienna, Hajduk Split and Anderlecht were all put to the sword, albeit some were more difficult to overcome than others. On this occasion the Scottish support acts were Steve Archibald who appeared in 11 out of the 12 Euro matches, Alan Brazil who joined Spurs from Ipswich Town in March 1983 and made five appearances in Europe, and Ally Dick, a Stirling-born schoolboy international who joined the north London club as an apprentice in 1981 (four appearances).

Archibald missed the opening match, a 6-0 away win against Drogheda, but in the return leg at White Hart Lane he scored one and Brazil netted a brace as the Lilywhites romped home 8-0 to go through 14-0 on aggregate. For Drogheda, there would be end-of-season comfort in winning the League of Ireland Cup.

In the second round, Spurs came up against old rivals Feyenoord, who now included a young Ruud Gullit, and in the home leg – for which pre-match entertainment included a skydiving display some 11 years before the arrival of Jürgen Klinsmann – Tottenham were 4-0 ahead at half-time through braces from Archibald and Irish international Tony Galvin before two second-half goals from the visitors, including one from Johan Cruyff in the twilight of his playing career, made things a little less comfortable for Keith Burkinshaw's men. In Rotterdam, however, Spurs achieved an impressive 2-0 win against the team who would go on to win the Dutch league and cup double that season.

Next up were Bayern Munich, who had eliminated Spurs at the second-round stage of the European Cup Winners' Cup the previous season. In a sub-zero Munich, the Rummenigge boys did their parents proud, Michael scoring and big brother Karl-Heinz skippering in a 1-0 first-leg victory. Back at the Lane, however, second-half goals from Archibald and Mark Falco saw Spurs through. Bayern's consolation prize that season would be winning the DFB-Pokal, their national cup.

At the last eight stage, Austria Vienna were defeated 2-0 in London with Archibald and Brazil scoring, while in the return leg a 2-2 draw was achieved thanks to Brazil's fourth goal of the competition plus one from 1978 World Cup winner Osvaldo Ardiles. Austria Vienna's consolation prize was the 1983/84 Austrian championship with city rivals Rapid finishing in runners-up spot on goal difference.

In the semi-finals, Tottenham travelled to the Adriatic port of Split and lost 2-1 to Hajduk who had finished second in the Yugoslav top flight the season previous. There was interesting half-time 'entertainment' when a Hajduk fan, in reference to Spurs' club symbol, the cockerel, ran into the centre circle with a live rooster and then proceeded to snap its neck. Hajduk were subsequently fined and ordered to play their next European tie at least 300km away from their home stadium. Just in case you were wondering, 1984 was the Chinese year of the rat. Back to the footie and in the return leg, a goal from Micky Hazard after just six minutes was enough to see Spurs through on the away goals rule. Hajduk would win the 1983/84 Yugoslav Cup.

And so to the final where Spurs would face a highly talented Anderlecht side choc full of internationals, who were the defending UEFA Cup holders but whose chairman had ensured that they had 'cheated' their way past Brian Clough's Nottingham Forest in the semi-finals. Glenn Hoddle missed the final due to fitness concerns and captain Steve Perryman's booking in the first leg meant he missed the return game. In that second leg Ally Dick came on as a substitute for Paul Miller in the 77th minute.

At the Constant Vanden Stock Stadium in Brussels the first leg finished 1-1 with Spurs having led from the 57th minute to the 85th. Back in London it swung the other way with Anderlecht leading 1-0 from the hour mark to the 84th minute. Extra time did not produce any more goals and just as would happen at the European Cup Final seven days later, to penalties it went with the English club triumphing. This time the goalkeeping hero was Tony Parks who saved two penalties as Spurs won 4-3 with Steve Archibald converting the fourth. Lord Alan Sugar, Sir Trevor McDonald, Sir Kenneth Branagh, Mark Wahlberg and Adele – your boys did rather well back in the day.

In defence of the trophy, Spurs would be eliminated by eventual winners Real Madrid at the quarter-final stage. Elsewhere in Spain in 1984/85, Steve Archibald was helping Terry Venables' Barcelona to their first La Liga title in 11 years.

* * *

After nine unsuccessful, often woeful, attempts, Everton finally got their hands on some European silverware when they won the **1984/85** Cup Winners' Cup. The tartan Toffees were strikers Graeme Sharp with four goals in eight appearances and Andy Gray with three appearances, two of which were alongside Sharp, and five goals. In the final, Everton for many people had also assumed the role of avenging angels when they defeated Rapid Vienna, who appeared to have conned their way past Celtic in the second round following a bottle-throwing incident at Parkhead which necessitated a third match, played at Old Trafford.

There was no flying start to Everton's campaign, however; indeed, in the first round they struggled to get past European debutantes University College Dublin – the club supported by *Father Ted* actor Dermot Morgan. The first leg in Dublin was goalless while back on Merseyside the tie against the Students was settled by a solitary goal from Sharp – Everton's 'starter for ten' as Bamber Gascoigne was wont to say.

In the second round, Everton had to travel further afield, to Czechoslovakia, to face Inter Bratislava where the Toffees won 1-0 before winning 3-0 at Goodison Park – Sharp netting the first goal in the 12th minute. In the last eight, there were also home and away victories against Fortuna Sittard – 3-0 in Liverpool thanks to Andy Gray's second-half hat-trick and 2-0 in the Netherlands.

The sternest test came in the semi-finals, against Bayern Munich. We don't know why it is but we've always savoured British victories against the always confident/sometimes arrogant teutonic titans from Bavaria. Anyway, a 0-0 draw was achieved at the Olympiastadion – advantage Everton. Thirty-eight minutes into the return game at Goodison, however, a goal from Dieter Hoeneß made it advantage Bayern going into the break. However, Goodison's greatest European night eventually materialised with three second-half goals from Graeme Sharp, Andy Gray and Berwick-born England international Trevor McGregor Steven. Auf wiedersehen, Klaus Augenthaler, Lothar Matthäus and co. Sorry, mustn't gloat.

For the final, the match programme said little about the players but a lot about host city Rotterdam plus too many adverts (a wee pet hate of ours) for the likes of Power Football Boots, Guinness, Camel cigarettes, Canon cameras, Coca-Cola, Bull computers, Gillette shavers, JVC video recorders etc., Seiko watches, Fujifilm and McDonald's.

Howard Kendall's Everton, who were now champions of England and whose cup-winning XI comprised five Englishmen, three Welsh, two Scots and one from the Republic of Ireland, completely dominated the final although we had to wait until the second half for the goals. Andy Gray and Trevor McSteven put Everton 2-0 up before that old warhorse Hans Krankl – whose music sideline also included a single release called 'Lonely Boy' – netted for Rapid five minutes from time. One minute later, however, it was 'Goodnight Vienna' when route one from Southall to Gray to Sharp to Sheedy was finished off by a powerful shot from the Irishman which went in via the underside of the crossbar just for effect, to make it 3-1 for Everton. And so the Cup Winners' Cup came back to England for the first time since 1971 – although it resided in Scotland in 1972 and 1983.

* * *

Fourteen days after Everton lifted the Cup Winners' Cup came the horror at the Heysel Stadium when the actual result of the football match, Juventus defeating Liverpool 1-0 in the final of the European Cup, became largely irrelevant. Consequently, all English clubs were banned from European competitions for a period of five years, Liverpool for six.

For a time, a debate ensued as to whether or not a blanket ban on English clubs was fair and justifiable. What can be said however is that as a result of the punishment, Everton (twice) and Arsenal missed out on opportunities to compete in the European Cup. Similarly, FA Cup or League Cup winners such as Coventry City, Luton Town, Norwich City, Oxford United and Wimbledon were also denied the thrill of European competitions.

* * *

Scotland topped the table of the 1981 British Championship with four points from two wins including a 1-0 victory over England at Wembley thanks to a penalty converted by Nottingham Forest winger John Robertson. However, that year's tournament was not completed due to civil disturbances in Northern Ireland.

Three years later, the curtain came down on the competition with all four nations tied on three points each after one win, one draw and one defeat, but with Northern Ireland as champions on goal difference. The final British Championship match took place between Scotland and England at Hampden Park on 26 May 1984 and it ended in a 1-1 draw. The four Anglo-Scots who got game time that day were Arthur Albiston of Manchester United, John Wark of Liverpool, Steve Archibald of Tottenham Hotspur and Mo Johnston of Watford. A century of British international football now consigned to the soccer dustbin of history. Shame.

The following year, Scotland beat England 1-0 at Hampden in the inaugural, but short-lived, Rous Cup – named after former FIFA president Sir Stanley Rous. The two Anglos who got to hold the trophy aloft that sunny afternoon were Gordon Strachan of Manchester United and Chelsea's David Speedie, who was making his full international debut. Eventually Brazil, Colombia and Chile were invited to participate in the end-of-season tournament but eventually apathy 'won' and in 1989 it ended. Anyway, there was always the World Cup, as Scotland made it five successive successful qualifying campaigns. Sigh.

Manager Jock Stein named 12 Anglo-Scots from across eight clubs in the 22-man squad he took to the 1982 World Cup in Spain. For Scotland's opening match against New Zealand, their starting line-up included no fewer than eight Anglos, six of whom had European Cup winners' medals in their collections – Alan Hansen, Graeme Souness and Kenny Dalglish of Liverpool and John Robertson and Frank Gray with Nottingham Forest (although Gray was now at Leeds) plus Allan Evans of that year's champions Aston Villa, winning his fourth and final cap. No other starting line-up at the finals featured more, although England had four versus Kuwait. The other two Anglos – John Wark and Alan Brazil – were 1981 UEFA Cup winners with Ipswich Town.

Scotland led New Zealand 3-0 at half-time, were pulled back to 3-2 (and yes we *were* bricking it) before getting a grip of themselves to run out 5-2 winners in Málaga – a brace from Wark plus goals from Dalglish,

Robertson and 1982 FA Cup winner Steve Archibald who replaced Brazil in the 53rd minute.

For Scotland's second group match, against Brazil in Seville – the game in which 'we made them angry' by having the temerity to score first – Asa Hartford of Manchester City made his 50th and final appearance for his country. It was of course a home Scot, David Narey of Dundee United, who netted a beauty against the tournament favourites, before they hit back to win 4-1.

In their third group match Scotland drew 2-2 with the USSR in Málaga to once again exit the competition early due to an inferior goal difference. Former Leeds and Manchester United striker Joe Jordan, who had just completed a season in Serie A with AC Milan, was brought into the team for what would be his 52nd and final cap. Jordan duly delivered to give Scotland the lead after 15 minutes – the third successive World Cup finals he had netted in – before defensive errors gifted the Soviets a 2-1 advantage. Two minutes from time Souness equalised but it was not enough. It never is.

By the time the 1986 finals came around, Scotland had lost Jock Stein in tragic circumstances at the end of a World Cup qualifying match against Wales in Cardiff. His assistant, the Aberdeen manager Alex Ferguson, took charge of the national team on a temporary basis.

Ferguson's 22-man squad for Mexico contained just seven Anglo-Scots in Arsenal's Charlie Nicholas, Everton striker Graeme Sharp, Steve Nicol of Liverpool, Frank McAvennie of West Ham United, and Manchester United duo Arthur Albiston and Gordon Strachan; Ferguson would move to Old Trafford in November 1986. That left 14 home Scots plus Steve Archibald of Barcelona. Liverpool player-manager Kenny Dalglish had withdrawn from the squad due to injury – it would have been his fourth successive World Cup finals.

Scotland's three matches produced a 1-0 defeat to Denmark with Nicholas being cynically crocked by Jan Bartram, and a 2-1 reverse against West Germany with Strachan giving Scotland the lead and Graeme Souness making his 54th and final appearance for his country, and a 0-0 draw with Uruguay as Nicol missed a glorious chance against the rough-house South Americans, so home we came, beating the postal services with their transatlantic deliveries.

At Hampden Park on 12 November 1986, Kenny Dalglish, Scotland's joint top scorer with Denis Law on 30 goals, won his 102nd and final cap – 60 of which were gained while with Liverpool – in a 3-0 European Championship win over Luxembourg. The home crowd of 35,078 were willing Dalglish to score and break the record but it wasn't to be. Incidentally, Dalglish's club-mate Alan Hansen won his 25th and penultimate Scotland cap that evening and to this day, the debate continues as to why the classy Clackmannanshire defender didn't win around twice that many caps.

For the 1990 World Cup, manager Andy Roxburgh went with 12 players from the Scottish Premier Division, two from the Bundesliga plus eight from England – Jim Leighton of Manchester United, skipper Roy Aitken from Newcastle United, Liverpool defender Gary Gillespie, Chelsea striker Gordon Durie, Everton midfielder Stuart McCall, Gary McAllister of Leicester, plus Robert Fleck and Bryan Gunn of Norwich. Of the Anglos only McAllister and Gunn would not see any game time while Leighton, overcoming the personal disappointment of being dropped for the 1990 FA Cup Final replay, Aitken and McCall would play in all three of Scotland's group matches. In getting Scotland to Italy, Leighton played in seven of the eight qualifiers while Nicol appeared in six.

The 'Italian Job' began with a 'Disaster for Scotland' – a 1-0 defeat against Costa Rica in Genoa. Five days later they got their act together however and defeated Sweden 2-1 with the goals coming from McCall and Mo Johnston, who was now with Rangers. In the third match, however, against Brazil in Turin, Scotland battled well but lost 1-0 and 24 hours and four other concluding group matches later it was confirmed that Roxburgh's hopefuls were one of the two third-placed teams out of six who would not make it through to the next round.

Sigh (again).

6

The Alternative Cult Heroes

By David Stuart

In 2004 BBC's *Football Focus* did a series on cult heroes and there was a book produced by Steve Boulton in support of it. George Best graces the cover and part of me thinks, surely George belonged to the world and not one wee part of it, so he is not really a cult hero. Then again, what do I know? Well, one thing I know is that no one under the age of 40 should get a say on these things. Your right to vote needs to be earned in years of agony etched into your faces as you've watched your team snatch defeat from the jaws of victory time and time again.

So I thought I'd run through some alternatives from the original list; no doubt fans of these clubs will never forgive me for casting aside their choices and replacing them with some Scottish dude or sometime dud.

Arsenal and Tony Adams. I get it, from schoolboy to captain in a great era, but for me too many titles and trophies won. Charlie George was a runner-up and he certainly was a true maverick, but it is of course the other Charlie I'm going for, Mr Nicholas. The fact that the great Viv Anderson named his only child after him is worthy of cult status alone, never mind his double against Liverpool in the 1987 League Cup Final.

Aston Villa and Paul McGrath, great choice. However, what about Charlie Aitken, 660 appearances for the club but only ever won the Third Division and the League Cup in his 15 years with the Villans? Then there's Alan Hutton who was cast out on loan three times and came back stronger in the end. But of course, I'm going for Super John McGinn!

Barnet weren't included in the book as they were adrift in the Conference at the time. I'm picking Dougie Freedman for hitting 27 goals in his 47 appearances for the Bees. That's what you want from a cult hero striker, a good record of banging the goals in.

Barnsley went for the great Ronnie Glavin. The former Jags player produced some great goals down Oakwell way. Anyway, he won the Scottish League Cup with Partick Thistle in 1971, so nuff said.

Bath City anyone? Shouldn't really be mentioned but former East Fife, Sunderland and Scotland player Charlie 'Cannonball' Fleming turned up there in 1958 and by the time he left in 1965, he had hit 216 goals in 300 games.

John McGinlay was runner-up in the Bolton list to the legendary Nat Lofthouse, and the 70s icon Frank Worthington was in there too. Who am I to tell the people of Bolton they got it wrong?

Stuart McCall won the Bradford title, and you won't get any arguments from me on that one.

There was a whole host of Scots at Bristol City in the 70s but it was the Polish ex-Celtic striker Dariusz 'Jacki' Dziekanowski who won it. Surely it should be Gerry Gow, the midfield hard man from Glasgow who played 375 games for the club and gets a mention in a Half Man Half Biscuit song. Sadly, the song is not called 'All I Want for Christmas is a Gerry Gow Panini 78 Sticker'.

Burnley runner-up was Ted McMinn which is not bad for the winger who only stayed for two seasons. I'm going for Andy Lochhead who scored 101 goals in 226 games for the club and because I forgot to mention him at Aston Villa. He hit four goals in the 1963 Boxing Day 6-1 massacre of Manchester United. Willie Morgan netted the other two; we'll get to him later.

At Bury I'm going for the 'Mighty Atom' Bobby Collins. Bobby broke his thigh bone aged 34 at Leeds. He still went on to have two seasons with the Gigg Lane mob in his late 30s, playing 75 games.

Chelsea. Plenty to choose from: Pat Nevin, Charlie Cooke, Billy Gilmour. However, I'm going for big Doug Rougvie. Not the best or most subtle of defenders but he's got a song. Chelsea were once 3-0 down to Sheffield Wednesday and came back to lead 4-3 until Doug gave away a penalty. The song goes 'Three goals down, four three up, Rougvie's gone and fucked it up'.

At Coventry City they went for David Speedie and despite his 'fiery' personality it should have gone to another Scot. The Cruyff turn, the Panenka penalty; the Willie Carr 'donkey kick' should roll off the tongue just as readily but alas it was banned. At a free kick Willie wedged the ball between his ankles and flicked it up for his team-mate Ernie Hunt to volley it into the Everton net. It is not like today where cameras are at every match so being able to do it on camera made it more special. It won *Match of the Day*'s goal of the season award too. Apparently, they did try it a few other times but not with the same outcome. We all tried it at school over the next few weeks after, and no doubt a few windaes were smashed in the process. However, those suits at FIFA banned it by the end of the season and so it slid into obscurity. Tommy Hutchison is of course a close runner-up.

Ted McMinn was runner-up in the Derby list too. Did his family do all the voting? I'd go for Archie Gemmill, just for being Archie Gemmill.

Everton, can't really argue with Neville Southall but for me it's a toss-up between Pat Nevin or James McFadden. Faddy scored *that* Scotland goal in Paris while with Everton.

Fulham, I'm going for a guy who played alongside the fans' choice of Johnny Haynes in Graham Leggat – 127 goals in 254 league games but it's for his hat-trick in three minutes from Boxing Day 1963 he gets the nod. It was the fastest threesome in English football until Sadio Mané of Southampton beat it in 2015.

Hartlepool didn't go for John McGovern, and instead chose Joe Allon. Although born in Montrose, McGovern grew up in the English north-east and joined his hometown team in 1966 when they were known as Hartlepools United. In charge was the duo of Brian Clough and Peter Taylor and the rest is history.

Huddersfield Town chose Iain Dunn, a guy I've never heard of but hey, sometimes that's the definition of a cult hero. I wonder, if the poll was done now, would Jordan Rhodes be included due to his 73 goals in 124 games in his first term with the Terriers?

Ipswich Town fans picked John Wark and in the words of that old Knight Templar geezer from *Indiana Jones and the Last Crusade*, 'You have chosen wisely.' I do wonder if sans moustache would they have voted the same. Cult heroes need a certain 'look' about them too.

Billy Bremner for Leeds with Gordon Strachan one of the runners-up. Ain't gonna rock that boat although surprised not to see Eddie Gray in there.

Leicester City *and* Liverpool – I'll cause controversy and throw in together and suggest Gary McAllister. I know he wasn't one of Leicester's Ice Kings (not to be confused with the Ice Warriors that Dr Who fought), the great team of the 60s, but he was a cracking player all the same.

At Liverpool he popped in aged 35 for two seasons and left clutching a handful of medals. Of course, I could have picked him for Leeds too.

Manchester City, never a team overly blessed with Scots at times. However, for this one I'm going for Jim Tolmie as he's my wife's second cousin. Although I've been married for 35 years, and I've never met him.

Manchester United. Best, Cantona and Keane. I'm going for Willie Morgan. Sadly, Willie only ever won the old Second Division title with United. Sometimes it's the players who carry you through the lean years who keep you going, and Willie came in just as Matt Busby's great 60s team was dissolving. However, with his flowing locks 'Willie on the wing' kept the crowds entertained in his time at Old Trafford. Of course, big Jim Holton is the runner-up for me.

Middlesbrough and Bernie Slaven was the choice and a true cult choice that one. The man was a legend on Teesside and continues to be so. Born in Paisley but played for the Republic of Ireland via the 'grandparents rule'.

Millwall. Do you think I'm brave enough to tell the fans' choice, the scary Terry Hurlock, it's not him? Nope, not me.

Newcastle United and I'll go for Tony Green. Tony's time at St James' Park was brought to a premature end due to injury and surely one of the other criteria for a true cult hero is the players you believe could have been one of the greats. 'If only'.

Norwich City went to Bryan Gunn, the goalie not the manager. At one point Bryan was named as Sheriff of Norwich, and of course Kenny McLean, the 'mayor' of Norwich, would be a good shout too. Robert Fleck was a runner-up but my affinity with Norwich began with Jimmy Bone of the Thistle moving to Carrow Road in the early 70s. The affinity doesn't actually go much beyond looking out for their scores on a Saturday. Jimmy helped the Canaries gain promotion to the top flight for the first time in 1972 and scored their first goal in the top tier. That'll do for me.

Nottingham Forest and the fans went for the winner of two League Cups, Stuart Pearce. Bunch of under-40s no doubt. The only answer is of course runner-up John Robertson, winner of two European Cups.

Notts County went with another legend of old in Tommy Lawton, can't argue with that but good to see Don Masson in there too.

As did Preston North End with Tom Finney. Alex Bruce was one of the runners-up and is second only to Sir Tom in the all-time scorer stakes for the Lilywhites. Good enough for me although full-backs Graham Alexander and Callum Davidson would be in the mix too.

QPR with Stan Bowles is a no-brainer and Rodney Marsh as a runner-up is too but Don Masson in that period of 1976/77 was immense for QPR and Scotland. If only Tommy Docherty didn't sign him (and Bruce Rioch too).

Rotherham saw ex-Rangers and Killie striker Bobby Williamson as a runner-up. Bobby hit a rich vein of form at Millmoor, scoring 49 goals in 93 games.

Tony Currie, like Frank Worthington and Stan Bowles, is a 70s icon and was the Sheffield United choice, and I can't better that.

Sheffield Wednesday and I'm not overly enthused about anyone although Jim McCalliog once signed a football card for me, but he was a Wolves player on the card. It is good to see that Barry Bannan continues to ply his trade at Hillsborough though and has made over 400 appearances for the Owls.

Being a Scottish football card collector in the 70s there's only one choice for me at Southampton and that is keeper Eric Martin. A&BC always filled out Scottish card sets with Anglos and for some reason Eric Martin appeared in four straight sets without anyone knowing who he was. Apparently, he did play for Cowdenbeath and Dunfermline and in his eight years at the Dell he played 248 league games but was never cited for a Scotland cap at any level. However, my alternate take on a football standing is Joe Jordan.

Sunderland and I'm going for Bobby Kerr, the diminutive leader of the team that won the FA Cup in 1973 and played over 400 games for the Wearside club.

For Spurs there's plenty to go around whether the double-winning side of Bill Brown, Dave Mackay and John White or Steve Archibald who formed a great partnership with Garth Crooks in the early 80s. However, my choice is Alan Gilzean, an early hero of mine.

Tranmere and it's Pat Nevin for me although Steve Mungall, who played over 500 games for the club, is worth a shout too.

Watford. It can only be Mo Johnston although I was heartbroken when Watford bought him from Thistle. The Jags' promotion run was going well with him up front and fell apart immediately after he departed. As for Watford, he blitzed it with 23 goals in only 38 league games in his short time there, helping the club to the FA Cup Final too.

West Brom. Cyrille Regis is a great choice and Willie Johnston in there too as a runner-up. That was a great era for the club, and I can't surpass them.

West Ham. Frank McAvennie, like his cohort Mo Johnston, had a great start down south, hitting 26 league goals in his first season at Upton Park, and gets my tartan-tinted choice for that. Christian Dailly is a great shout too as is Ray 'Tonka' Stewart.

Wigan and I'd have to go for the extremely talented Shaun Maloney who helped them to the FA Cup win in 2013. Lee McCulloch and Gary Teale are my runners-up.

Wolves and did I tell you that Jim McCalliog once signed a football card for me? More recently, Colin Cameron was an underrated player for both club and country, and one-season wonder left-back Barry Douglas, who scored five goals and made 14 assists, is a good shout too.

York City were also not included, due to plummeting out of the Football League. However, my wildcard choice is ex-Jag Manny Panther, just for having one of the great footballing names.

7

1990/91–1999/2000

Overview

In the 1990s, the internet took hold while mobile phones became smaller, cheaper and more personal. Sales of personal computers, dishwashers, widescreen (now multi-channel) televisions, DVDs and digital cameras also increased significantly. The National Lottery was launched in 1994 and while it has generated millions of pounds for countless deserving causes and projects (including grassroots and women's football), it has had a significantly detrimental effect on the football pools competitions.

In the world of entertainment, there were a couple of classic footie movies, *When Saturday Comes* (1996) starring Sean Bean and Pete Postlethwaite, and *Fever Pitch* (1997) starring Colin Firth and Ruth Gemmell. The former film sees Bean's character, a brewery worker, realise his dream and play for Sheffield United, while the latter is based loosely on Nick Hornby's best-selling memoir, *Fever Pitch: A Fan's Life*, which is all about love versus supporting Arsenal.

Hugh Cornwell left the Stranglers in August 1990, however the music world gave us Blur, Oasis and Pulp plus Take That, East 17, Spice Girls and All Saints – 'Cool Britannia' apparently.

In 1999, ex-Leicester City, Everton, Barcelona, Tottenham Hotspur and England striker Gary Lineker replaced Desmond Lynam as the main presenter on *Match of the Day*. From 1992 until 2014, one of the main pundits on the show was ex-Partick Thistle, Liverpool and Scotland defender Alan 'You can't win anything with kids' Hansen.

In 1991 the profession of football agents, which had been around for decades, was officially recognised when FIFA established the first official licensing system.

In the 1990s the transfer market started to get a bit carried away with itself. In July 1991 Aston Villa midfielder David Platt headed to

Alex Ferguson of Manchester United and George Graham of Arsenal were to dominate the early 90s period of English football.

Bari in Italy for £5.5m. In January 1995 striker Andy Cole moved from Newcastle United to Manchester United for £7m and just over a year later in July 1996 another forward, Alan Shearer, departed Blackburn Rovers, where he collected a Premier League winners' medal in 1994/95, to join his hometown club Newcastle United under Kevin Keegan for £15m, a world record at the time.

In the aftermath of the Hillsborough disaster, the 1990 Report by Lord Justice Taylor led to several safety improvements in the largest English football grounds, notably the elimination of fenced standing terraces in favour of all-seater stadia in the top two tiers. A massive stadium revamping/rebuilding exercise ensued although some redevelopment and modernisation of British grounds had been introduced following the Bradford City stadium fire in 1985 in which 56 spectators lost their lives.

The Bosman ruling of December 1995 by the European Court of Justice banned restrictions on European players within national leagues and allowed players in the EU to move to another club at the end of a contract without a transfer fee being paid. Essentially, footballers were permitted to join other clubs for free following the expiration of their contract. The effect was profound, but sadly the ruling did not bring wealth or happiness for the eponymous Belgian midfielder, Jean-Marc Bosman.

The Premier League was created in 1992 following the decision of clubs in the First Division, England's top tier from 1888 to 1992, to break away from the Football League, although relegation and promotion between the Premier League and the Football League has remained in place. The top tier reduced in number from 22 to 20 clubs but at the same time took advantage of the sale of extremely lucrative television rights to Sky Sports.

In the 1990s, Scottish influence in English football went into something of a decline, at least at the top level, with the notable exceptions of the achievements of the Manchester United manager Alex Ferguson and to a lesser extent, Arsenal and Spurs boss George Graham plus Kenny Dalglish at Blackburn. Seven of the ten champions had Anglos within their ranks, however the overall number of actual appearances made by Scottish players had dropped considerably when compared to previous decades. In the FA Cup only eight of the 20 finalists utilised the services of Scots while in the League Cup it was nine out of 20. Season 1994/95 was a last hurrah of sorts with champions Blackburn, FA Cup finalists

Everton and Manchester United, and League Cup runners-up Bolton Wanderers, who were also managed by Bruce Rioch, all featuring Scots. Thereafter, success stories became much more sporadic.

Trophy-wise, the balance of power shifted to Manchester United who successfully 'knocked Liverpool off their perch' in the collection of silverware with London clubs Arsenal and Chelsea also having a noticeably successful decade.

In season 1990/91 English clubs returned to European competitions but the decade saw just four successes – one European Cup and three Cup Winners' Cups – across three clubs: Arsenal, Chelsea and Manchester United. Anglo-Scottish footballers appeared in just two of the winning sides, although the aforementioned Ferguson and Graham oversaw three of the winning teams.

In 1992 the European Cup was rebranded as the UEFA Champions League and in 1997/98 the competition was expanded to include the runners-up of the top eight domestic leagues. The European 'greed genie' was now out of its bottle.

Trophy winners 1990/91 to 1999/2000

Successful clubs	League	FA Cup	League Cup	European	Total
Manchester United	6	3	1	2	12
Arsenal	2	2	1	1	6
Chelsea	-	2	1	1	4
Liverpool	-	1	1	-	2
Tottenham Hotspur	-	1	1	-	2
Aston Villa	-	-	2	-	2
Leicester City	-	-	2	-	2
Blackburn Rovers	1	-	-	-	1
Leeds United	1	-	-	-	1
Everton	-	1	-	-	1
Sheffield Wednesday	-	-	1	-	1
TOTALS	**10**	**10**	**10**	**4**	**34**

* * *

Scotland qualified for the finals of their first Euros, the 1992 tournament in Sweden, which was won by Denmark, the late replacements for war-torn Yugoslavia. Scotland then made it two-in-a-row by reaching Euro 96 – hosted by England but won by Germany – plus the 1998 World Cup in France which was won by the host nation. There was, however, play-off heartbreak for Euro 2000.

∗ ∗ ∗

Domestic competitions
1990/91

George Graham's Arsenal won the league once more, amassing 83 points, seven ahead of nearest rivals Liverpool. Prior to Kenny Dalglish's surprise resignation, Liverpool had been five points ahead in February. As before, there were no Scots in the Arsenal line-up over the season.

The FA Cup was won by Tottenham Hotspur, beating Nottingham Forest 2-1 after extra time. Scotland under-21 striker Lee Glover, who had been on the bench for the 1989 League Cup Final, played in this match and was part of the Forest squad that reached the League Cup Final in 1992.

The League Cup was won by Sheffield Wednesday of the Second Division, beating the much-fancied Manchester United. Irish international John Sheridan scored the only goal of the game. Wednesday had no Scots in their side. As for Fergie's United, Brian McClair, who had scored in the semi-final against Leeds, was fielded. McClair and United would have better luck in the final the following season.

1991/92

Leeds United were to top the table in what was to be the final Football League in its traditional form, as the following season would herald the arrival of the Premier League. They finished four points ahead of Manchester United with 82 points.

A pair of Scots were part of the make-up of the Leeds midfield: Gordon Strachan and Gary McAllister. Strachan had won the FA Cup with Manchester United in 1985 and moved to Leeds in 1989 for £200,000. Now into his 30s, Strachan had a renaissance in the Leeds side, playing some of the best football of his career. He inspired them to the Second Division title in 1989/90 where he netted 16 goals in 46 games. In winning the top-tier title, Strachan played in 36 games, scoring four times. However, Leeds and Strachan did struggle in the following seasons and Gordon left the Elland Road club (197/37) to join previous manager Ron Atkinson at Coventry in 1995. Ostensibly he was going there as assistant to Ron but was quickly promoted to player-manager. Gordon played his last match for Coventry aged 40 in 1997 (26/0). He would manage City for five years before moving to Southampton, whom he took to the 2003 FA Cup Final.

Gary McAllister, in comparison to the tenacious Strachan, was a more elegant, graceful player. He had started out at his hometown team Motherwell in 1981 (59/6). He and fellow midfielder Ally Mauchlen were bought by Leicester City for £350,000 in August 1985. City got their money's worth with Mauchlen making 239 appearances in a seven-year stay. As for Gary, he played 201 times, scoring 41 goals, before he headed to Leeds for £1m in July 1990. Gary played in all 42 matches of the title-winning season, scoring five goals. He also played in the 1996 League Cup Final.

The joint top goalscorers in the Second Division with 23 goals were both Scots, one with his Scotland career in front of him and the other with it in his past: Fort William-born Duncan Shearer, and from Glenrothes, David Speedie.

Shearer, of Swindon Town, had started out in the Highland League with Inverness side Clachnacuddin before moving to Chelsea in 1983. However, the striker pecking order back then was Kerry Dixon and one David Speedie. Opportunities were few (2/1) and so after three years Duncan moved on to Huddersfield Town (83/38). With the goals flowing, Swindon manager Lou Macari laid out £250,000 for Shearer. The goals continued as he hit 79 in 164 games for the Robins. Kenny Dalglish and Blackburn paid £800,000 for Shearer in March 1992 but within months (6/1), he was on his way back north to Aberdeen. He was idolised by the fans at Pittodrie and his time there would see him capped for Scotland. He remained there until 1997 (152/54) before ending his playing days at Inverness Caledonian Thistle (55/17).

The pugnacious David Speedie of Blackburn had started out at Barnsley in 1978 (21/0). By 1980 he was playing in the Fourth Division for Darlington (88/21), and his second season there saw him hit 17 goals in 44 games. Chelsea manager John Neal spent £80,000 on Speedie in May 1982, and he won the Second Division title with the club in 1983/84. However, a fall-out with new manager John Hollins saw Speedie leave Stamford Bridge prematurely (162/47). He moved to Coventry for £750,000 and spent four seasons at the club (122/31) before moving to Kenny Dalglish's Liverpool for £625,000 in January 1991. A month later Kenny quit his post and Speedie was not favoured by the incoming Graeme Souness, so it was time to move again (12/6).

Don Mackay of Blackburn bought him for £500,000 in August 1991. By October Mackay was gone and Dalglish was in place. Speedie hit 23 goals in 36 games that season but with Blackburn gaining promotion via the play-offs, he was offloaded to Southampton. Dalglish had bought Alan Shearer from the Saints for £3.6m and sold Speedie to them for £400,000. It didn't work out at the Dell for Speedie, and his career dropped off from there (11/0). Loan spells followed at Birmingham (10/2), West Brom (7/2), and West Ham (11/4). Season 1993/94 was spent at Filbert Street with Leicester, but injury saw his professional career end there (37/12). David then spent years turning out for various non-league clubs.

Although his time as manager of Liverpool did not work out too well, Graeme Souness's side won the 1992 FA Cup, beating Sunderland 2-0 in the final. Ironically despite winning five titles with the club and numerous other trophies as a player, this was to be his only FA Cup triumph either on the pitch or from the dugout.

Steve Nicol was to remain at Anfield for a few seasons more, but this was to be his last trophy. Steve left Anfield (343/36) having won four titles, three FA Cups and the European Cup to join Notts County in 1995 (32/2) whom he managed briefly before spells with Sheffield Wednesday (49/0), West Brom on loan (9/0) and Doncaster Rovers (25/0). He then headed Stateside with Boston Bulldogs (41/0) and went on to manage New England Revolution for nine years.

Ray Houghton also played in the final but was to bow out at Anfield (153/28) for Aston Villa shortly after, for £900,000. There he was to win the League Cup in 1994.

The defeated Sunderland side fielded no Scots.

The League Cup went to Alex Ferguson's Manchester United, beating Brian Clough's Nottingham Forest 1-0. This was to be United's first League Cup triumph, with Brian McClair hitting the 14th-minute winner.

As for Forest, in their midfield was son of former Scotland legend Archie – Scot Gemmill. Archie had won two titles under Clough, one at Derby and one at Forest (Clough's son Nigel also played in the losing final). Scot started out as a youth at Forest, progressing to making his first-team debut in March 1991. He remained at the City Ground (245/21) for a turbulent eight years as the team became a veritable yo-yo club – relegation thrice, promotion twice. He moved to Everton for £250,000 in March 1999 (97/5) which initially went well but by 2003/04 he was out of the picture and had a loan spell at Preston North End (7/1) before a permanent move to Leicester City in 2004. He only spent two years with City (17/0) before going into coaching at Oxford and playing one game. Although he spent some time in New Zealand, Scot has primarily been known for his work in the Scotland setup at under-17 and under-21 levels.

Lee Glover spent the match on the bench as he had been for the 1989 final. By the time of the 1992 final he had been on loan three times: Leicester (5/1), Barnsley (8/0) and Luton for one game. He left Forest (76/9) in 1994 for Port Vale (52/7). Then it was Rotherham for four seasons (85/29) with a loan spell at Huddersfield in 1997 (11/0). The turn of the century saw him at Macclesfield (85/18) then Mansfield (2/0) and Burton Albion (9/2) before moving into management with non-league Corby Town and Grantham Town.

1992/93

Alex Ferguson won the first Premier League and then went on to win another 12 before retiring. United won the title with 84 points, ten clear of second-placed Aston Villa.

Brian McClair played in all 42 matches, scoring nine goals, in what was to be the first of his four title wins.

The other Scot in the United squad that season was Alex's son, Darren Ferguson. Midfielder Darren played in 15 games without scoring. Born in Glasgow, Darren had joined the United setup in 1990 and was to have four seasons with the Red Devils (28/0). He joined Wolves in 1994, spending five years with them, all in the First Division (117/4). Part of 1999 was spent with Sparta Rotterdam (14/1) before heading to Wrexham. He captained them to promotion to the Second Division and also won the Football League Trophy with the Welsh club (301/51). Darren moved into management with Peterborough United in 2007 and indeed has managed them on four occasions, with spells at Preston and Doncaster Rovers also.

The FA Cup and League Cup were both won by George Graham's Arsenal. These were to be the last domestic trophies Graham was to win with the Gunners. He was to win the Cup Winners' Cup the following season but having been found to have taken a couple of 'bungs' from an agent he was dismissed shortly after. George went on to win the League Cup with Tottenham in 1999.

Both finals were against Sheffield Wednesday, and both were won 2-1 although the FA Cup was taken to a second game. Nary a Scot was fielded by either team.

1993/94

Manchester United retained the title with 92 points, eight clear of Kenny Dalglish's Blackburn in second place. Brian McClair played in 26 matches but 14 were as sub, contributing just the one goal. Darren Ferguson played in only three.

Youth player Colin McKee made his one and only United appearance that season too. He had signed in 1987, turning professional in 1992. Glasgow-born Colin had a loan spell at Bury (2/0) before heading north to Kilmarnock for £350,000 along with defender Neil Whitworth. At Killie he played 76 matches, scoring 12 goals, but his career just petered out after that. Over a two-year period, he played for Partick Thistle (1/0), Falkirk (4/0), Queen of the South (2/0), Ross County (1/0), Stirling Albion (2/0), Víkingur (8/0) and finally Queen's Park (7/0) before heading into Junior football.

United also achieved the double by beating Chelsea 4-0 in the FA Cup Final at Wembley. Brian McClair came on in the 86th minute with United three goals to the good. Three minutes into injury time and he tapped in the fourth after Paul Ince set him up.

In the Chelsea line-up were three Scots: Craig Burley, John Spencer and future manager Steve Clarke. Saltcoats-born Clarke started out at St Mirren in 1982 (200/7) having been signed from Beith Juniors. Chelsea paid out £422,000 for his services in January 1987. Steve was to remain at Stamford Bridge until 1998, winning the FA Cup in 1997 and the League Cup and UEFA Cup in 1998.

Ayr-born Craig Burley is the nephew of former Ipswich player and Scotland manager George Burley. He joined Chelsea as a youth, signing professionally in 1989. Craig made his debut in 1991. It was under Glenn Hoddle that the midfielder began to get more game time and his final year at Chelsea came under former team-mate Ruud Gullit. Burley had played in the 1997 FA Cup quarter-final and semi-final but was left out of the squad for the final. By the summer he left Chelsea (113/7) for Celtic at a cost of £2.5m and enjoyed a couple of years there (64/20). Craig returned to England with Derby for £3m in December 1999 and spent four seasons with them (73/10). After that came short spells at Dundee (2/0), Preston (4/0) and Walsall (5/0). Craig quite quickly then made the move into the media and at the time of writing worked with ESPN in the United States.

Forward John Spencer was born in Glasgow and though a Catholic signed for Rangers in 1982 as a youth, progressing to the professional ranks in 1988. There was little opportunity for a first-team place under Graeme Souness, so he had two loan spells: one with Morton (4/1) and then with Lai Sun in Hong Kong (24/20). He left Ibrox in 1992 (13/2) when Chelsea paid £450,000 for him. John spent five years at Stamford Bridge (103/36) before going on loan to QPR in 1996 (25/17). In November 1997 the transfer was made permanent (23/5) for £2.5m but a year later John was on the move to Everton initially as a loanee (6/0) and then as a £1.5m signing. However, things didn't work out (3/0) and once more he was on loan; this time to Motherwell (21/7) where he became a permanent signing in 1999 for £600,000. By 2001 with Motherwell in financial trouble Spencer (33/11) was offloaded to Colorado Rapids. John eventually moved into coaching Stateside and has had posts with Houston Dynamo, Portland Timbers, the Rapids and finally with San Jose Earthquakes in 2017.

The League Cup was won by Ron Atkinson's Aston Villa, denying Manchester United a treble. Scots Irishman Ray Houghton, having joined Villa from Liverpool in August 1992, was in the winners' midfield. He spent two full seasons with the club (95/6), moving to Crystal Palace in March 1995. After Palace (73/7) he joined Reading (43/1), ending his playing days at Stevenage Borough.

Brian McClair was once again a late sub, coming on in the 83rd minute with United 2-1 down, but Villa would extend their lead to win 3-1.

1994/95

Kenny Dalglish's Blackburn won the Premier League, one point ahead of Manchester United with 89 points. At the heart of their defence, playing in 38 games and notching up four goals, was Colin Hendry.

Hendry had started out with his hometown Highland League side Keith and then Junior club Islavale before moving to Dundee in 1983. After four years at Dens Park (41/2) he moved to Blackburn to be reunited with former Dundee manager Don Mackay. In his first season he scored the only goal in the 1987 Full Members' Cup Final.

In November 1989, however, Hendry left Blackburn (102/22) for Manchester City (63/5) for £700,000 but newly installed Rovers manager Dalglish bought him back for the same fee two years later. Hendry spent the next seven years at Ewood Park (235/12) but neither he nor the club were to reach the same heights of a title win again. A £4m move to Rangers (22/0) in 1998 was made, but by 2000 he was back south again with Coventry for £750,000. His time with the Sky Blues didn't work out well (11/0) and spells with Bolton (25/3), Preston (2/0) and finally Blackpool (14/0) followed. He went into management with the Seasiders; however his tenure did not last long nor did his reign at Clyde in 2007.

Kevin Gallacher only played in one game for Rovers that season due to two successive broken legs. Clydebank-born Gallacher started out at Jim McLean's Dundee United (131/26). He scored v Barcelona in the 1986/87 UEFA Cup to give his side the lead in the first leg of the quarter-final and played in the losing final against IFK Göteborg. He transferred to Coventry in January 1990 for £950,000 and spent three years at Highfield Road (100/28). Blackburn paid £3.5m for Kevin in March 1993 and once he overcame the fractures, he began to get among the goals. Injuries in his final few seasons saw him miss much of the 1998/99 season. Blackburn were relegated and Gallacher left Ewood Park (144/46) for Bobby Robson's Newcastle United. After a couple of seasons at St James' Park (39/4) Kevin ended his career with short spells at Preston (5/1), Sheffield Wednesday (4/0) and Huddersfield (7/0).

Top of the scoring charts in the Third Division was Dougie Freedman of Barnet with 24 goals. Glaswegian Dougie had joined QPR as a youth player and was given a free transfer to Barnet. He hit his 24 goals in his first season. Crystal Palace came in for Dougie as the 1995/96 campaign was barely started, paying Barnet £800,000 (47/27). Dougie spent two years at Palace (90/31) before Wolves bought him for £800,000. The 1997/98 season was spent at Molineux (29/10) before heading to Nottingham Forest (70/18) for an increased fee of £900,000. The new century marked a return to Palace for £600,000. Dougie spent the next eight years with the club (237/64) and collected his two Scotland caps during this period too. There was a short loan spell at Leeds in 2008 (11/5) before he finished his career at Southend United (36/6). He has had management spells with Palace, Bolton and Forest since.

The FA Cup was won by Everton, beating Manchester United 1-0 thanks to a Paul Rideout goal. Coming on as a sub for the Toffees in the second half was the much-loved and much-maligned Duncan Ferguson. He was a full-on player, which was sometimes glorious to see as he soared above defenders to bullet-head the ball into the net, or notorious when he grappled with opposition players. He had started out with Dundee United in 1990 (77/28) but moved to Rangers for a then British record of £4m. Things didn't work out so well for him at Ibrox (14/2) and a head-butt on a Raith Rovers player eventually led to a prison sentence. He was loaned out to Everton initially (9/2) in 1994 and later moved for £3.75m. Ferguson was idolised by the Goodison crowd (107/35) for his aggressive play. Ruud Gullit's Newcastle paid out £8m for 'Big Dunc' in November 1998 where he was to take part in the 1999 FA Cup Final.

The League Cup Final was won by Liverpool, now managed by Roy Evans, defeating Bruce Rioch's Bolton Wanderers 2-1. It had only been a couple of years since Bolton had defeated Liverpool, under Graeme Souness, 2-0 at Anfield in the FA Cup. The scorers that day were John McGinlay and his striking partner Andy Walker.

Inverness-born McGinlay was still in the Bolton line-up. It took a while for John's career to really start. He had been playing in the Highland League with Fort William and Nairn as well as Elgin City with stops at North Shore United in New Zealand and Yeovil Town in Somerset. Eventually, he ended up at Shrewsbury Town in 1989 in his mid-20s. At Shrewsbury the goals started to flow (60/27). A period at Bury (25/9), then Millwall followed initially on loan (34/10) before signing for Bolton. Bruce Rioch had already managed at Millwall and Middlesbrough and was to field an exciting Bolton side that produced giant-killing exploits and soon took the team to the second tier. McGinlay's goals were a big part of it, initially with Andy Walker, who had joined Bolton from Celtic. Walker only stayed for a couple of years before heading back to Celtic but had his share of goals too (67/44).

McGinlay, over his five years, hit 87 in 192 games before joining Bradford City in November 1997 for £625,000. The move to Bradford was injury-strewn (17/3) and John's career petered out with Oldham (7/1) and then spells in the US, playing and coaching in Cincinnati.

As for Rioch, he went on to manage Arsenal where his first signing was Dennis Bergkamp, but he was sacked after only one season. Since then, Bruce has managed Norwich, Wigan and worked in Denmark too.

1995/96

Alex Ferguson's group of 'kids' won the Premier League with 82 points, four ahead of challengers Newcastle. Brian McClair was used sparingly, playing in 22 matches with ten of those coming off the bench, contributing three goals.

United also won the FA Cup, beating Liverpool 1-0 thanks to an Eric Cantona goal. Fergie was the only Scot involved in the final with McClair being left out.

Duncan Ferguson in the thick of it v Chelsea in November 1994. John McGinlay (right), a Bolton legend but fondly remembered by Scotland fans for his goal v Sweden in 1996.

Aston Villa won the League Cup with a convincing 3-0 win over Leeds. Gary McAllister captained the Leeds side, in what was to be his last season with the club (231/31) having won the title with them in 1991/92. He moved to Coventry City, teaming up with former team-mate Gordon Strachan, for £3m. Four years later he moved from City (119/20) to Liverpool where he was to win three trophies in 2000/01.

The only other Scot involved in the final was Andy Gray, the son of former Leeds full-back Frank Gray. Andy had come through the youth setup at Elland Road, progressing to the first team by 1995. His career is perhaps a typical of the era to come for many following the Bosman ruling as Andy ran through a gamut of teams after leaving Leeds in 1998 (22/0). His playing career lasted for around 18 years with stops at Nottingham Forest (64/1), Bradford (77/20), Sheffield United (58/25), Sunderland (21/1), Burnley (60/25), Charlton (44/9), Barnsley (96/21) and Leeds again (8/1) before finishing up at Bradford (15/1) in 2013/14. The forward also had loan spells at Bury, Preston and Oldham as well as 'try before you buy' ones at Burnley and Charlton. His league tally is 490 games and 108 goals.

1996/97

Manchester United retained the title with 75 points, seven clear of Newcastle, Arsenal and Liverpool all on 68. Brian McClair only started four games, without scoring, and making 15 appearances as a substitute. He was often used by Fergie to see out games with his calming influence. This was to be his final trophy having won the title four times, the FA Cup twice as well as the League Cup. Brian ended his playing career at Old Trafford the following season (355/88), returning to Motherwell for an 11-game spell. He has since been involved in coaching at United and at one point was the SFA's performance director.

The FA Cup was won by Chelsea, beating Middlesbrough 2-0. The only Scot was Chelsea's Stevie Clarke, still holding that right-back berth in a team full of stars such as Dan Petrescu, Frank Leboeuf and the two Italians, Roberto Di Matteo and Gianfranco Zola. Clarke had been part of the team that lost the FA Cup Final to Manchester United in 1994. He was to win two more trophies with Chelsea the following year.

Martin O'Neill's Leicester also defeated Middlesbrough in the League Cup Final 1-0 after a replay, without any Scots being fielded by either side.

1997/98

Arsenal, managed by Arsène Wenger, dominated the season, winning the Premier League and FA Cup. Central defender Scott Marshall had joined Arsenal aged 15 in 1988, signing on a few years later. His father and grandfather, Gordon Marshall Jnr. and Gordon Marshall, were goalkeepers in their time. However, first-team appearances were hard to come by and he was farmed out on loan to Rotherham (10/1), Oxford (no appearances) and Sheffield United (17/0). Scott played three games in the title season, two as sub, and left Highbury in August 1998 (25/1). A brief stop at Southampton (2/0) and a loan to Celtic (1/0) followed before four years at Brentford (75/3). Retiring after the 2003/04 season with Wycombe (8/0), Scott has had various coaching roles over the years and was caretaker manager at Villa, Reading and Colchester too.

Although no Scots played in the FA Cup Final as Arsenal beat Newcastle 2-0, the Magpies were managed by Kenny Dalglish. Kenny had taken Blackburn to the summit of the Premier League in 1994/95 but had chosen to move position and became director of football afterwards. Stepping down a year later, he took over at Newcastle in January 1997. Although he lost this final, Kenny was to return to Wembley for the FA Cup and League Cup finals as manager of Liverpool in 2011/12.

The League Cup Final was to see Stevie Clarke as the only Scot as Chelsea overcame Middlesbrough once more in a final to lift the trophy. Stevie came on in the 75th minute with the scores level. Extra time saw Chelsea emerge as 2-0 winners. He was also to win the Cup Winners' Cup in what was to be his final season. After 11 years at the club (330/7) Stevie left to join former team-mate Ruud Gullit as assistant at Newcastle. His coaching career has been quite varied with spells as a coach or assistant to Bobby Robson, José Mourinho, Avram Grant, Gianfranco Zola and Kenny Dalglish. He has since gone on to manage West Brom, Kilmarnock and of course the Scotland national side.

1998/99

Alex Ferguson's Manchester United had their greatest season with the Champions League, Premier League and FA Cup all won for a glorious treble. The league was close though, winning with 79 points, one ahead of Arsenal.

There were no Scots involved in these triumphs although Alex Notman was a squad member but his only United game came in the

League Cup that year as a substitute in a defeat to Tottenham, denying the chance of a quadruple for Fergie's side.

Forward Notman was born in Dalkeith, the same Midlothian town that future player Darren Fletcher hailed from. He went on loan to Aberdeen (2/0) and then Sheffield United (10/3) before moving to Norwich in 2000 for £250,000. Sadly, injury would see his career come to a premature end at 24 (54/1). Alex would go on to play non-league football with King's Lynn and others before playing in the Highland League with Formartine United.

Manchester United won the FA Cup, beating Ruud Gullit's Newcastle 2-0 at Wembley. Among the three subs used by Newcastle were Scots Duncan Ferguson and Stephen Glass. Ferguson had won the FA Cup in 1995 with Everton but shortly after his move to St James' Park in November 1998 he had been blighted by a hernia injury. After a second season at Newcastle (30/8) he was welcomed back to Everton for £3.75m. Although loved at Goodison, his aggression did lead to eight red cards in his Premier League career, which came to an end in 2006 after choosing to retire early. He spent five years in Spain before returning to Everton as a youth coach and then moving up to first-team coach and caretaker boss at one point, He has since taken charge at Forest Green Rovers and Inverness Caledonian Thistle.

Midfielder Stephen Glass was born in Dundee and started his career at Aberdeen. After being loaned out to short-lived Junior side Crombie Sports, Glass made his breakthrough in 1994/95, playing in 21 league games. Stephen won the Scottish League Cup with the Dons the following season. He left in 1998 (108/9) for Newcastle for £650,000. He was to play at St James' Park for three seasons (43/7) but niggling injuries hampered his playing time. He signed on at Watford in 2001 and played a couple of seasons there (64/4). Back in Scotland he played first for Hibernian (86/3) and then Dunfermline (69/9) before heading Stateside for a season with Carolina Railhawks. Since then, Stephen has been involved in coaching at Shamrock Rovers, Atlanta United and then as manager at Aberdeen for a brief period.

The League Cup was won by Tottenham Hotspur, by now managed by George Graham. After his dismissal from Arsenal and the serving of his 'bung' ban, George took over at Leeds in 1996. In September 1998 he moved to Tottenham and soon won the League Cup but he wasn't to last long at White Hart Lane, being dismissed by the new owners in March 2001. George never returned to football management after this.

Runners-up Leicester had two Scots in their line-up. Matt Elliott is probably as English as you can get but qualified for Scotland through his Scottish grandmother. However, anytime he played for Scotland he gave his all, and he was part of the World Cup 1998 squad. Matt had started out in non-league football before signing on at Charlton in 1988 where he only made one league appearance.

The central defender then moved on to Torquay for three years (124/15) before heading to Scunthorpe initially on loan (8/1), then signing a more permanent deal in March 1992 (53/7). Over three years were then spent at Oxford United (148/21) when Leicester bought him for £1.6m in 1997. Matt would captain Leicester for their League Cup triumph in 2000.

Stuart Campbell was an unused sub on the bench for the Foxes. Born in that most Scottish of English towns, Corby, Stuart joined from his hometown team in 1997. More often used as a sub at Filbert Street (37/0), the midfielder had a loan spell at Birmingham City (2/0) before going to Grimsby first on loan (38/2) and then permanently for £200,000 in 2001. Three years were spent with the Mariners (117/10) before moving to Bristol Rovers. Stuart captained Rovers during his seven-season period at the club before being released in 2011 (288/3). At the tail end of his last season Stuart took over as caretaker manager but couldn't save the side from relegation. He finished his career in the US with Tampa Bay Rowdies and has done some coaching there too.

1999/2000

Fergie's United retained the Premier League title with no Scots involved in the playing side. They won 91 points, a massive 18 in front of second-placed Arsenal.

Chelsea won the FA Cup with no Scots and only one Englishman, captain Dennis Wise, in their starting line-up, beating Aston Villa 1-0 thanks to a Roberto Di Matteo goal. Villa did have more players from the home nations involved but no Scots.

Matt Elliott captained Leicester to victory in the League Cup Final over Tranmere Rovers. Having scored the only goal in the semi-final win over Villa, he netted both goals for Leicester as they ran out 2-1 winners. Matt spent another four years with the Foxes (245/26) although he was loaned out to Ipswich in 2004 (10/0). He retired early due to a knee injury in January 2005.

Brian McClair was bought for £850,000 from Celtic in July 1987 and spent over ten years at Old Trafford.

Stevie Clarke spent over ten years with Chelsea after his move from St Mirren in January 1987 for £422,000.

* * *

European and international competitions

Season **1990/91** saw English clubs return to European competitions after a five-year ban, and it was Alex Ferguson's Manchester United who immediately restarted the collection of silverware by winning the European Cup Winners' Cup, defeating Johan Cruyff's Barcelona 2-1 in the final at the Stadion Feijenoord in Rotterdam. It was, however, only the second European trophy for the Old Trafford outfit, won some 23 years after their Wembley 1968 success. For Alex Ferguson, it was also his second European trophy having guided Aberdeen to Cup Winners' Cup glory in 1982/83.

United's starting line-up in the final was still what you could call a 'traditional' British and Irish affair – comprising seven Englishmen including skipper Bryan Robson and Paul Ince, two Welshmen in Clayton Blackmore and Mark Hughes, the latter netting both of their goals in the final, Irish full-back Denis Irwin and Scottish international striker Brian McClair, who also appeared in all games leading up to the final. For their part, the Barcelona starting XI consisted of nine Spaniards and Danish striker Michael Laudrup plus Dutch midfielder Ronald Koeman – whose goal in the final came after the brace by the avenging ex-Camp Nou man Sparky.

United had a 'businesslike' run to the final, beating Pécsi Munkás in the first round, 2-0 at Old Trafford and 1-0 in Hungary with McClair the scorer. Next up were Wrexham, the runners-up to Hereford United in the 1990 Welsh Cup Final. United won comfortably, 3-0 at Old Trafford with McClair scoring the opening goal and 2-0 in North Wales. Where was Deadpool when you needed him?

There was a bit of a hiccup in the quarter-finals however when Montpellier visited Manchester and fought out a 1-1 draw, and this after McClair had given United the lead in the first minute. In Occitania, however, the hosts were less than fragrant (sorry) and United won 2-0 with a howler by the goalkeeper plus a penalty despite Montpellier having the services of future United defender/Slaven Bilić slapper Laurent Blanc (Larry White if you prefer) and creative Colombian midfield playmaker Carlos Valderrama with his distinctive, huge blond Afro-hairstyle. For those who like to categorise everything, apparently CV had type IV curly hair; we think Christian Dailly was type III.

Anyway, in the semi-finals United travelled to a Poland that was no longer behind the Iron Curtain. During English clubs' absence from

UEFA competitions, Europe had changed dramatically with the collapse of communist regimes throughout the eastern part of the continent. Legia Warsaw, who were the main official club of the Polish Army, were the opposition and United defeated them 3-1 with McClair scoring the first (an associated match ticket was sold at auction for £440 in February 2024). In the return game at Old Trafford, however, United had to be content with a flat 1-1 draw, but through they went to face and overcome Barcelona in what was the Catalan club's fifth Cup Winners' Cup final.

United's success though did not signal a return to the English dominance of silverware of the late 1970s and early 1980s – in defence of the Cup Winners' Cup, the Red Devils were beaten by Atlético Madrid in the second round.

As for player nationalities, the times they were a-changing – big style.

* * *

In **1993/94** Arsenal, skippered by Tony Adams, landed their second European trophy when they defeated the holders, a Parma side that would supply Italy with five members of their 1994 USA World Cup squad, in the final of the Cup Winners' Cup in Copenhagen – England international Alan Smith the scorer after 20 minutes. It was 1-0 to the Arsenal who were managed by former Scotland international George Graham and included future Scotland international Paul Dickov on the bench as an unused substitute.

* * *

In **1994/95** Arsenal came close to becoming the first team (indeed, they would have been the *only* team; the competition was discontinued in 1999) to successfully defend the Cup Winners' Cup when they again reached the final, this time in Paris, only to lose to 2-1 to Real Zaragoza of Spain after extra time. Arsenal's caretaker manager at the time was Stewart Houston, the Dunoon-born former Manchester United and Scotland left-back. George Graham had left their employ three months earlier 'under a bit of a cloud'.

* * *

In **1997/98** Chelsea became the last British club to win the Cup Winners' Cup when they defeated VfB Stuttgart 1-0 in the final in Stockholm with Super Stevie Clarke at right-back, his final game for the west London outfit. For company Clarke had cosmopolitan colleagues including the likes of Frank Leboeuf (France), Dan Petrescu (Romania), Gus Poyet (Uruguay) and match-winner Gianfranco Zola (Italy) who netted seconds after replacing Tore André Flo (Norway) in the 71st minute. Skippered by Crazy Gang member Dennis Wise with Gianluca Vialli as player-manager, the good times were back at the Bridge and the frequency of winning silverware would increase in the early part of the 21st century.

Chelsea's route to a second Cup Winners' Cup triumph began with a 4-0 aggregate win over Slovan Bratislava (2-0 in London and 2-0 in the relatively 'new' Slovakia – Czechoslovakia having been peacefully dissolved on 31 December 1992). In the first leg of the second round they were on the receiving end of a surprise 3-2 defeat by Tromsø in the snowy northern Norwegian city, sitting 350km above the Arctic Circle. However, in the return match the Blues duly defrosted and won 7-1 with Vialli netting a hat-trick.

In the quarter-finals there were impressive back-to-back victories against Real Betis, 2-1 in Seville and 3-1 at Stamford Bridge. Their semi-final opponents were Vicenza, who had won their first Coppa Italia the season previous. Around 40 miles west of Venice, Chelsea lost the first leg 1-0 but prevailed 3-1 at the Bridge. Chelsea would then add the Cup Winners' Cup to the League Cup that was also won that season.

Steve Clarke's Euro run began in the second round while most of Chelsea's goals came from their Italian triumvirate of Vialli (five), Zola (four) and Roberto Di Matteo (three). Chelsea's success came in the penultimate season of the Cup Winners' Cup competition as it was abolished in 1999 and merged with the UEFA Cup.

The *final* final would be played at Villa Park on 19 May 1999 with Lazio triumphing over RCD Mallorca, who had eliminated Chelsea, in the semi-finals. The tournament ran for 39 seasons in total with English clubs being the most successful with eight titles spread across seven clubs and 13 final appearances overall. Barcelona, however, were the most successful club with three wins in five finals.

* * *

Despite being managed by Alex Ferguson, there were no Scots in the Manchester United side (Premier League runners-up in 1997/98) that achieved a stunning late, late 2-1 victory over Bayern Munich (1997/98 Bundesliga runners-up) to win the **1998/99** Champions League Final in

Barcelona. Fergie time. Sheringham. Solskjaer. Superb. European victory number three for the Red Devils and Europe's top club trophy returning to England for the first time since 1984.

In defence of their crown, United lost out to eventual winners Real Madrid at the quarter-final stage the following year.

* * *

In **1999/2000** Arsenal, managed by Arsène Wenger, reached their fourth European final – the UEFA Cup – but this time Copenhagen wasn't so wonderful as the Gunners lost in the Danish capital to Galatasaray, 4-1 on penalties after the game finished goalless. Ray Parlour was the only Gunner to net and Galatasaray's success was the first European trophy for a Turkish club.

* * *

In the 1990s, Sweden, England and France provided the stages for Scotland's three appearances at the finals of major international competitions – but yet again, we somehow failed to win any of them!

There were only eight nations at Sweden in 1992 but alas, the dream final of Scotland v England failed to materialise with both teams being eliminated at the group stage. Scotland had reached Sweden by virtue of topping a qualifying group ahead of Switzerland, Romania, Bulgaria and San Marino but in Scandinavia they finished third behind the Netherlands and a reunified Germany, although ahead of the former Soviet Union who were cunningly disguised as the Commonwealth of Independent States (CIS).

Scotland were unlucky to lose against the Netherlands, 1-0 with Gordon Durie of Tottenham Hotspur winning his 20th cap, and world champions Germany, 2-0 with the under-appreciated Pat Nevin of Everton getting game time, before deservedly defeating the CIS 3-0 with goals from Paul McStay of Celtic, Brian McClair of Manchester United and Gary McAllister of Leeds.

They say every picture tells a story, and in Panini's Euro 92 sticker album, the impish-looking image of Leeds' Gordon Strachan sits proudly next to that of Kevin Gallacher of Coventry City, but alas after having played in four of the qualifying matches, scoring away to San Marino, and two warm-up matches to take his cap tally to 50, and helping the Elland Road club clinch the final top-flight First Division title, the fiery midfielder retired from international football due to a long-term back injury, aged 35. Strachan would, however, continue his club football with Leeds and Coventry for another five years.

Kevin Gallacher won 53 Scotland caps between 1988 and 2001 and played at the 1992 and 1996 European Championships, as well as the 1998 World Cup finals – the latter two when he was with Blackburn. He scored nine goals for his country, six of them in qualifying for France 98, including a double against Austria at Celtic Park.

To make it over the border to Euro 96, however, Craig Brown's Scotland finished a strong second behind Russia but ahead of Greece, Finland, the Faroe Islands and San Marino. Goalscoring heroes included John McGinlay of Bolton, Colin Calderwood of Tottenham and Pat Nevin of Tranmere. At the Euros, Scotland did well in Birmingham, drawing 0-0 with the Netherlands and defeating Switzerland 1-0, both at Villa Park. Unfortunately, sandwiched in the middle was a game at Wembley which was lost, 2-0 against England, the pivotal moment being Gary McAllister's penalty miss with England leading 1-0. Of course, everyone knows that the skipper from Leeds wasn't to blame – it was that dastardly psychic-magician Uri Geller who made the ball wobble just before Gary struck it.

Just as Euro 96 expanded to include 16 teams, so France 98 increased to 32, which meant that although Scotland qualified for both, they were now getting further and further away from the final itself. Just a thought.

Anyway, to reach France, Scotland qualified as Europe's best second-placed team behind Austria but ahead of Sweden, who had finished third in 1994, Latvia, Estonia and Belarus. A key match was Scotland's 1-0 win over Sweden at Ibrox with John McGinlay netting after just eight minutes and skipper Colin Hendry of Blackburn marshalling his troops for a successful but nerve-wracking, rearguard action.

Scotland travelled around France quite a bit – Paris, Bordeaux and Saint-Étienne – but couldn't find a win at any locale before disappearing into a Gallic triangle. At the Stade de France in the opening game of the tournament against Brazil, the defending champions 'fluked it' 2-1, with five Anglos – Colin Calderwood of Spurs and Christian Dailly of Derby plus Blackburn trio Hendry, Gallacher and Billy McKinlay – giving their all on the big stage. A 1-1 draw with Norway at the Parc Lescure followed before it all went horribly wrong at the Stade Geoffroy-Guichard as the Scots crashed 3-0 to Morocco. Au revoir! Au revoir! Au revoir!

Scotland then came up agonisingly short in trying to make it to what would have been a third successive European Championship finals. After finishing second in the Euro 2000 qualifiers to the Czech Republic but ahead of Bosnia-Herzegovina, Lithuania, Estonia and the Faroe Islands, Scotland lost to England in a two-legged play-off, going down 2-0 at Hampden before giving it a right go at a soon to be replaced 'old' Wembley and winning 1-0.

Premier League Wimbledon's Neil Sullivan had replaced Jim Leighton in goal for Scotland while John Collins, the penalty hero against Brazil in 1998, was now with Everton but it was his Goodison Park club-mate Don Hutchison who netted at Wembley on 17 November 1999 to give Scotland their most recent victory against the 'auld enemy'. David Weir concluded an Everton threesome and there was also the Blackburn duo of Callum Davidson and Christian Dailly.

Born in Sutton, Greater London, Sullivan would win a total of 28 Scotland caps between 1997 and 2003 (13 at Wimbledon, 15 at Tottenham). In his final international appearance as a Womble – in that qualifying second leg – Sullivan became only the third Scotland goalkeeper not to concede a goal against England at Wembley, following on from David Cumming of Middlesbrough in 1938 and Alan Rough of Partick Thistle in 1981. David Marshall of Derby became the fourth in 2021.

Between 1997 and 2008, Christian Dailly would win 67 caps and net six times for his country. His last cap came while with Rangers but his preceding 66 were all achieved with clubs south of the border – Derby (14), Blackburn (12) and West Ham (40).

The Dundee-born centre-back was so popular with the Scotland and West Ham supporters that he inspired 'The Christian Dailly Song' – sung to the tune of the Andy Williams classic 'Can't Take My Eyes Off You'. The revised lyrics went like this, 'Oh Christian Dailly you are the love of my life. Oh Christian Dailly I'd let you make love to [or equivalent] my wife. Oh Christian Dailly I want curly hair too.' They really don't write them like that any more.

The 1990s brought to a conclusion a 'golden age' for Scottish international football dating back to the early 1970s although we suppose 'golden' is a relative term – perhaps 'shiny' would be a better adjective.

8

Early 21st Century

Overview

Smartphones have become integral to our way of life. A cloud-based, virtual assistant called Alexa has inveigled her way into our homes. Electric vehicles (including driverless cars), giant wind-turbines dotted across the landscape and artificial intelligence are the way ahead. Cue the theme tune from *Terminator 3: Rise of the Machines*.

In 2014 the Scottish electorate said 'No' to full political independence from the UK. In 2016 the UK electorate said 'No' to continued membership of the European Union. In 2018 the International Football Board formally said 'Yes' to the use of Video Assistant Referees (VAR). Tears for Fears were right – it's a mad world. It's also a world which in 2020 and 2021 nearly came a cropper when the global, and often fatal, coronavirus pandemic resulted in much of the planet going into lockdown and/or imposing travel, social and business restrictions. Football was not exempt and in England season 2019/20 was suspended in March for three months before being concluded behind closed doors. Season 2020/21 was also largely played behind closed doors but ultimately with restricted attendances permitted, though with no away fans allowed as the situation slowly returned to some sort of normality. Full attendance returned in 2021/22 and a lasting effect was the increase in the maximum number of substitutes permitted from three to five.

Back to keeping it light, and the movie world in the early 21st century has been dominated by escapist blockbusters from the Harry Potter and Lord of the Rings series as well as superheroes from the Marvel and DC Comics universes. That said, there has still been room for some soccer classics such as *Mean Machine* (2001) starring Wimbledon method actor Vinnie Jones as a retired footballer but now prison inmate, as well as *Bend It Like Beckham* (2002) and *The Damned United* (2009). The latter movie was based on Brian Clough's 44-day tenure as manager of Leeds United in 1974 and included former Greenock Morton footballer turned successful actor Martin Compston playing the part of Scottish international John O'Hare. Furthermore, Eddie Gray was portrayed by his son Stuart Gray, another former footballer who had played for Greenock Morton as well as Celtic, Reading, Rushden & Diamonds and Oxford United.

On 3 January 2020 the BBC aired a 50th-anniversary special of the long-running quiz show *A Question of Sport*. The 1,255th episode included former Sunderland, Rangers and Scotland striker Ally McCoist who had been a team captain from 1997 to 2006. Back in the 1980s, another popular footballing team captain on the show had been Liverpool's Emlyn Hughes. As for *Match of the Day* it became Gary Lineker's fiefdom, faithfully supported by pundits such as Alan Shearer and Ian Wright. In an ever-changing media world, however, the TV honours have had to be shared among the terrestrial channels as well as with the likes of Sky Sports, Eurosport, BT Sport, ESPN and Al Jazeera Sport (rebrandings and mergers add to the fun) plus numerous dedicated football club channels such as MUTV.

An excellent theatrical production among a growing trend of theatrical football-related productions was *You'll Never Walk Alone – The History of Liverpool FC* in words and music by Nicky Allt which this author caught and enjoyed in 2011, the dodgy Scottish accents of the actors portraying Bill Shankly and Kenny Dalglish notwithstanding.

Into the literary world, and in 2002 there was founded Pitch Publishing which has become the UK's leading and most prolific sports publisher, and for an outfit based in the deep south (of England) the number of Scottish football titles within its vast catalogue is pretty impressive (geographically speaking, Pitch Publishing is closer to Paris and Brussels than Partick or Bute!). In 2020 *World Soccer* magazine, also based on the English south coast, celebrated its 60th anniversary while 2024 saw the 30th anniversary of *FourFourTwo*.

Three impressive paper and print success stories against a backdrop of an ongoing electronic, online onslaught and a growing demand for immediacy of information which has seen some clubs cease production of their matchday programmes.

For its part, English football has become an extremely attractive, multi-national, global concern in which British and Irish players and managers now often struggle to make their presence felt. As such, Scottish appearances on the winners' rostrums are now something of a rarity but are still to be cherished nonetheless, perhaps even more so.

In the first 24 seasons of the new millennium, from 2000/01 to 2023/24, Scots have featured in nine title-winning squads, although for four of these the connection is tenuous at best – goalkeeper Andy Goram's two appearances and Michael Stewart's three for Manchester United in 2000/01. In terms of FA Cup finalists successful or otherwise, the number is 16 out of 48 and for League Cup finalists it is 14. In Europe, English clubs have recorded 11 winning campaigns so far with Scots featuring in just two of those finals – both with Liverpool.

From season 2002/03 UEFA enforced the creation of two transfer windows in summer and winter as the money involved in the transfer market got ridiculous, or obscene depending on your point of view. In July 2002 Leeds United defender Rio Ferdinand crossed the Pennines to Manchester United for £29.1m. In September 2013 Welsh midfielder Gareth Bale joined Real Madrid from Spurs for a world record £85.3m and in the summer 2023 transfer window Premier League clubs spent an aggregate total of over £2bn.

The vast bulk of on-field success, however, has been restricted to five extremely wealthy clubs – Arsenal, Chelsea, Liverpool, Manchester City and Manchester United. In the 2000s Manchester United won the most domestic trophies with nine (five Premier League titles, one FA Cup and three League Cups) while their not-so-noisy neighbours Manchester City won nowt! Indeed, as at 2010, City's most recent trophy success was the 1975/76 League Cup win. In the 2010s, however, it was City who topped the domestic silverware table with four Premier Leagues, two FA Cups and five League Cups. This included an unprecedented domestic treble in 2018/19. City's success has continued into the 2020s with them winning six of the 12 competitions at the time of writing plus a Champions League trophy in 2022/23 just for good measure.

There are arguably two main reasons for this sea-change – United's Alex Ferguson retiring from football management at end of season 2012/13, while in August 2008 City were purchased by Abu Dhabi United Group and investment in players went through the proverbial roof and into the stratosphere, culminating with the appointment of the phenomenally successful Pep Guardiola as their manager in 2016.

Chelsea also enjoyed a gloriously successful era under the ownership of Russian oligarch Roman Abramovich from 2003 to 2022 as the undernoted summary of trophy winners testifies. The winning combination was 'megabucks' player investment plus a steady stream of high-profile and highly talented managers, with Portugal's José 'The Special One' Mourinho arguably the pick of the bunch.

Meanwhile, over in north London, Frenchman Arsène Wenger also delivered an impressive number of trophies during his spell as manager of Arsenal (which ran from 1996 to 2018) without having access to the same size of 'war chest' as Manchester City or Chelsea. Liverpool's 21st-century trophy haul is impressive in overall number and in Europe but currently includes just the one Premier League title – Jürgen Klopp's Covid-disrupted but ultimately successful 2019/20 campaign.

So far, the 21st century, which is almost one quarter complete, has seen 'giants' such as Tottenham Hotspur lift but one trophy, the 2007/08 League Cup, while the likes of Aston Villa, Everton and Leeds have yet to win silverware and of course Newcastle United's 50-plus years' famine continues. Maybe the Magpies need to start collecting some more Scottish signatures. Just a suggestion. Ironically, Aston Villa, skippered by John McGinn, finishing fourth in the Premier League in 2023/24 and qualifying for the Champions League for the first time since 1982/83 was viewed as something of a 'breakthrough'.

As if to emphasise the changing times, the original Wembley Stadium closed in October 2000, and was then demolished and replaced on the same site with no twin towers but a 134m-high arch, two partially retractable roof structures and 90,000 seats. It opened in 2007 with Cardiff's Millennium Stadium hosting seven League Cup finals from 2001 to 2007 inclusive, and six FA Cup finals from 2001 to 2006.

Trophy winners 2000/01 to 2023/2024

Successful clubs	League	FA Cup	League Cup	European	Total
Manchester City	8	3	6	1	18
Chelsea	5	5	3	4	17
Manchester United	7	3	5	2	17
Liverpool	1	3	5	3	12
Arsenal	2	7	-	-	9
Leicester City	1	1	-	-	2
West Ham United	-	-	-	1	1
Portsmouth	-	1	-	-	1
Wigan Athletic	-	1	-	-	1
Birmingham City	-	-	1	-	1

Blackburn Rovers	-	-	1	-	1
Middlesbrough	-	-	1	-	1
Swansea City	-	-	1	-	1
Tottenham Hotspur	-	-	1	-	1
TOTALS	**24**	**24**	**24**	**11**	**83**

* * *

For the Scotland national team, much of the first quarter of the 21st century can be labelled 'The Wilderness Years' – as a result of six unsuccessful World Cup qualifying campaigns and four failed attempts to reach the Euros. Conversely the highlights have been winning the 2006 Kirin Cup (ahem!) plus appearances at the finals of the 2020 and 2024 European Championships. God bless managers Walter Smith, Alex McLeish and Steve Clarke!

Helping the Tartan Army get through these wilderness years, the Scotland women's team qualified for the Euros of 2017 and World Cup in 2019. Indeed, the dramatic growth of women's football in the early part of the 21st century both at club and country level is a success story in its own right.

* * *

Domestic competitions
2000/01

The first full season of the 21st century saw little change with Alex Ferguson's Manchester United winning the championship on 80 points, ten clear of Arsenal. Two Scots featured for United over the season in a limited capacity.

Goalkeeper Andy Goram was brought in on loan from Motherwell, playing in two games at the tail end of the campaign. Andy was born in Bury, the town his father Lewis had settled in after his own goalkeeping career had ended.

Andy's career began in earnest at Oldham (195/0) where he spent six years and won his first four Scotland caps. A £325,000 move to Hibs (138/1) followed in 1987 then Rangers paid out £1m for Andy in 1991. Andy won five titles, three Scottish Cups and two League Cups in his time at Ibrox. He left at the end of the 1997/98, and prior to his exit it had been disclosed that he suffered from mental health issues. He had short spells with Notts County (1/0) and Sheffield United (7/0) before Motherwell took him on for a longer term (57/0). In March 2001, with both of his keepers struggling for fitness, Ferguson needed an experienced goalie for cover and so Andy was brought in for three months, costing £100,000. The following seasons saw Andy play for Hamilton (1/0), Coventry (7/0), Oldham (4/0), Queen of the South (19/0) and finally Elgin City (5/0). Afterwards Andy went into goalkeeper coaching but sadly passed away in July 2022 due to oesophageal cancer.

The other Scot involved was Edinburgh-born Michael Stewart. Signed professionally in 1998, Stewart made his debut in October 2000 but was only to make two more league appearances that year. He made three appearances the following season but only one after that. He went out on loan to Nottingham Forest (13/0) and Hearts (17/0) before being let go. In 2005 he joined Hibernian (54/2) before returning to Tynecastle and Hearts in 2007 (87/12). A move to Turkish club Gençlerbirliği in 2010 quickly fell apart and Michael ended his career at Charlton (9/0). He has since gone on to a career in television with BBC Scotland.

The League Cup and FA Cup were won by Liverpool with Gary McAllister being the only Scot fielded in both finals.

McAllister had been in the losing Leeds side in the 1995 League Cup Final. He had been a surprising signing at Liverpool by Gérard Houllier given that he was 35 at the time but he was to win five trophies with the club in his two years at Anfield: the FA Cup, League Cup, UEFA Cup, Charity Shield and UEFA Super Cup.

The League Cup was won by defeating Birmingham on penalties after a 1-1 draw. Gary had come on in the 78th minute and took Liverpool's first spot-kick, which he duly dispatched. He was also used as a late sub in the 60th minute of the FA Cup Final as Liverpool faced Arsenal. The Gunners took the lead shortly after, but a McAllister free kick wasn't cleared and Michael Owen latched on to it to equalise in the 83rd minute. Five minutes later Owen hit the winning goal.

After two great years at Anfield (55/5), Gary returned to Coventry as player-manager but resigned in April 2004 (55/10). He became Leeds manager in 2008 but was sacked in his second season. Gary has since been assistant manager at Middlesbrough, Villa (twice), Liverpool and Rangers.

2001/02

Arsenal lifted the Premier League and also won the FA Cup, beating Chelsea 2-0 in the final.

Scots were to be involved in the League Cup Final as Graeme Souness's Blackburn beat Tottenham 2-1 at the Millennium Stadium in Cardiff. Souness had won the FA Cup in 1992 as manager of Liverpool but by January 1994 he had resigned his post. In the next few years, he managed at Galatasaray, Southampton, Benfica and Torino, and in March 2000 he took over at Blackburn. His time at Blackburn saw him oversee the League Cup win and some decent Premier League standings; however, he left in September 2004 for Newcastle. Things didn't work out so well on Tyneside and he was sacked in December 2005. Graeme has never returned to management but is a regular contributor to football shows on TV.

On the playing side, Neil Sullivan was between the sticks for Spurs. Born in Sutton, Neil qualified for Scotland through his Scottish grandmother. He joined Wimbledon as a youth in 1986 and by the time he left for Spurs in 2000 he had amassed 181 appearances for the Dons. His three years at Tottenham (64/0) were followed by a stint at Chelsea as emergency cover (4/0). Neil signed for Leeds in 2004 (95/0) before moving to Doncaster initially on two loan spells (three appearances in his first, 13 in his second). Signing permanently, Neil won the League One title and the Football League Trophy with Rovers (186/0). There was also a loan spell at AFC Wimbledon (20/0). Neil hung up his gloves in 2013 but went on to goalkeeper coaching at Leeds and Hull.

2002/03

Manchester United won the league on 83 points, five clear of Arsenal. Michael Stewart made his final United appearance as a substitute in a Champions League match.

Arsenal won the FA Cup Final thanks to a Robert Pires goal. Opponents Southampton were managed by Gordon Strachan and had Edinburgh-born Paul Telfer at right-back. After Strachan had won the First Division with Leeds in 1991, he moved on to Coventry in 1995 where he was soon in charge. Dismissed at the start of the 2001/02 season, he took over at Southampton shortly after. Strachan left St Mary's for a break from football in February 2004. He later went on to manage Celtic, Middlesbrough and then Scotland.

Telfer started his career at Luton Town (144/19) in 1988, leaving in 1995 for Coventry. There he was soon working with Strachan as his boss (191/6). He was one of Strachan's first signings both at Southampton

(127/1) and Celtic (57/1). He cut his career at Celtic short but returned to football after a few months with Bournemouth (18/0). He briefly played with Leeds in 2008 (14/0) before finishing his playing days with Slough and then Sutton United.

Manchester United lost 2-0 to Liverpool in the League Cup Final with no Scots in either squad.

2003/04

The see-saw title race tipped towards Arsenal this season, going the Premier League season unbeaten and topping the table with 90 points, 11 clear of Chelsea in second place

The FA Cup was won by Manchester United beating Millwall 3-0 in the final in Cardiff. In their midfield was 20-year-old Darren Fletcher, from Dalkeith. Darren had joined the United youth setup aged 11 and had broken through in this season, playing in 22 league games and the final. He was to win five titles with the club although this was to be his only FA Cup success.

Peter Sweeney was the only Scot in the Millwall line-up. Glasgow-born Peter grew up in London from the age of three, joining Millwall as a youth, and made his debut for the first team in 2002. The midfielder left the Den (59/5) for Stoke City (35/2) in 2005 and was loaned out to Yeovil Town (8/0) and Walsall (7/0) during his three seasons with the Potters. A move to Leeds in 2008 (9/0) was followed by a loan spell and permanent signing at Grimsby (8/0; 40/4). After 2010 he played for Bury (82/5) and AFC Wimbledon (29/0) before moving into non-league football.

The League Cup was won by Middlesbrough, beating Bolton 2-1 in a Scot-free match.

2004/05

The José Mourinho bandwagon had rolled into town and Chelsea took the title on 95 points, 12 clear of Arsenal. In the 89th minute of the final game of the season, away at Newcastle, Mourinho gave Steven Watt his only Chelsea league appearance. The Aberdonian defender had been out on loan at Barnsley (3/1) before this. He moved to Swansea (3/0) in 2006, where a shoulder injury halted his progress. He went on loan to Inverness Caledonian Thistle which only saw him play in a cup match, and he signed for Highland rivals Ross County in 2008 (43/1). The 2010/11 season was spent at Grimsby (25/2) before turning out for several non-league sides.

Manchester United's Darren Fletcher, a winner in the 2004 FA Cup Final.

West Ham's Christian Dailly, a runner-up in 2006.

Arsenal won the FA Cup, beating Manchester United on penalties after a 0-0 draw. Darren Fletcher was substituted in the 91st minute so never took part in the shoot-out.

The League Cup was won by Chelsea, beating Liverpool 3-2 after extra time.

2005/06

Chelsea retained the Premier League title on 91 points, eight clear of Manchester United.

Liverpool were to win the FA Cup, defeating West Ham on penalties after a 3-3 draw. Dundee-born Christian Dailly came on for the Hammers in the 77th minute of the match. Dailly had made his debut for Dundee United aged 16 in 1990, initially playing as a forward. Following on to play at the heart of the defence by the time he left Tannadice in 1996 (143/18) for Derby County for what would eventually be £1m.

He spent two years with Derby (67/4) before a £5.35m move to Blackburn in August 1998 (70/4). He suffered relegation with Blackburn and did not see eye-to-eye with newly installed manager Graeme Souness, so a £1.75m move to West Ham was precipitated in January 2001. The 2001/02 season saw Christian play every minute of every league game although injuries would curtail some of his appearances over the next few seasons. At the start of 2007/08 he was loaned out to Southampton (11/0) and by January he left the Hammers (158/3) for Rangers. He spent 18 months at Ibrox (21/2) with moves to Charlton (76/1) and Portsmouth (1/0) to follow, and he finished his career at Southend (3/0) in 2012.

The League Cup was won by Manchester United, hammering Wigan Athletic 4-0. Darren Fletcher was not included in the United squad, but Wigan had two Scots on show – Gary Teale and Lee McCulloch. Both had been part of Wigan's rise from the third tier to the Premier League.

Glasgow-born Teale started his career at Clydebank in 1996 (84/16) before moving to Ayr United for three seasons (104/13). Wigan paid out, eventually due to add-ons, £400,000 for the winger in January 2002. After two promotions and that final, Teale left (162/8) for Derby five years later for £600,000. During his time with Derby (87/4), Gary was loaned out to Plymouth Argyle (12/0) and Barnsley (3/0). He spent season 2010/11 with Sheffield Wednesday (41/2) before heading back to Scotland to play with St Mirren where he won the 2013 Scottish League Cup (85/0). He took over as manager at St Mirren for the last half of the 2014/15 season but left the club in the summer and retired from football.

Lee McCulloch, from Bellshill, started out at Motherwell in 1994 making his debut in August 1996. The midfielder with an eye for goal (124/21) was bought by Wigan for £700,000 in March 2001. Lee, like Teale, won two promotions and was to come on as a substitute for Wigan in the League Cup Final (224/44). He left for Rangers in July 2007 at a cost of £2.25m. His time at Rangers would see him savour the highs of three top-tier title wins and play in the 2008 UEFA Cup Final but also suffer their fall from grace in 2012. Lee, however, remained with the club and played his part in their return to the top flight (209/52). He left in 2015 for a coaching position with Kilmarnock, making one appearance for the Ayrshire club, and he went on to manage them also.

2006/07

Alex Ferguson's United won the title with 89 points, six clear of second-placed Chelsea. Darren Fletcher played 24 matches, scoring three goals. Darren also played in the 1-0 FA Cup Final defeat to Chelsea. Chelsea also won the League Cup, beating Arsenal 2-1.

2007/08

The title was retained by United by two points over Chelsea with a total of 87. Darren Fletcher was utilised less this season, playing in 16 games but only starting five.

The FA Cup Final was won by Portsmouth, beating Cardiff City thanks to a goal from Nwankwo Kanu. Three Scots were fielded by Cardiff.

At right-back was Kevin McNaughton who spent nine years at the club. Dundee-born Kevin made his debut for Aberdeen aged 18 and went on to play at Pittodrie for seven years (175/3). He signed for Cardiff in May 2006 and became a regular fixture in the defence. Kevin was also part of the team that lost the 2012 League Cup Final.

In midfield was Aberdeen-born Gavin Rae, who began his career at Dundee. After eight years at Dens Park (223/26), Rae moved to Rangers in January 2004, but his time at Ibrox was hampered by injuries (28/3). He joined Cardiff in June 2007 and was to remain with them until 2011 (130/7). The next few years saw a return to Dundee (13/3), then to hometown team Aberdeen (47/3) and back to Dundee (14/1) before finishing his career in Australia where he has also been involved in coaching.

Coming on as a second-half sub in the final was Steven Thompson. The Paisley-born striker started off at Dundee United in 1996, spending five years at Tannadice (133/18). He moved to Ibrox in December 2002 for £200,000 and spent just over three years at Rangers (62/17). Cardiff signed him for £250,000 in January 2007, but he left the Bluebirds in September 2008 (97/16). Working under former Dundee United team-mate Owen Coyle at Burnley saw Steven net 11 goals as the Turf Moor side gained promotion to the top tier. Released after three years (83/13), Steven ended his playing career at his hometown club St Mirren (154/44). He won the 2013 League Cup with the club and since retiring in 2016 has been a fixture of BBC Scotland's football coverage.

The League Cup was won by Tottenham, beating Chelsea 2-1 after extra time. Playing in only his third game since signing the month before was Alan Hutton. Glasgow-born Hutton started out at Rangers, making his debut in 2002. It took a few years for the free-flowing full-back to establish himself (94/2) but by the time Spurs came in for him in January 2008 the price was a reported £9m. His time at White Hart Lane saw him in and out of favour and latterly Kyle Walker was often picked ahead of him (51/2). Hutton went out on loan to Sunderland (11/0) and finally moved on to Aston Villa in August 2011. There, he was to play in the 2015 FA Cup Final.

2008/09

Darren Fletcher played 26 games, starting 25, and scored three goals as Fergie's side won the title for the third year in a row. They finished on 90 points, four ahead of Liverpool.

The FA Cup was won by Chelsea, defeating Everton 1-0 at Wembley. Everton were managed by Davie Moyes. As a player Moyes took a circuitous route to finally play for Preston, the side he would go into management with. Starting at Celtic in 1980 (24/0), then on to Cambridge United (79/1), Bristol City (83/3), Shrewsbury Town (96/1), Dunfermline (105/1), and Hamilton (5/0), he finished playing in 1998 after five years at Preston (143/5).

His management career has seen him in charge at Preston, Everton, Manchester United, Real Sociedad, Sunderland and latterly West Ham, where he won the UEFA Europa Conference League in 2023.

Sir Alex was the only Scot involved in the League Cup Final as United beat Spurs on penalties, after a 0-0 draw.

2009/10

Carlo Ancelotti's Chelsea wrenched the Premier League trophy from United, winning with 86 points, one ahead of Ferguson's side.

Chelsea managed the double by beating Portsmouth 1-0 in the FA Cup Final thanks to a Didier Drogba goal. On the Portsmouth bench that day was Richard Hughes. Glasgow-born Hughes was brought up in Italy and as a youth was attached to Italian club Atalanta. Returning to the UK, he spent five years at Arsenal. Unable to make the grade, aged 19 he signed on at Bournemouth where he quickly established himself (131/14). The midfielder moved to Portsmouth in 2002 for £50,000. He spent nine years at Fratton Park (131/1), with a loan spell in 2003 at Grimsby (12/1). He did retire at this point but returned to Bournemouth for two more seasons (26/1). He has since gone on to be the technical director at Bournemouth and recently took over as the sporting director at Liverpool.

Alex Ferguson's Manchester United won the League Cup, beating Aston Villa 2-1 with Darren Fletcher playing the 90 minutes.

2010/11

Manchester United returned to the summit of the Premier League with 80 points, nine clear of Chelsea and Manchester City. Darren Fletcher played in 26 matches in total, scoring twice.

Top scorer in League One was Peterborough striker Craig Mackail-Smith with 27 goals. Watford-born Craig qualified for Scotland through his Edinburgh-born grandmother. By the time he had signed for the Posh, Craig had already played for St Albans City, Arlesey Town and Dagenham & Redbridge. In four seasons with Peterborough, he hit 80 goals in 185 appearances. Brighton shelled out £2.5m for Craig in July 2011 but he didn't hit his previous heights and left in 2015 (109/21). He then spent two years at Luton (35/4) with a loan spell to Peterborough (18/5). Craig then went to Wycombe (62/11) with loan periods at Notts County (16/3) and Stevenage (18/0), finishing his career at non-league Bedford Town in 2023.

Manchester City beat Stoke City 1-0 to lift the FA Cup. Neither side fielded any Scots.

Birmingham City won the League Cup, defeating Arsenal 2-1. City were managed by Alex McLeish, who had been part of Alex Ferguson's Aberdeen side that dominated Scottish football in the early 80s. His management career started at Motherwell, then Hibernian before taking over at Rangers. He had won two titles, two Scottish Cups and three League Cups at Ibrox but left the club at the end of the 2005/06 season. He landed the Scotland job in January 2007 but by November he had taken over at Birmingham.

His time at St Andrew's saw the team relegated then promoted and this cup success. Alex went on to manage city rivals Aston Villa, Nottingham Forest, Genk in Belgium and Zamalek in Egypt before a poor return to the Scotland post.

Barry Ferguson was the only Scot on the playing side. Ferguson had started out as a youth at Rangers, debuting in May 1997. In his two periods with the Ibrox club he was to win five titles, five Scottish Cups and five League Cups (288/44). His first spell in England came in August 2003 when Graeme Souness's Blackburn paid £7.5m for him. After a 16-month stay at Ewood Park (36/3) Ferguson returned to Ibrox for £4.75m.

Alex McLeish brought Ferguson to Birmingham in July 2009, and he spent two seasons with the club (72/0) before moving on to Blackpool (80/1) with a loan spell at Fleetwood Town in 2012 (6/0). Barry played once for Clyde, during his tenure as manager from 2014 to 2017. He has since managed Kelty Hearts and Alloa.

A James McFadden goal had opened Birmingham's account in the League Cup run against Rochdale in August 2010 but due to an anterior cruciate ligament injury McFadden's City career was ended prematurely. Having previously been with Motherwell (63/26) and Everton (109/11), Birmingham paid £5m for McFadden in 2008. However, his injury put paid to his career in general, leaving St Andrew's at the end of the 2010/11 season (82/13). The next few seasons saw him play at Everton (7/0), Sunderland (3/0), Motherwell (40/9), St Johnstone (16/1), Motherwell (9/2) and finally Queen of the South (11/0). Faddy retired in January 2018 and has worked in the Scottish football media since.

2011/12

Manchester City under Roberto Mancini won the Premier League in their final match with Sergio Agüero's winning injury-time goal giving them the title over city rivals United on goal difference.

Top scorer in League One was Jordan Rhodes of Huddersfield Town with 36 goals. Oldham-born Rhodes qualified for Scotland through being schooled there while his father Andy played for Dunfermline, St Johnstone and Airdrie. Although a prolific scorer, Jordan had been the subject of several high-profile transfers without getting the chance to make a real impact in top-tier football. Starting off at Ipswich in 2007 (10/1) with loan spells at Oxford (4/0), Rochdale (5/2) and Brentford (14/7), a £350,000 move to Huddersfield in July 2009 saw the goals start to flow, hitting 73 in 124 league games. Blackburn splashed out £8m and the goals kept a-comin' although Rovers could not achieve promotion to the Premier League (159/83).

A move to Middlesbrough occurred in February 2016 and Jordan was to win promotion with the club that season. However, he was given limited game time in the Premier League and his time at the Riverside fizzled out (24/6). A loan spell and then permanent signing at Sheffield Wednesday followed (18/3 and then 83/15). He was loaned out to Norwich (36/6) before returning to Huddersfield in 2021 (55/8). Loaned out once more, to Blackpool (29/15), Jordan has since signed on for another year with the Lancashire club.

Kenny Dalglish, after winning the title with Blackburn in 1994/95, had tried his hand at managing Newcastle for 18 months from January 1997. He had also been involved with Celtic as director of football and following John Barnes's sacking he took over as manager for six months from January 2000. He returned to Liverpool in 2009 with a role in the youth academy but by October 2010 he was once again in charge at Anfield. He led the Reds to the finals of the FA Cup and League Cup in 2011/12 but was dismissed by the club at the end of the season.

The FA Cup was lost 2-1 to Chelsea with no Scots other than Dalglish himself involved.

Charlie Adam was part of the Liverpool side that won the League Cup by beating Cardiff City on penalties after a 2-2 draw. Dundee-born Adam had started out at Rangers, making his debut in April 2004. Within his time at Ibrox (61/13) he had three loan spells: Ross County (11/2), St Mirren (29/5) and Blackpool (13/2). The latter paid £500,000 for Charlie in August 2009. He had two great seasons with Blackpool, gaining promotion via the play-offs into the Premier League. Despite his endeavours he couldn't prevent the Seasiders from being relegated in 2010/11 (78/28). Liverpool paid £6.75m for Charlie the following season but he was only to have one term with the club (28/2). He spent several years at Stoke (156/19) before moving on to Reading (21/2) and finishing up with hometown club Dundee (49/7) in 2022.

Cardiff had three Scots starting and a further two on the bench, and were managed by Malky Mackay. In his playing days defender Mackay had been with Queen's Park (70/6), Celtic (34/4), Norwich City (213/15) and West Ham (18/2), finishing with Watford (52/3). It was at Vicarage Road that he first took over in a caretaker role before going on to manage the club. He moved on to Cardiff in June 2011 and won the Championship title in 2012/13. Just over a year later he was dismissed and following the revelations of racist, sexist and homophobic ccontent in texts, his career has been blighted to a certain extent. However, he has been in management roles at Wigan and Ross County as well as being the SFA's performance director.

On the playing side, Kevin McNaughton, who had appeared in the 2008 FA Cup Final, was still at right-back. He played 400 games overall for the Welsh club with 254 in the league, scoring a solitary goal. He had two loan spells at Bolton (13/1 and 9/0) before leaving for Bolton in 2015 (2/0). Kevin moved back to Scotland and Inverness (9/0) in 2016 before finishing up coaching at Forfar (10/0).

In midfield was Inverness-born Don Cowie, who had started out at Ross County in 2000 (156/17). He moved to Inverness Caledonian Thistle in 2007 (59/12) then headed south to Watford in January 2009. He teamed up with Malky Mackay there (88/9) and followed him to Cardiff (86/6). His last club in England was Wigan (37/0) before joining Hearts in 2016 (72/3) and finishing up back at Ross County (38/2). Don converted his penalty in the cup final shoot-out.

Up front for Cardiff was Kenny Miller, who missed the first penalty for the Bluebirds. This was Kenny's third stint in English football; he had earlier played at Hibs (45/12), Stenhousemuir on loan (11/8) and Rangers (30/8) and following a loan spell he joined Wolves for £3m. He scored in the 2003 play-off final as Wolves beat Sheffield United to go into the Premier League. His five years at Wolves were his longest period at any club (169/52) but it was followed by a slew of clubs: Celtic (33/11), Derby County (30/4), Rangers (81/49), Bursaspor in Turkey (15/5) and then Cardiff (43/10). Vancouver Whitecaps, Rangers (again), Livingston, Dundee and finally Partick Thistle were to follow before hanging up his boots aged 40.

On the bench was keeper David Marshall. David, in his early days at Celtic, was a half-time substitute in a UEFA Cup tie against Barcelona after the dismissal of first-choice keeper Rab Douglas. Marshall held Barça at bay and did so in the return leg too. However, he couldn't hold down the number one spot and three years later in 2007 he left Celtic (51/0) for Norwich City initially on loan (2/0). He had two years at Carrow Road (92/0) before a £500,000 move to Cardiff in May 2009. Seven seasons were spent with Cardiff and at one point he captained the side (264/0). Hull City paid £5m for Marshall in August 2016 (61/0). Following on, David turned out for Derby (33/0), QPR (11/0) and finished up with Hibs (71/0), retiring in June 2024.

Irvine-born Craig Conway began his career at Ayr United (61/7) in 2003. By 2006/07 he was plying his trade at Dundee United (137/13), where he won the Scottish Cup in 2010. Winger Craig hit a double in the 3-0 victory over Ross County in a man-of-the-match performance. In June 2011 he signed on at Cardiff but despite scoring in two earlier rounds of the cup run he was benched for the final. He helped Cardiff to the Championship title in 2011/12 (58/5) but at the start of the following season he was loaned out to Brighton (13/1). January 2014 saw him sign with Blackburn where he spent five years (178/13). Moves to Salford City (20/0) and St Johnstone (28/3) saw out his career, retiring in June 2022.

2012/13

Manchester United won the Premier League with Sir Alex announcing his retirement at the end of the season. He had been in charge for over 26 years and had won 13 titles, five FA Cups and four League Cups as well as three European successes.

Darren Fletcher only made three appearances that season and only eight the season before. He had been quite seriously ill with ulcerative colitis and was to need surgery. He eventually recovered but by February 2015 he had left Old Trafford (223/18) on a free transfer to West Brom where he played consistently (91/4) for over two seasons. His final club was Stoke (38/2), announcing his retirement in 2019.

The FA Cup was won by Wigan, defeating Manchester City 1-0 in the final. Three Scots were fielded in the Wigan team and two were on the bench.

Midfielder James McCarthy was born in Glasgow, but went on to play for the Republic of Ireland. He started his career at Hamilton where he turned out for the club the day before his 16th birthday in November 2006. He spent three seasons there (95/13) before Wigan signed him for £1.2m. James had four seasons at Wigan (120/7) before moving to Everton the summer after the FA Cup win for £13m. Injuries, including a broken leg suffered in January 2018, limited McCarthy's game time over his five years at Goodison (108/6) and he then moved to Crystal Palace in 2019 (49/0). James latterly signed for Celtic in 2021, but his four-year contract was terminated a year early in 2024 having made only 12 league appearances.

Alongside him in the midfield was his former Hamilton team-mate James McArthur. James broke into the Hamilton side in 2005 and spent five years at New Douglas Park (168/10). Wigan paid out £500,000 for him in 2010. September 2014 saw James sign for Crystal Palace where he was to play in the 2016 FA Cup Final.

Malaysia-born Shaun Maloney grew up in Aberdeen but joined Celtic as a youth in 1999, making his debut in April 2001. In season 2005/06 he won both the SFA Player of the Year and Young Player of the Year awards. However, his first term with Celtic came to an end in 2007 (104/26). Having signed a pre-contract agreement to join Aston Villa in the summer of 2007, Celtic allowed him to leave in the January for £1m. Former Celtic boss Martin O'Neill was in charge at Villa Park, but Shaun never really settled there (30/5) and headed back to Parkhead in August 2008 for £3m. However, he left again in 2011 after a frustrating time with injury and form (54/13). Joining Wigan for £850,000, Shaun was always a scorer of great goals and he hit the opener in the 2-0 win over Millwall in the FA Cup semi-final. He also provided the cross for Ben Watson's late winner in the final. Maloney left Wigan for Chicago Fire in 2015 (14/3) and finished his playing career with two years at Hull City (28/2). Shaun has since gone into coaching, spending some years with former Wigan manager Roberto Martínez as coach to the Belgian national side. He has also managed Hibernian and Wigan.

Wigan club captain Gary Caldwell was on the bench due to injury, but at the end of the final he and match captain Emmerson Boyce lifted the trophy jointly. Caldwell had started his days at Newcastle and although capped by Berti Vogts he never played a match for the Magpies. After loan spells at Darlington (4/0), Hibernian (11/0), Coventry (36/0) and Derby (9/0) he joined Hibernian permanently in 2004. He spent a couple of years at Easter Road (88/5) before moving to Celtic (105/6) in 2006. He joined

Wigan in 2010 and retired from the game in 2015 due to a hip injury (102/6). He has since gone into management with Wigan, Chesterfield, Partick Thistle and Exeter.

Also on the bench was Fraser Fyvie. Aberdeen-born Fraser broke into his hometown team aged 16 in 2009 but the following season his progress was halted as a cruciate ligament injury ruled him out for almost a year. He returned the following season and established himself in the team (58/2) before he moved south to Wigan. A transfer fee of around £500,000 was paid but his time at Wigan did not work out well. Loans at Yeovil (2/0) and Shrewsbury (4/0) were not successful either and he left Wigan in 2015 having only played in one league match, moving on to Hibernian (54/2) where the highlight was to be the 2016 Scottish Cup Final win over Rangers. However, by 2017 he was playing for Dundee United (32/4) and was with Cove Rangers at the time of writing.

The League Cup was won by Swansea, thrashing Bradford City 5-0 in the final. Goalkeeper Jon McLaughlin started on the bench for the Yorkshire club. Edinburgh-born Jon had joined Bradford after playing non-league football in Harrogate in 2008. With Swansea three to the good in the final, keeper Matt Duke was sent off in the 56th minute for a foul. Jon's first touch of the ball was to pick it out the net as Swansea scored from the resultant penalty. He played at Bradford for six years (125/0) before heading to Burton Albion in 2014 (133/0). After a trial, Hearts took him on for a season (33/0) followed by a few years at Rangers ostensibly as backup keeper (29/0) and likewise Swansea.

2013/14

Manchester City won the Premier League, two points clear of Liverpool with 86 points.

Top scorer in the championship was Ross McCormack of Leeds United with 28 goals. Runner-up to Ross was Jordan Rhodes of Blackburn who hit 25 for his club.

McCormack had begun his career with Rangers in 2004, but opportunities were hard to come by (11/2). After a loan move to Doncaster (19/5) Ross signed with Motherwell in 2006. Two seasons were spent at Fir Park (48/10) as there would be with Cardiff (74/25). He moved to Leeds in 2010 for £350,000, spending four years at Elland Road (144/53). Fulham spent £11m on Ross in July 2014 (89/38) and this was followed with Aston Villa paying out £12m in August 2016, but things fell apart at Villa Park. Ross's fitness was called into question as he missed some training sessions. This led to him being loaned out to Nottingham Forest (7/1), to Australia with Melbourne City (17/14) and Central Coast Mariners (5/1), as well as back to Scotland with Motherwell. He was let go by Villa in 2019 (20/3) and most recently played in non-league football.

The FA Cup was won by Arsenal, beating Hull City 3-2 in extra time. In goal for the Humberside club was Allan McGregor, whose career was bookended by two periods at Rangers. Although he made his debut for the club in 2002, he was farmed out to first St Johnstone (20/0), then Dunfermline (26/0) before becoming first choice at Ibrox (205/0). When the club went into liquidation in 2012, McGregor chose to end his contract and headed to Turkey and Beşiktaş (27/0). He signed for Hull in 2013 for £1.5m and spent five years at the club (141/0) with a loan spell at Cardiff in 2017 (19/0) included. He returned to Ibrox in 2018, playing until he retired in 2023 (141/0).

Winger George Boyd came on as a substitute in the 102nd minute of the final. His career had begun with a five-year spell with Stevenage Borough of the Conference from 2002 to 2007 (111/24) before moving to Peterborough for a fee of £260,000. George won two consecutive promotions with the Posh (263/64) but was loaned out to Nottingham Forest in 2010 (6/1) and then to Hull in 2013 (13/4). His loan spell saw Hull win promotion to the Premier League and George signed for the Tigers permanently in May 2013 (30/2). Burnley swooped for George a year later, laying out a reported £3m for his services. Although relegated during his time at Turf Moor (115/12), George helped Burnley back into the top flight in 2015/16. Following on, he played for Sheffield Wednesday (40/3), returned to Peterborough (22/0) and finished professionally with Salford City (11/0) in 2021.

The League Cup was won by Manchester City, beating Sunderland 3-1. Playing right-back for Sunderland was Salford-born Phil Bardsley who spent five years professionally at Manchester United (8/0) where he was a serial loanee. From 2004 to 2008 he played for Royal Antwerp in Belgium (6/0), Burnley (6/0), Rangers (5/1), Aston Villa (13/0) and Sheffield United (16/0), then he moved to Sunderland for an initial fee of £850,000 in January 2008. He was with the Black Cats until 2014 (174/7), moving to Stoke City (51/0) and Burnley afterwards (57/0). He played a couple of matches with Stockport County before calling time on his career.

Coming off the bench in the 60th minute was striker Steven Fletcher. His career had begun at Hibernian, signing professionally in 2004 where he scored twice in the League Cup Final victory of 2007 (156/43). Burnley laid out £3m for Steven in 2009 but he only stayed for one season as they were relegated (35/8), moving to Wolves for a reported £6.5m. Wolves were relegated in his second season and once again Steven was transferred (61/22) – Sunderland came in with a £12m bid and he moved to the Stadium of Light in August 2012. By January 2016 he was out on loan to Marseille (12/2) and let go by Sunderland that summer (94/23). He then spent four years at Sheffield Wednesday in the Championship (124/36), moving to Stoke in August 2020 (72/12) and then Dundee United for a season (33/9). At the time of writing he was playing for the Hollywood glamour side Wrexham.

2014/15

Chelsea won the Premier League title and the League Cup, beating Tottenham 2-0 in the final.

The FA Cup was won by Arsenal, pumping Aston Villa 4-0. Alan Hutton, who had won the League Cup with Spurs in 2008, had joined Villa at the start of the 2011/12 season but quickly saw himself frozen out at Villa Park. He was loaned to Nottingham Forest (7/0), Mallorca (17/0) and then Bolton (9/0). Alan remarkably resurrected his career at Villa, gaining a new three-year contract in 2015 which was eventually extended to 2019. Released that year, Alan called time on his career shortly after (185/3).

2015/16

Claudio Ranieri's Leicester City won the Premier League, employing no Scots. Manchester City won the League Cup over Liverpool on penalties using the same 'tactic'.

The FA Cup was won by Manchester United, defeating Crystal Palace 2-1 after extra time. In the Palace line-up was midfielder James McArthur who had won the cup with Wigan in 2013. James had signed for Palace in 2014 for £7m. Initially on a three-year contract, he stayed at Selhurst Park for nine seasons – all in the Premier League – before retiring from the game in August 2023 (240/17).

2016/17

Chelsea, Arsenal and Manchester United won the title, FA Cup and League Cup respectively with no Scottish involvement.

2017/18

Manchester City won the Premier League and League Cup, with no Scots.

Scottish interest was in the FA Cup where Scott McTominay sat on the bench for Manchester United in their 1-0 defeat to Chelsea. Lancaster-born McTominay had joined the United academy aged six in 2002, eventually making his first-team debut in 2017. He would go on to win the League Cup with United in 2023 and the FA Cup in 2024.

2018/19

Manchester City dominated the season, winning the domestic treble in England, but without any Scottish involvement.

2019/20

Jürgen Klopp's Liverpool won the Covid-impacted Premier League. At left-back was Andy Robertson, playing in 36 games, scoring two goals and making 12 assists. After being let go by Celtic as a youth, Glaswegian Andy joined Queen's Park, making his debut in 2012 (34/2). Within a season he was on his way to Dundee United (36/3) and within another to Hull for £2.85m. He spent three seasons at Hull, experiencing relegation and promotion (99/3). Liverpool bought him for £8m ostensibly as backup but once Andy was given his run in the first team he did not look back. As well as winning the Champions League in 2019, Andy has won the FA Cup and the League Cup twice as of the summer of 2024.

The FA Cup was won by Arsenal, beating Chelsea 2-1. At left-back for Arsenal was Kieran Tierney. Born on the Isle of Man, Tierney was raised in Wishaw and joined Celtic as a youth. Making his league debut in April 2015, he became their first-choice left-back the following season. He won four titles, two Scottish Cups and two League Cups in his time with Celtic (102/5). Arsenal paid out a reported fee of £25m for Kieran in August 2019. It is fair to say his time at the Emirates Stadium hasn't gone to plan despite a good start. He spent season 2023/24 at Real Sociedad (20/0) but suffered two hamstring injuries in his time there. He has played 91 league games for Arsenal netting thrice, it is unlikely he will play many more.

Manchester City beat Aston Villa 2-1 in a League Cup Final with no Scottish presence.

2020/21

Manchester City won the Premier League and League Cup with the City of Manchester Stadium continuing to be a Scot-free zone.

Leicester City, managed by former and future Celtic manager Brendan Rodgers, won the FA Cup, beating Chelsea 1-0. On the Chelsea bench was Billy Gilmour. Irvine-born Gilmour had been part of the Rangers youth academy when Chelsea swooped for the then 15-year-old with a hefty cheque, reportedly £500,000, in May 2017. Billy made his senior debut in 2019 and was loaned out to Norwich in 2021/22 (24/0). After making only 11 league appearances for Chelsea he transferred to Brighton in September 2022. He left Brighton (46/0) for Napoli in August 2024 for a reported fee of more than £12m.

2021/22

Manchester City retained the Premier League title. The FA Cup and League Cup were both contested by Liverpool and Chelsea. Both matches went to penalties after 0-0 draws with Liverpool winning each one. Andy Robertson competed in both and took one of the penalties in the League Cup win.

2022/23

Once more Manchester City won the Premier League. They also won the FA Cup, beating Manchester United 2-1. Scott McTominay came on for United as a late substitute in the 83rd minute.

United, however, won the League Cup, beating Newcastle 2-0. McTominay again started on the bench, coming on in the 69th minute. Coming on in the 91st minute for Newcastle was midfielder Matt Ritchie, winner of 16 caps for Scotland. Gosport-born Matt had joined Portsmouth as a youth in 2002 and signed on to the club in 2008. Over the next few years he was loaned out to Dagenham & Redbridge (37/11), Notts County (16/3) and Swindon Town (16/3). He made his Premier League debut for Pompey in April 2010 (7/0). However, he soon moved to Swindon full-time in January 2011 (91/23). Joining Bournemouth in January 2013 for £400,000, Matt helped his side gain promotion to the Championship and then win that league in 2014/15 (130/31). In July 2016 he signed with newly relegated Newcastle and helped them win the Championship too. Ritchie remained with Newcastle for seven years (187/20). August 2024 saw him return to Portsmouth and during the 2024/25 season he reached his milestone 500th career league appearance.

2023/24

Manchester City once more won the Premier League, although in fourth place and earning Champions League football for the first time since the 1982/83 season were Aston Villa, led by team captain Super John McGinn. From Clydebank, John started out across the river in Paisley with St Mirren in 2012 as did his older brothers Stephen and Paul. John was part of the St Mirren side that won the League Cup in 2013. He left St Mirren (87/4) to sign with Hibs in 2015, winning the Scottish Cup with them in 2016. After three seasons (101/12) McGinn moved to Villa in 2018 where he has now played over 200 games and scored the winning goal in the 2019 Championship play-off final.

Again, the FA Cup Final was an all-Manchester affair, but it was to be United who prevailed, winning 2-1. Scott McTominay played almost all the match. As his prominence in the Scotland side has risen it was not matched in United colours at times. Some fans loved him, seeing him as one of their own, while others often scapegoated him, and managers never knew where to play him. It was no surprise that in August 2024 he moved on to Napoli for a reported £25.4m after over 20 years attached to United (178/19).

The League Cup was won by Liverpool, beating Chelsea 1-0 in extra time. Andy Robertson played in the match and made his 200th league appearance for Liverpool in September 2023.

* * *

European and international competitions

In **2000/01** the UEFA Cup returned to England for the first time since Spurs' 1984 triumph. From season 1997/98 onwards UEFA Cup finals became one-match affairs and in the Westfalenstadion in Dortmund, Gérard Houllier's Liverpool defeated Alavés of Spain 5-4 in a thrilling game that was decided using the golden goal rule 26 minutes into extra time. Sole Anglo-Scot Gary McAllister was the man of the match in a starting line-up which also contained five Englishmen. It was the Anfield club's third UEFA Cup triumph, their seventh Euro success overall and their first since 1984, and it also gave them a unique treble that season having already won the League Cup and FA Cup.

Due to the expansion of UEFA membership in the 1990s, and the inclusion of clubs eliminated from the early stages of the Champions League, the UEFA Cup had an additional knockout round to negotiate, as well as a sizeable preliminary round for clubs from countries with a lower UEFA ranking – which did not include England. McAllister would play in nine of Liverpool's 13 Euro matches, although five of them would be as a substitute.

Gary did not appear in the first round in which Liverpool edged it against Rapid Bucureşti, winning 1-0 in Romania then drawing 0-0 at Anfield, however substitute appearances were made in both the home and away wins against Slovan Liberec in the second round, 1-0 on Merseyside and 3-2 in the Czech Republic.

In the third round McAllister appeared as a substitute in both the matches against Olympiakos, 2-2 in Athens and a 2-0 home win in Liverpool. In the fourth round, however, he started both legs against Roma, commencing with the Stadio Olimpico, the venue for Liverpool's European Cup Final triumphs of 1977 and 1984 – and a 2-0 victory resulted. Back in England the Reds slipped to a 1-0 home defeat but progressed 2-1 on aggregate.

McAllister was missing from the quarter-finals, a 0-0 draw away to Porto and a 2-0 win at Anfield, but he had a key role in the semis against Barcelona. The 180 minutes of football produced but one goal, and it came from our Gary when he converted a penalty in the 44th minute of the second leg at Anfield. A Patrick Kluivert handball from a corner had given Big Mac the opportunity to send the ball past future Liverpool goalie Pepe Reina. The Barça team also included the likes of Rivaldo, Emmanuel Petit, Marc Overmars, Carles Puyol and skipper Pep Guardiola.

The opponents in the final were another Spanish outfit, the relative unknowns of Deportivo Alavés from the Basque city of Vitoria-Gasteiz, some 60km south-east of Bilbao. Alavés were European debutantes having qualified for the UEFA Cup by virtue of their sixth-placed finish in La Liga the previous season but on 16 May 2001 what a game of football they contributed to. Marcus Babbel started the scoring after three minutes then it was 2-0 to Liverpool through Steven Gerrard. Alavés got one back before McAllister's penalty made it 3-1 by half-time. The Spaniards were level four minutes into the second half after a quick-fire double, Robbie Fowler made it 4-3, but Alavés equalised at 4-4 with two minutes remaining. There were only four minutes of extra time remaining when an own goal, the golden goal, by the unfortunate Delfi Geli made it 5-4 to Liverpool and the trophy went back to Anfield with praise coming from all around for the performance of former Motherwell man McAllister, aged 36.

In winning the UEFA Cup, Liverpool, who had also finished third in the Premier League, automatically qualified for the 2001/02 Champions League where they progressed beyond the group stage to the knockout rounds before losing to Hampden-bound Bayer Leverkusen, so no parachuting back to defend their UEFA Cup. It was so much simpler back in the day – when you lost, you were out, irrespective of the stage of the competition, no second chances unless, like Rapid Vienna in the 1984/85 Cup Winners' Cup, you won a dodgy appeal. OK, rant over.

* * *

Liverpool also provided England's next 21st-century Euro success when they lifted the **2004/05** Champions League trophy in another dramatic final – this time coming back from 3-0 down to AC Milan at half-time in Istanbul to level the game at 3-3 before winning on penalties. No Scots appeared in this 50th final of the competition, however; indeed only two Englishmen, Jamie Carragher and skipper Steven Gerrard, made it into Rafael Benítez's starting line-up.

The following season, Liverpool were eliminated by Benfica in the last 16, so no parachuting etc etc.

* * *

In **2007/08** Manchester United won their third Champions League/ European Cup, beating Chelsea on penalties in the final in Moscow with Scotland skipper Darren Fletcher being an unused substitute. Earlier in the competition, however, Fletcher managed to make six appearances including four in the group stages – the 4-2 away and 4-0 home wins against Dynamo Kiev, the 2-1 home victory versus Sporting Lisbon and the 1-1 draw away to Roma. He also played in the 1-0 win over Lyon in the second leg of the last 16 at Old Trafford, while in the second leg of the semi-final against Barcelona at Old Trafford, Fletcher came on as a late substitute for goal hero Paul Scholes as United ran out 1-0 winners.

Alex Ferguson's attempt to retain the Champions League came unstuck in the 2009 final in Rome when United lost 2-0 to Pep Guardiola's Lionel Messi-inspired Barcelona.

* * *

In **2011/12** Chelsea won the Champions League for the first time, defeating Bayern Munich in the final in their opponents' own Allianz Arena with four Englishmen making the starting line-up but no Scots. The Blues were the fifth English club to lift Europe's premier trophy and the first from the 'deep south'.

* * *

In defence of their Champions League crown, Chelsea crashed out at the group stage but they did go on to win the **2012/13** Europa League, beating Benfica in Amsterdam, and in so doing became the fourth club – after Juventus, Ajax and Bayern Munich – and the first English team to win all three major UEFA club titles. Chelsea's winning 11 comprised three players each from England, Brazil, and Spain plus one apiece from the Czech Republic and Serbia.

The following season, Chelsea did not defend their Europa League title but instead competed in the Champions League, reaching the semi-final before losing to Atlético Madrid, who in turn lost in the final to their city rivals Real.

* * *

When José Mourinho's multi-national Manchester United – nine different countries were represented, although not Scotland – defeated Ajax in the final of the **2016/17** Europa League, the Red Devils became the fifth club to win all three major UEFA club titles. It was also United's fifth European trophy overall.

Europa League glory meant that the following season United went straight into the group stages of the Champions League, where they were eliminated in the last 16 by Sevilla.

* * *

In **2018/19** Chelsea won the Europa League for the second time, in a London derby like no other. Maurizio Sarri's team triumphed 4-1 over Unai Emery's Arsenal having travelled 4,000 miles by air for the showdown in Baku, Azerbaijan. Of the 22 players who started the game there was but one Englishman – Arsenal midfielder Ainsley Cory Maitland-Niles.

Again, Chelsea did not defend the Europa League but instead competed in the 2019/20 Champions League, losing to Bayern Munich in the last 16.

* * *

Three days after Arsenal lost out to Chelsea in the 2019 Europa League Final, their rivals from the north of the capital, Tottenham Hotspur, lost 2-0 in the **2018/19** Champions League Final in Madrid, to a Liverpool side which included Glaswegian left-back Andy Robertson. Robertson became only the second Scot this millennium to play in a winning European final, following on from fellow Red Gary McAllister in the UEFA Cup 18 years previous. Andy was also the first Scot to lift Europe's premier club prize since Paul Lambert was a member of Borussia Dortmund's 1997 winning side.

Liverpool went straight into the group stage as a result of finishing fourth in the Premier League in 2017/18 and were joined by French champions Paris Saint-Germain, Serie A runners-up Napoli, and Red Star Belgrade, the Serbian champions who had to successfully negotiate a play-off round to reach the group stage.

In Group C Liverpool won all three home games but lost all three away matches, qualifying for the last 16 by finishing in second place behind PSG, though ahead of Napoli on the basis of total goals scored after points won, the head-to-head record and goal difference could not separate the English and Italian rivals.

In the last 16 Liverpool faced Bayern Munich (Neuer, Ribery, Lewandowski et al) – the fourth time they had clashed in European competitions – and after the first leg, a 0-0 draw at Anfield, things looked good for Bavaria's finest. But slap my lederhosen and deep-fry my bratwurst, did Liverpool then not go to the Allianz Arena and win 3-1!

Andy Robertson missed both quarter-final victories against Porto – 2-0 at home and 4-1 in Portugal – partly due to picking up three yellow cards in the tournament, though reappeared for the epic semi-final encounter against Barcelona. Liverpool lost 3-0 at the Camp Nou to one goal from Luis Suárez plus two from Lionel Messi, but won 4-0 at Anfield to reach their second successive Champions League Final. Apparently the bookmakers' odds against that result were 50/1. Wow!

Scotland captain Andy Robertson was bought from Hull City in July 2017 for £8m, expected to be the second choice left-back and has now played over 300 games for Liverpool.

And so to the grand finale at Atlético Madrid's Estadio Metropolitano on 1 June. A significant Scottish presence as part of a predominantly British and Irish squad at Anfield was now a thing of the past. As such, Andy Robertson's team-mates in the final starting XI included three from Brazil, two from the Netherlands, two from England – skipper Jordan Henderson and Trent Alexander-Arnold – plus one each from Cameroon, Egypt and Senegal.

Tottenham, who had finished third in the Premier League in 2017/18, featured five Englishmen including returning striker Harry Kane after injury, plus international stars from Belgium (two), France (two), Denmark and South Korea.

Mo Salah gave Liverpool the lead from the penalty spot after just 106 seconds following Moussa Sissoko's handball in the box, while substitute Divock Origi netted the second three minutes from time. Spurs had the greater amount of possession and more shots on target but it was Liverpool who lifted the trophy for the sixth time, their ninth European crown overall – the first silverware at Anfield for manager Jürgen Klopp.

In defence of their prize, Liverpool were eliminated at the last-16 stage in February 2020, somewhat ironically by Atlético Madrid. In the European champions' first home game of the 2019/20 campaign Andy Robertson scored his first European goal in a 4-3 victory against Austrian champions Red Bull Salzburg. 'Doe, a deer' as Andy's fans in the Tartan Army like to sing.

* * *

In **2020/21** Thomas Tuchel's Chelsea upset the odds to defeat Pep Guardiola's Manchester City 1-0 in Porto in front of a Covid-restricted crowd of 14,110. It was Chelsea's sixth European success, made up of two Champions Leagues, two Cup Winners' Cups and two Europa Leagues, with four of the finals taking place in the 21st century.

Irvine-born midfielder Billy Gilmour was an unused substitute for Chelsea, but earlier in the competition he got some game time in two Group E matches – as a late sub for Jorginho in the 4-0 away win against Seville and in the starting line-up in the 1-1 draw against Russian outfit Krasnodar at Stamford Bridge.

The following season Chelsea lost out to eventual winners Real Madrid in the quarter-finals.

* * *

West Ham United won the **2022/23** Europa Conference League – the second season of UEFA's new tertiary club competition – by defeating Fiorentina 2-1 in the final in Prague. It was the Hammers' second success in Europe, the first being their Cup Winners' Cup win 58 years earlier, and they were managed by Glaswegian David Moyes.

Earlier in his career, Moyes had played at centre-back for Celtic, winning the Premier Division in 1981/82, Cambridge United, Bristol City where he won the Associate Members' Cup in 1985/86, Shrewsbury Town, Dunfermline Athletic, Hamilton Academical and Preston North End, where he won the Third Division in 1995/96. He then went on to manage Preston to the Second Division championship in 1999/2000, Everton, Manchester United, Real Sociedad, Sunderland and then West Ham in 2017, initially for six months to guide the East End outfit to Premier League safety, before returning in December 2019.

Needless to say, the Hammers did not defend their trophy the following season but instead were 'promoted' to the group stages of the second-tier Europa League. Moyes's Magnificos made it to the quarter-finals where they were beaten by Bayer Leverkusen, who had just been crowned German champions for the first time. Leverkusen also went on to win the German Cup, completing an undefeated domestic double in the process.

* * *

On 10 June, three days after West Ham's Conference League triumph, Pep Guardiola's Manchester City lifted the **2022/23** Champions League trophy by defeating Inter Milan 1-0 in Istanbul. Like West Ham, it was City's second European success and came 53 years after their Cup Winners' Cup glory. In so doing, City became the sixth English club, and the 23rd club overall, to land the big one.

In 2023/24, however, City failed to emulate Liverpool and Nottingham Forest, bowing out of the Champions League to Real Madrid at the quarter-final stage. Methinks it's time for Pep to start recruiting some Scottish footballers – I reckon an Erin Cuthbert would have helped the Sky Blues overcome *Los Blancos*. There, I said it.

* * *

Since the turn of the century there have also been several near-misses for English clubs in Europe. Beaten finalists include Arsenal in the 2006 Champions League, Middlesbrough in the 2006 UEFA Cup with future Championship winner with West Bromwich Albion and 46-cap Scotland midfielder James Morrison in the starting line-up, Liverpool in the 2007 Champions League, Manchester United in the 2009 Champions League when Darren Fletcher missed out having been sent off in the semi-final second leg against Arsenal, Fulham in the 2010 UEFA Cup, Manchester United in the 2011 Champions League when Fletcher was an unused substitute, Liverpool in the 2016 Europa League, Liverpool in the 2018 Champions League with Andy Robertson in the starting line-up, Manchester United in the 2021 Europa League with Scott McTominay in the starting line-up, and Liverpool in the 2022 Champions League when Robertson again made the starting line-up, his third appearance in a Champions League Final.

* * *

The 'Wilderness Years' applied even more so to Scottish representation at major international tournaments. Indeed, it was June 2021 before Scotland appeared at the finals of a 21st-century major competition thanks to a dramatic Nations League back-door route to the Covid-delayed 2020 European Championship. Prior to that, the closest Scotland came to appearing on the big stage was when they lost out to the Netherlands in a play-off to reach Euro 2004. After winning the first leg 1-0 at Hampden Park with Everton's James McFadden netting, Scotland crashed to a 6-0 defeat in Amsterdam – they were probably not the first bunch of Scots laddies to get their arses felt on an evening in the Dutch capital but it stung nonetheless.

Walter Smith provided some light relief when he took a largely experimental squad of players to Japan in May 2006 to compete in the Kirin Cup – an international competition organised since 1992 by the Kirin Brewing Company involving hosts Japan and usually two other invited teams. Along with Scotland, other winners include Argentina, Hungary, France, Peru and Japan.

Scotland defeated Bulgaria 5-1 in their opening match at the Kobe Wing Stadium in Kobe, and then drew 0-0 with Japan in the Saitama Stadium in Saitama to lift the trophy – Bulgaria having beaten the hosts 2-1 in the first game in Osaka.

Cardiff City's Neil Alexander was between the sticks for both of Scotland's matches while Graeme Murty of Reading, Darren Fletcher of Manchester United, Everton trio Gary Naysmith, James McFadden and skipper David Weir, plus Gary Teale and Lee McCulloch of Wigan Athletic, also appeared against Bulgaria and Japan. Over 30 Everton players have represented Scotland while at Goodison Park with Weir topping the list, 43 of his 69 caps coming on Merseyside. Conversely, Graeme Murty is the Berkshire club's only full Scotland international.

More and more, Scotland were utilising the services of Anglo-Scots from 'less fashionable' or lower-division clubs plus overseas 'curios' like Russia's Lokomotiv Moscow (Gary O'Connor, 2006 and 2007), Bursaspor of Turkey (Kenny Miller, 2011), Canadian club Vancouver Whitecaps (Kenny Miller, 2012 and 2013) and Sporting Kansas City in the USA (Johnny Russell, 2018 and 2019).

Of course, Kenny Miller's Scotland career, which ran from 2001 to 2013 and included 69 caps and 18 goals, also encompassed several UK clubs – Rangers, Wolverhampton Wanderers, Celtic, Derby and Cardiff. Miller was almost always first-choice, playing either on his own up-front or as part of a two-man attack. He also had a tendency to score important goals against some of the so-called major footballing nations.

A big shout-out also for Darren Fletcher who shone throughout those mostly dark years for Scotland. Between 2003 and 2017 the elegant midfielder won a total of 80 caps, 66 while with Manchester United, 12 at West Bromwich Albion and two with Stoke City. Fletcher, who captained his country 34 times, could possibly have 'done the ton' caps-wise had his playing career not been disrupted due to health problems caused by ulcerative colitis. In his second appearance for Scotland, he netted a second-half volley to give his team a 1-0 win over Lithuania at Hampden Park to take Scotland through to those Euro 2004 play-offs.

Another great Scot who missed out on playing at the Euros or World Cup finals was James McFadden who, between 2002 and 2010, won 48 caps (four with Motherwell, 38 with Everton and six at Birmingham) and scored 15 goals including the worldie winner against France in Paris in a 2007 Euro qualifier.

Scotland's return to the big stage came about at Euro 2020 though, and speaking as a collector, one of the bonuses of Scotland qualifying for a major finals was the reappearance of images of our players in the associated Panini or Topps sticker albums.

For the Euro 2020 album, 16 of the 20 Scotland players included made the actual squad and 14 of them, including ten Anglos – David Marshall (Derby), Andy Robertson (Liverpool), Scott McTominay (Manchester United), Kieran Tierney (Arsenal), John McGinn (Aston Villa), Lyndon Dykes (QPR), Liam Cooper (Leeds), Stuart Armstrong (Southampton), Ryan Fraser (Newcastle United) and Scott McKenna (Nottingham Forest) – got actual game time.

Action also went to Ché Adams of Southampton, Chelsea's Billy Gilmour, and Grant Hanley of Norwich – skilful, photogenic players who somehow were not featured in the sticker album!

Time to spare a thought for Sheffield United's Oliver McBurnie who played in both of Scotland's Euro 2020 play-off matches, behind closed doors at home to Israel and away to Serbia. He scored in the penalty shoot-out win in the latter game in Belgrade and made the dizzy heights of inclusion in a Panini album but then missed the tournament itself due to injury, and subsequently disappeared from the international scene.

On the actual field of play, the results at the surreal finals – restricted stadium capacities, allocated stadium entry time slots for spectators and face masks everywhere – were somewhat disappointing. Two defeats at Hampden Park, 2-0 to the Czech Republic and 3-1 against Croatia, sandwiched a creditable 0-0 draw at Wembley against an England side that went all the way to the final itself before running out of steam against Italy.

It was a much more impressive qualification campaign for the 2024 European Championship, however, coming second behind Spain but qualifying ahead of Norway, Cyprus and Georgia with two games to spare. The 'regular' heroes included Scott McTominay with eight appearances and seven goals, John McGinn with three in eight, Lyndon Dykes with one in eight, Ryan Christie of Bournemouth with eight goalless appearances, Watford's Ryan Porteous with one in seven, Kenny McLean of Norwich with the same record, six goalless outings each from Andy Robertson, Aaron Hickey of Brentford and Nathan Patterson of Everton, and one in six from Southampton's Stuart Armstrong, plus goalkeeper Angus Gunn of Norwich with six appearances.

All of the aforementioned made it into the Topps Euro 24 sticker album, however injuries unfortunately prevented Dykes, Hickey and Patterson from actually making it on to the plane to Germany. The 26-man squad that did travel comprised 14 Anglo-Scots made up of five from Premier League clubs and nine from the Championship, eight from Scottish clubs and four from overseas – Denmark, Spain, Saudi Arabia and the USA. In terms of game time, a total of 14 players – nine Anglos, three of whom were from second-tier Norwich – appeared in all three matches at the finals with eight of them, including five Anglos, starting all three games. Eighteen of the 26 squad players – 11 of them Anglos – appeared in at least one match.

Perhaps too much was expected from the Aston Villa hero who merits praise in song from supporters of club and country alike, 'We've got McGinn, Super John McGinn, I just don't think you understand. He's Unai Emery's/Steve Clarke's man, he's better than Zidane, We've got Super John McGinn.'

Sadly, someone brought Kryptonite to the Euros although the entire Scotland team had a disappointing time of it in Deutschland, suffering 'stage fright' in the tournament's opening match against Germany in Munich – 5-1 to the hosts who at least had the decency to net one for Scotland. A spirited 1-1 draw with Switzerland in Cologne followed with Scott McTominay giving Scotland the lead, which was held for 13 first-half minutes before the dark blues teed up Xherdan Shaqiri's equaliser. In the third match, in Stuttgart, Scotland waited until late on before throwing the lightweight, stainless steel version of a kitchen sink at Hungary who hit back with the ultimate sucker-punch – a winning goal ten minutes into stoppage time.

Spain would be crowned European champions for the fourth time after defeating England 2-1 in the final, the superb Spaniards winning all seven of their matches in Germany. Spain were of course rather impressive in the qualifying campaign as well, winning seven out of eight ties – their only defeat being a 2-0 reverse at Hampden Park on 28 March 2023 with Scott McTominay scoring an *encantador doble* (delightful double). I just had to get that one in.

It was Steve Clarke, a successful assistant manager to José Mourinho at Chelsea in the early 2000s, who guided Scotland to successive appearances at the Euro finals. Clarke, somewhat surprisingly, picked up only six caps during his playing career, all won while at Stamford Bridge.

Clarke also steered Scotland to promotion to League A of the UEFA Nations League, topping Group B1 ahead of Ukraine, the Republic of Ireland and Armenia in 2022/23 – coincidentally, the same season in which Gareth Southgate's England were relegated from League A.

Scotland's stint at the top table then saw Clarke's side narrowly miss out on a place in the Nations League quarter-finals and included a recall for veteran Hearts goalkeeper Craig Gordon who won 17 of his 70-plus caps while with Sunderland. Gordon had joined the Black Cats from the Tynecastle outfit in August 2007 for £9m, which at the time was the highest fee a British club had ever paid for a goalkeeper. Craig made around 100 appearances for Sunderland over an injury-interrupted five seasons.

Now we must wait and see if Scotland can qualify for the 2026 World Cup in Canada, the USA and Mexico, which would be their first such finals since France 1998. One thing is for sure: if qualification is secured it will be achieved via a significant contribution from the Anglo-Scottish players.

* * *

Women to the fore

This one chapter cannot, of course, begin to do justice to women's football but it does seek to recognise the relatively recent rapid growth in importance with regard to its place within the English game and the contributions made by Anglo-Scottish players.

The Women's Super League (WSL), the highest league of women's football in England, was established in 2010 and now consists of 12 fully professional teams. It replaced the FA Women's Premier League National Division which had been running since 1991/92.

The inaugural winners of the WSL were Arsenal in 2011, and when the Gunners retained the title the following year, their Scottish midfielder Kim Little was the competition's top goalscorer with 11. In 2012/13 Aberdeen-born Little became the first recipient of the PFA Women's Players' Player of the Year award. Currently Chelsea have won the most WSL titles with seven, then it's Arsenal on three, Liverpool on two and Manchester City with one.

The Women's FA Challenge Cup has been running since 1970/71 and currently Arsenal have the most successes with 14, followed by Southampton with eight, Doncaster Belles on six, Chelsea on five and Manchester City with three, with 13 other sides enjoying cup glory – Manchester United's first triumph coming in 2024 when they defeated a Tottenham Hotspur side that included Scottish international Martha Thomas in the final.

Julie Fleeting and Kim Little have over 250 Scotland caps between them, and were a big part of Arsenal's dominance of the women's game in the early part of this century.

The FA Women's League Cup was inaugurated in 2011 – in its previous format it was known as the FA Women's Premier League Cup. To date there have been but three successful sides – Arsenal with seven wins, Manchester City with four and Chelsea on two.

So far, only Arsenal have achieved success in Europe when they defeated Umeå of Sweden 1-0 on aggregate in the two-legged final of the 2007 UEFA Women's Cup, which ran from 2001 to 2009 before being replaced by the UEFA Women's Champions League. Julie Fleeting was the tournament's top scorer with nine goals. On 16 May 2021 Chelsea lost out in the Champions League Final to Barcelona in Gothenburg, behind closed doors during the Covid pandemic, with Irvine-born Erin Cuthbert getting game time late on. Thirteen days later the Chelsea men's team won their Champions League Final against Manchester City in front of a restricted attendance in Porto. What a unique 'double' for the London club that could have been.

Super striker Julie Fleeting is arguably Scottish women's football's most successful export. Fleeting started out at Ayr United Ladies in 1996, reaching Arsenal in 2004 via San Diego and Dingwall. Nine glorious years at the north London club brought eight league winners' medals plus five FA Cups and three League Cups as well as the aforementioned European success. The domestic treble was also secured in 2006/07. In March 2013 the Ayrshire lass, whose father Jim Fleeting was a professional player and manager, returned to Scotland to enjoy further glory with Glasgow City.

Fleeting scored an aggregate total of six goals, including a hat-trick against Charlton Athletic in 2004, across four FA Cup finals for Arsenal, while Kim Little has netted in three. The dynamic duo got a goal apiece in the 2-0 win over Bristol Academy in the 2011 final at the Ricoh Arena in Coventry, with Glaswegian Jen Beattie also getting on as a second-half sub for Fleeting. Arsenal's 2-1 win over Sunderland in the 2009 final at Derby County's Pride Park Stadium also featured three Scots in Little, Suzanne Grant and Natalie Ross.

Little, an attacking midfielder from Aberdeenshire, started off at Hibernian Ladies, helping the Edinburgh club to the domestic treble in 2006/07 before signing for Arsenal in March 2008, aged 17. She has enjoyed two successful spells for Arsenal – leaving in November 2013 before returning in 2017. In between she played for Seattle Reign and Melbourne City. Her Gunners collection of winners' medals includes five in the league, three in the FA Cup and six in the League Cup (including

2024 as skipper) and encompassing the domestic treble of 2008/09. In 2023/24, at the sold-out WSL fixture against Manchester United at the Emirates Stadium, Little received a trophy pre-match to mark her 300th Gunners appearance before going on to score in the 3-1 home victory.

Jen Beattie is the daughter of former Scotland and British Lions rugby union player John Beattie but fortunately for fans of *real* fitba, Jen turned her back on the 'dark side' and chose association football instead. Like Little, Beattie has enjoyed two successful spells at Arsenal, with additional glory at Manchester City sandwiched in between.

Jen first joined Arsenal from Celtic Ladies in July 2009, spending four seasons in north London and collecting one league, two FA Cup and two League Cup winners' medals before heading to Montpellier HS in France for two seasons. In July 2015 Beattie returned to England, to Manchester City where she added a further five gongs to her collection with a repeat of the quintet won earlier at Arsenal. In 2019 the doughty defender rejoined the Gunners and in 2023 she came on as a late sub as they triumphed 3-1 over Chelsea in the League Cup Final at Selhurst Park.

Arsenal have been a popular club for several other Scottish women footballers including Kirkcaldy-born left-back Emma Mitchell who won the league three times, two FA Cups and three League Cups between 2013 and 2020, Inverness-born striker Suzanne Grant who joined Arsenal in February 2009 and helped them win the treble that season including scoring on her debut in the 5-0 League Cup Final win against Doncaster Rovers Belles, and Natalie Ross from Aberdeen whose success was restricted by an ankle injury to just the 2009 FA Cup.

Yet another Scottish medal winner at Arsenal was Perth-born Lisa Evans. Evans started out at Glasgow City where she picked up nine trophies in four seasons before moving to Germany where she won the Bundesliga with Bayern Munich in 2015/16. In June 2017 Evans signed for Arsenal where she played in defence or attack and was in the starting line-up in the 2018 League Cup-winning side as well as being a regular when the Gunners won the WSL in 2018/19. In an FA Cup tie in 2020, Evans scored a hat-trick against north London rivals Tottenham Hotspur before moving to West Ham United the following year.

A significant contributor to Chelsea's haul of trophies has been Scotland midfielder/striker Erin Cuthbert. Cuthbert had spells with Rangers and Glasgow City, helping the latter to the Scottish treble in 2015, before moving to west London in December 2016 where she has helped the Blues to seven league titles, including five in a row from 2019/20 to 2023/24, four FA Cup successes and one League Cup – part of the English treble in 2020/21. In February 2018, aged 19, she scored her first hat-trick for Chelsea in the 10-0 demolition of London Bees in an FA Cup tie. Cuthbert also netted Chelsea's second goal in the 3-2 win over Manchester City in the 2022 FA Cup Final at Wembley.

Former Hibernian midfielder Caroline Weir's most successful time was while at Manchester City from 2018 to 2022, although in 2014, as a non-playing substitute with Arsenal, she picked up an FA Cup winners' medal. There followed spells at Bristol Academy and Liverpool before moving to Manchester and winning two FA Cups and two League Cups – netting a brace against Chelsea in the 2022 final at AFC Wimbledon's Plough Lane, which ended 3-1 for the Citizens. In July 2022 Weir signed for Real Madrid and a month later she scored the goal for the Spanish giants which eliminated Manchester City from the UEFA Champions League.

Another former Hibs midfielder, Claire Emslie, also played for Manchester City in their successful 2018/19 FA Cup and League Cup finals. In the summer of 2019 she moved to Orlando Pride and then Melbourne City before returning to the WSL with Everton.

The Women's Super League has gone from strength to strength, from increased media exposure to use of larger stadia accommodating significantly higher attendances. A popular culture breakthrough came about in December 2023 when Panini, in partnership with the Football Association, officially launched the first Barclays WSL sticker collection at Manchester's National Football Museum. The WSL had almost 100 players representing their countries at the 2023 Women's World Cup – more than any other league in the world – and it is hoped that the sticker collection will help the women's game to continue to grow.

Panini, which has been publishing sticker albums since 1970, first created a women's football collection for the 2011 World Cup. In 2022 it launched its first women's domestic football collection for Spain's top-flight competition, Liga F. To date, the Scotland squad has featured in albums for the finals of two major international competitions.

As for those footballers included within the groundbreaking WSL sticker album, Scottish shout-outs for Arsenal captain Kim Little and Aston Villa skipper Rachel Corsie (both foils!) plus Kirsty Hanson (Aston Villa), Abi Harrison, Jamie-Lee Napier and Amy Rodgers (all Bristol City), Erin Cuthbert (Chelsea), Lucy Hope (Everton), Sophie Howard

(Leicester City), Jenna Clark (Liverpool), Emma Watson (Manchester United), Martha Thomas (Tottenham Hotspur) and Lisa Evans and Kirsty Smith (both West Ham).

So can the lasses sustain their significant presence and contribution south of the border? Their contribution to Scotland's national sporting pride cannot be overstated so we certainly hope so.

* * *

At international level, two smashing highlights for Scotland were qualification for the 2017 European Championship in the Netherlands and the 2019 World Cup in France – both coming at a time when the Scotland men's national team were struggling to escape from their long-running 'Wilderness Years'.

Scotland's first successful qualification campaign came by way of being one of the six best runners-up out of eight qualifying groups. They finished behind Iceland on goal difference having earned the same points total, and ahead of Slovenia, Belarus and Macedonia. Across all the qualifying groups, Manchester City striker Jane Ross, who hails from Rothesay, Isle of Bute, was joint top scorer with ten goals.

At Euro 2017 Scotland found themselves in Group D alongside England, Portugal and Spain. There were 16 finalists, the same number as when England would host and triumph at Euro 2022.

Scotland had the misfortune to open against the vastly experienced and much-fancied England and in Utrecht on 19 July they were overwhelmed 6-0. Having three of the regular back four – Emma Mitchell, Jen Beattie and Hayley Lauder – all sidelined through injury didn't help. Neither did having Jane Ross crocked following a challenge from England skipper Steph Houghton.

Four days later against Portugal in Rotterdam, Scotland were worthy of a draw – a second-half equaliser from Chelsea's Erin Cuthbert had given us belief – before conceding a second goal to go down 2-1 with Liverpool's Caroline Weir hitting the post late on. Scotland could still have made it through to the quarter-finals if they had managed to beat Spain in Deventer by two goals or more so their 1-0 win on 27 July, with Caroline Weir netting, was not quite enough. Bloody typical Scotland though!

Of the 23 players Scotland took to the Netherlands, eight were home Scots and seven were Anglo-Scots (defenders Chloe Arthur and Frankie Brown of Bristol City; midfielders Erin Cuthbert and Caroline Weir of

Chelsea and Liverpool respectively; and strikers Lisa Evans, Jane Ross and Christie Murray of Arsenal, Manchester City and Doncaster Rovers Belles). The squad also included four players who plied their trade in Sweden plus one each from Germany, Iceland, Italy and the USA. In terms of game time at the finals, Cuthbert, Evans and Weir appeared at some point in all three matches while Arthur and Brown faced England and Spain with Ross on against the English.

Twenty-four nations competed at the 2019 World Cup in France – the number of finalists would increase to 32 in 2023 – and in Group D Scotland were up against England (again), Japan and Argentina.

This time Scotland's route to the finals was as a result of topping their qualifying group ahead of Switzerland, Poland, Albania and Belarus and our top scorers were Erin Cuthbert and Jane Ross, who moved from Manchester City to West Ham in July 2018, with four apiece and with both appearing in all eight qualifying matches. Anglo-Scots were now in the majority in the squad for the finals with 12 (three from Manchester City, two each from Arsenal and Manchester United, plus one apiece from Birmingham City, Chelsea, Liverpool, Reading and West Ham) compared to seven home Scots, two from Sweden and one each from Italy and the USA.

Again, Scotland opened with a game against the 'auld enemy' (or noisy neighbours if you prefer) and despite what the Stranglers might sing, on 9 June it was not 'nice in Nice'. That said, although Phil Neville's England won the match, Scotland gave a much better account of themselves than at Euro 2017. Trailing 2-0 at half-time, Manchester City's Claire Emslie pulled one back in the 79th minute but an equaliser proved elusive. There were eight Anglo-Scots in that starting line-up plus two from Glasgow City and skipper Rachel Corsie of Utah Royals. Another three Anglos also appeared as substitutes.

Indeed, seven Anglo-Scottish players would play in all three of Scotland's group matches – Lisa Evans, Kim Little, Erin Cuthbert, Jen Beattie, Claire Emslie, Caroline Weir and Kirsty Smith.

Five days later in Rennes, recent history repeated itself with Scotland giving their opponents, 2015 runners-up Japan, two soft goals of a start before Fiorentina's Lana Clelland netted two minutes from time. Just like the previous game the opposition were the recipients of a soft penalty award, while Scotland had two good shouts for a penalty ignored by team VAR. Different gender, same rotten luck.

JEN BEATTIE

SCO

FRANCE
2019

1,77
13-5-199
Manchester City WFC (EN

CLAIRE EMSLIE

SCO

FRANCE
2019

LISA EVANS

SCO

FRANCE
2019

1,66 m
21-5-1992
Arsenal WFC (ENG)

CAROLINE WEIR

SCO

1,73 m
20-6-1995
Manchester City WFC (ENG)

All four played in all three of Scotland's games at the Women's World Cup in France 2019. Claire Emslie scored Scotland's first ever goal in the finals.

Erin Cuthbert of Chelsea who has won six full titles with the London club. Rachel Corsie has played in England with Notts County, Birmingham and Aston Villa.

And so to the Parc des Princes in Paris on 19 June for the game against Argentina. Goals from Kim Little on 19 minutes, Jen Beattie on 49 and Erin Cuthbert on 69 meant Scotland were coasting it.

Leading 3-0 with 20 minutes to go, Shelley Kerr's Scotland were set to book a place in the last 16 – and then we blew it by conceding on 74, 79 and 90+4 minutes when even a one-goal victory would have allowed us to remain in the competition. The equaliser was particularly cruel – a penalty awarded via VAR was saved by Lee Alexander only for another VAR review resulting in the North Korean referee ordering a retake after the Glasgow City keeper was adjudged to have moved off her line. Florencia Bonsegundo made no mistake second time around and 3-3 it finished in front of a crowd of 28,000. Holy heartbreak Batman.

Unfortunately, Scotland's qualifying campaigns for Euro 2022 and the 2023 World Cup did not go according to plan, and so they failed to appear in England (ironically) and Australia/New Zealand as well as in the associated Panini sticker albums. However, in July 2024 at the conclusion of the first phase of the qualifying process for Euro 2025, to be held in Switzerland, Scotland topped Group B1 ahead of Serbia, Slovakia and Israel to advance to the play-offs as well as win promotion to League A of the 2025/26 UEFA Nations League. Five of Scotland's goals came from Martha Thomas of Spurs while Claire Emslie of Angel City netted four, Aston Villa's Kirsty Hanson contributed two, plus there was one apiece from Chelsea Cornet of Rangers and Leicester's Sophie Howard.

In the Euro play-offs, Scotland defeated Hungary 5-0 on aggregate at the semi-final stage, the result including two goals from Thomas and one from Cuthbert. Against Finland in the play-off final, a 0-0 draw in the first leg at Easter Road was followed by a 2-0 defeat in Helsinki with Scotland being refused a good penalty claim and later hitting the upright. Of course, we've all seen this 'movie' before. Never mind, roll on the 2027 World Cup finals so we can visit Brazil instead of Switzerland.

As an aside, at the 2012 London Olympics football competition the Team GB side included Kim Little, along with fellow Scot Ifeoma Dieke of Vittsjö GIK of Sweden, while at the Tokyo 2020 Games, postponed until 2021 due to the Covid pandemic, Little and Caroline Weir were the two Scots in the British line-up. In each tournament Great Britain were eliminated at the quarter-final stage.

And finally, no fewer than 16 female players have won 100 or more caps for Scotland and almost all of them have played some of their club football south of the border. They include the likes of Jen Beattie, Rachel Corsie, Lisa Evans, Kim Little and Caroline Weir plus goalkeeper Gemma Fay who won some of her incredible haul of 203 caps between 1998 and 2017 while playing for Brighton & Hove Albion and Leeds United, and Julie Fleeting, Scotland's most prolific goalscorer with 116 in 121 international appearances. Superb achievements.

Appendix 1

The 500 club

There are currently 58 Scottish and Scotland-aligned players who have played in 500 or more league games for English clubs. There are a handful still oot there kickin' a baw and have an asterisk next to their name. The cut-off date for details is 2 December 2024, so by the time you read this some of these guys will have moved further up the charts.

At the time of writing Matt Ritchie of Portsmouth was only a handful of matches away from joining the list.

Listings are only for English clubs and only for league appearances; Ted MacDougall is not listed as having played for Liverpool and Steve Mungall is not listed as having played for Motherwell.

833 Graham Alexander (defender, born Coventry). Years active 1990 to 2012. Clubs – Scunthorpe, Luton, Preston, Burnley, Preston.

794 Tommy Hutchison (midfielder, born Cardenden). Years active 1967 to 1991. Clubs – Blackpool, Coventry, Manchester City, Burnley, Swansea.

744 Asa Hartford (midfielder, born Clydebank). Years active 1967 to 1991. Clubs – West Brom, Manchester City, Nottingham Forest, Everton, Manchester City, Norwich, Bolton, Stockport, Oldham, Shrewsbury.

 700 Steve Howard (striker, born Durham). Years active 1995 to 2014. Clubs – Hartlepool, Northampton, Luton, Derby, Leicester, Hartlepool, Sheffield Wednesday.

 661 Gary McAllister (midfielder, born Motherwell). Years active 1985 to 2004. Clubs – Leicester, Leeds, Coventry, Liverpool, Coventry.

653 Billy Bremner (midfielder, born Raploch, Stirling). Years active 1959 to 1982. Clubs – Leeds, Hull, Doncaster.

641 John Wark (midfielder, born Glasgow). Years active 1974 to 1997. Clubs – Ipswich, Liverpool, Ipswich, Middlesbrough, Ipswich.

NORWICH CITY

W.B.A.

BACK-FOUR

ALISTAIR ROBERTSON

BIRMINGHAM

ARSENAL

MID-FIEL

ALAN CAMPBELL

CENTRE-BACK

FRANK McLINTOCK

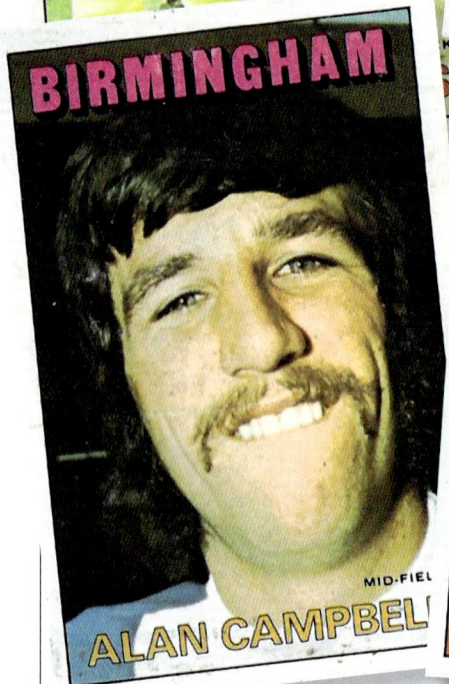

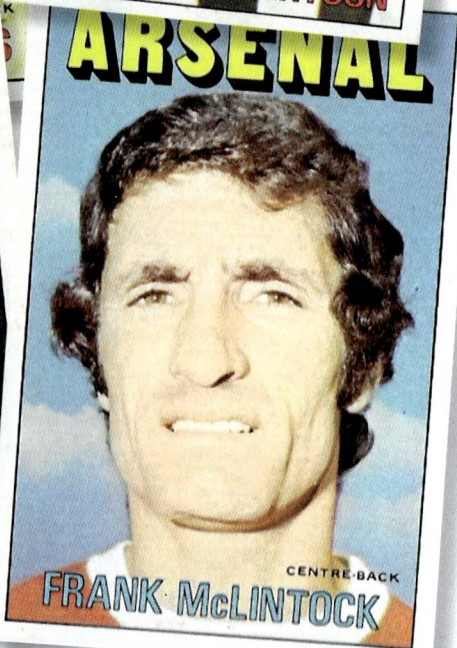

Members of the 500+ club

632 Colin Calderwood (defender, born Stranraer). Years active 1981 to 2001. Clubs – Mansfield, Swindon, Tottenham Hotspur, Aston Villa, Nottingham Forest, Notts County.

 631 Willie Morgan (winger, born Glasgow). Years active 1962 to 1982. Clubs – Burnley, Manchester United, Bolton, Blackpool.

616 Jack Ashurst (defender, born Renton). Years active 1972 to 1993. Clubs – Sunderland, Blackpool, Carlisle, Leeds, Doncaster, Rochdale.

614 Bob McKinlay (defender, born Lochgelly). Years active 1951 to 1970. Clubs – Nottingham Forest.

613 Ally Robertson (defender, born Philpstoun, West Lothian). Years active 1969 to 1990. Clubs – West Brom, Wolves.

609 Frank McLintock (defender, born Glasgow). Years active 1959 to 1977. Clubs – Leicester, Arsenal, Queens Park Rangers.

608 Frank Gray (defender, born Glasgow). Years active 1972 to 1992. Clubs – Leeds, Nottingham Forest, Leeds, Sunderland, Darlington.

602 Jimmy Scoular (defender, born Livingston Station). Years active 1946 to 1964. Clubs – Portsmouth, Newcastle, Bradford Park Avenue.

596 John MacPhail (defender, born Dundee). Years active 1978 to 1995. Clubs – Sheffield United, York, Bristol City, Sunderland, Hartlepool.

595* Chris Martin (forward, born Beccles, Norfolk). Years active 2006 to present day. Clubs – Norwich, Luton, Crystal Palace, Swindon, Derby, Fulham, Reading, Hull, Bristol City, Queens Park Rangers, Bristol Rovers.

595 Don Masson (midfielder, born Banchory). Years active 1964 to 1982. Clubs – Middlesbrough, Notts County, Queens Park Rangers, Derby, Notts County.

595 George Wood (goalkeeper, born Douglas, Lanarkshire). Years active 1971 to 1991. Clubs – Blackpool, Everton, Arsenal, Crystal Palace, Cardiff, Blackpool, Hereford.

592 Archie Gemmill (midfielder, born Paisley). Years active 1967 to 1984. Clubs – Preston, Derby, Nottingham Forest, Birmingham, Wigan, Derby.

591 Willie Donachie (defender, born Glasgow). Years active 1969 to 1991. Clubs – Manchester City, Norwich, Burnley, Oldham.

588 Matt Elliott (defender, born Wandsworth). Years active 1988 to 2005. Clubs – Charlton, Torquay, Scunthorpe, Oxford, Leicester, Ipswich.

578 Colin Methven (defender, born India). Years active 1979 to 1993. Clubs – Wigan, Blackpool, Carlisle, Walsall.

TOM HUTCHISON

COVENTRY

JOHN McGOVERN

NOTTINGHAM FOREST

WILLIE DONACHIE

MANCHESTER CITY

GEORGE WOOD

EVERTON

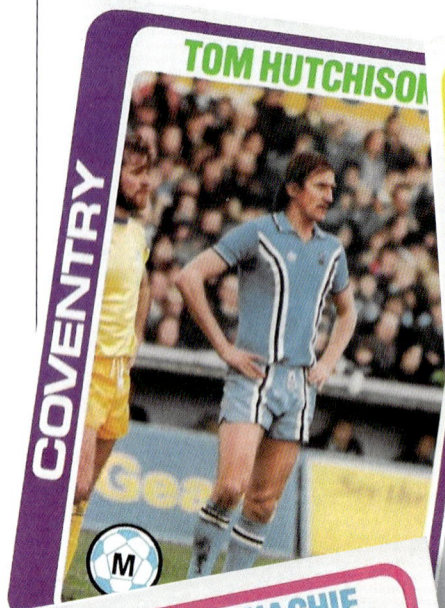

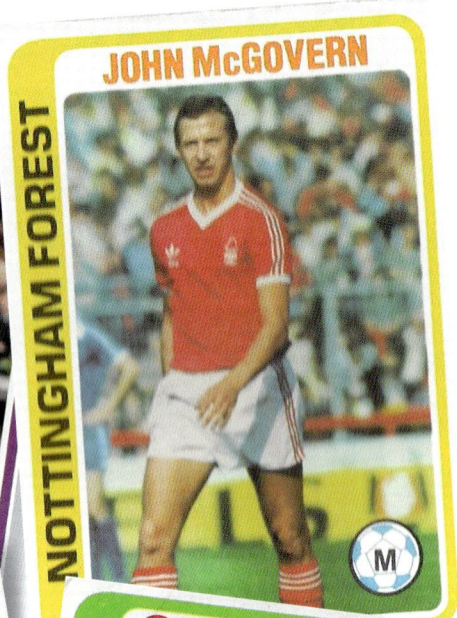

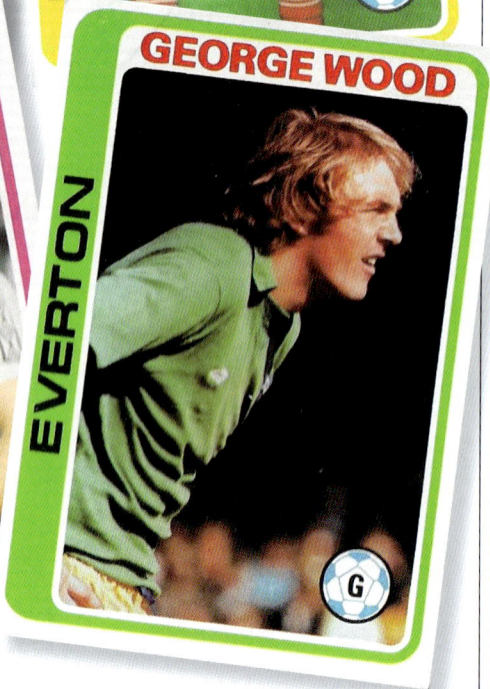

Members of the 500+ club

576 Ray Houghton (midfielder, born Glasgow but represented Republic of Ireland). Years active 1981 to 1999. Clubs – West Ham, Fulham, Oxford, Liverpool, Aston Villa, Crystal Palace, Reading.

575 Andy Liddell (forward, born Leeds). Years active 1991 to 2010. Clubs – Barnsley, Wigan, Sheffield United, Oldham, Rotherham.

572 Duncan Forbes (defender, born Edinburgh). Years active 1961 to 1981. Clubs – Colchester, Norwich, Torquay.

571 Alan Campbell (midfielder, born Arbroath). Years active 1965 to 1982. Clubs – Charlton, Birmingham, Cardiff, Carlisle.

571 Jim Cannon (defender, born Glasgow). Years active 1972 to 1988. Clubs – Crystal Palace.

570 Jordan Rhodes* (striker, born Oldham). Years active 2007 to present day. Clubs – Ipswich, Oxford, Rochdale, Brentford, Huddersfield, Blackburn, Middlesbrough, Sheffield Wednesday, Norwich, Huddersfield, Blackpool.

569 Stuart McCall (midfielder, born Leeds). Years active 1982 to 2004. Clubs – Bradford, Everton, Bradford, Sheffield United.

567 Ian Miller (midfielder, born Perth). Years active 1973 to 1991. Clubs – Bury, Doncaster, Swindon, Blackburn, Port Vale, Scunthorpe.

564 Joe Jakub (midfielder, born Falkirk). Years active 1975 to 1995. Clubs – Burnley, Bury, Chester, Burnley, Chester, Wigan Athletic.

562 Bruce Rioch (midfielder, born Aldershot). Years active 1964 to 1984. Clubs – Luton, Aston Villa, Derby, Everton, Derby, Birmingham, Sheffield United, Torquay.

561 Charlie Aitken (defender, born Edinburgh). Years active 1960 to 1976. Clubs – Aston Villa.

560 Neil Sullivan (goalkeeper, born Sutton). Years active 1990 to 2013. Clubs – Wimbledon, Crystal Palace, Tottenham Hotspur, Chelsea, Leeds, Doncaster, AFC Wimbledon.

556 Neil McNab (midfielder, born Greenock). Years active 1973 to 1994. Clubs – Tottenham Hotspur, Bolton, Brighton, Leeds, Manchester City, Tranmere, Huddersfield, Darlington.

555 Peter Lorimer (midfielder, born Dundee). Years active 1962 to 1986. Clubs – Leeds, York, Leeds.

551 Paul Gallagher (midfielder, born Glasgow). Years active 2002 to 2021. Clubs – Blackburn, Stoke, Preston, Stoke, Plymouth, Leicester, Sheffield United, Preston.

551 Ron Wylie (forward, born Glasgow). Years active 1950 to 1971. Clubs – Notts County, Aston Villa, Birmingham.

GRAHAM ALEXANDER

STUART McCALL

GARY McALLISTER

jimmy scoular

Right-half

NEWCASTLE UNITED
& SCOTLAND

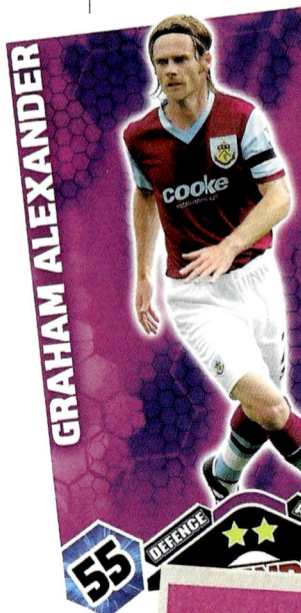

*Members of the
500+ club*

548 Bobby Doyle (midfielder, born Dumbarton). Years active 1972 to 1987. Clubs – Barnsley, Peterborough, Blackpool, Portsmouth, Hull.

539 Jim McNab (midfielder, born Denny). Years active 1958 to 1976. Clubs – Sunderland, Preston, Stockport.

535 Ted MacDougall (forward, born Inverness). Years active 1967 to 1981. Clubs – York, Bournemouth, Manchester United, West Ham, Norwich, Southampton, Bournemouth, Blackpool.

535 John McGovern (midfielder, born Montrose). Years active 1965 to 1984. Clubs – Hartlepool, Derby, Leeds, Nottingham Forest, Bolton.

535 Charlie Wright (goalkeeper, born Glasgow). Years active 1958 to 1973. Clubs – Workington, Grimsby, Charlton, Bolton.

528 Johnny McNichol (forward, born Kilmarnock). Years active 1948 to 1963. Clubs – Brighton, Chelsea, Crystal Palace.

523 Barry Bannan* (midfielder, born Airdrie). Years active 2008 to present day. Clubs – Aston Villa, Derby, Blackpool, Leeds, Crystal Palace, Bolton, Sheffield Wednesday.

520 Dougie Freedman (forward, born Glasgow). Years active 1994 to 2010. Clubs – Barnet, Crystal Palace, Wolves, Nottingham Forest, Crystal Palace, Leeds, Southend.

520 Les Massie (forward, born Aberdeen). Years active 1956 to 1971. Clubs – Huddersfield, Darlington, Halifax, Bradford Park Avenue, Workington.

519 David Speedie (forward, born Glenrothes). Years active 1978 to 1994. Clubs – Barnsley, Darlington, Chelsea, Coventry, Liverpool, Blackburn, Southampton, Birmingham, West Brom, West Ham, Leicester.

518 John Hendrie (midfielder, born Lennoxtown). Years active 1981 to 1999. Clubs – Coventry, Hereford, Bradford, Newcastle, Leeds, Middlesbrough, Barnsley.

515 Tommy Craig (midfielder, born Glasgow). Years active 1968 to 1985. Clubs – Sheffield Wednesday, Newcastle, Aston Villa, Swansea, Carlisle.

515 Jimmy Gabriel (defender, born Dundee). Years active 1959 to 1974. Clubs – Everton, Southampton, Bournemouth, Swindon, Brentford.

512 Matt Phillips* (forward, born Aylesbury). Years active 2007 to present day. Clubs – Wycombe, Blackpool, Sheffield United, Queens Park Rangers, West Brom, Oxford.

512 Steve Mungall (defender, born Bellshill). Years active 1979 to 1996. Clubs – Tranmere.

510 Lee Peacock (forward, born Paisley). Years active 1993 to 2010. Clubs – Carlisle, Mansfield, Manchester City, Bristol City, Sheffield Wednesday, Swindon.

503 Paul Devlin (midfielder, born Birmingham). Years active 1991 to 2006. Clubs – Notts County, Birmingham, Sheffield United, Notts County, Birmingham, Watford, Walsall.

502 David Marshall (goalkeeper, born Glasgow). Years active 2005 to 2022. Clubs – Norwich, Cardiff, Hull, Wigan, Derby, Queens Park Rangers.

501 George Burley (defender, born Cumnock). Years active 1973 to 1995. Clubs – Ipswich, Sunderland, Gillingham, Colchester.

500 George Boyd (midfielder, born Chatham). Years active 2006 to 2021. Clubs – Peterborough, Nottingham Forest, Hull, Burnley, Sheffield Wednesday, Peterborough, Salford.

MANCHESTER UNITED

Willie Morgan
OUTSIDE RIGHT

COVENTRY CITY

WOLVERHAMPTON WANDERERS

Jim McCalliog
INSIDE RIGHT

SOUTHAMPTON

Eric Martin
GOALKEEPER

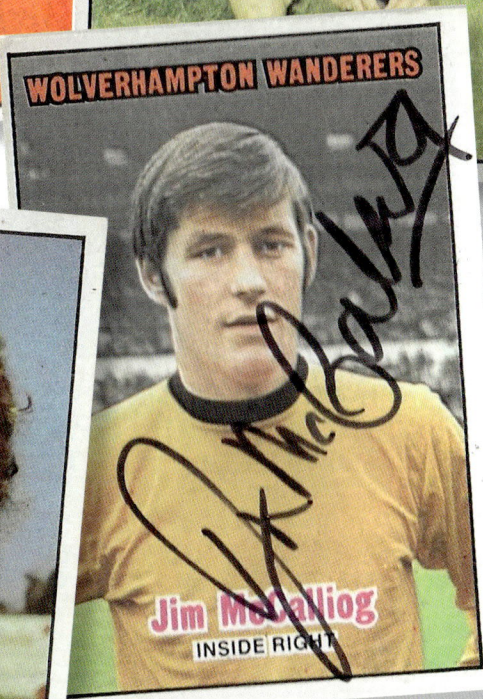

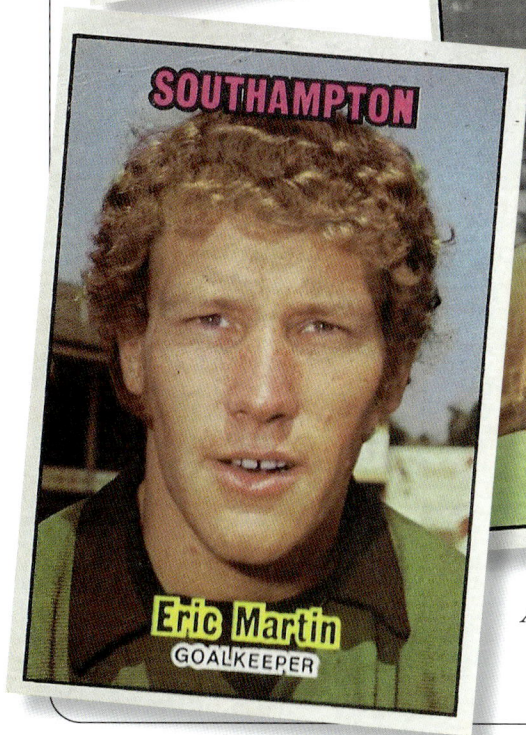

Alternative Cult Heroes

Appendix 2

Major goalscoring achievements in England by Scottish footballers

Top goalscorers in England's top flight

Season	Player (Club)	Goals	Apps	League finish
1889/90	Jimmy Ross (Preston North End)	24	22	1st
1891/92	John Campbell (Sunderland)	32	26	1st
1892/93	John Campbell (Sunderland)	31	30	1st
1894/95	John Campbell (Sunderland)	22	30	1st
1895/96	Johnny Campbell (Aston Villa)*	20	30	1st
1906/07	Alex Young (Everton)	28	38	3rd
1911/12	David McLean (Sheffield Wed)**	25	38	5th
1912/13	David McLean (Sheffield Wed)	30	38	3rd
1914/15	Bobby Parker (Everton)	35	38	1st
1921/22	Andrew Wilson (Middlesbrough)	31	42	8th
1928/29	Dave Halliday (Sunderland)	43	42	4th
1948/49	Willie Moir (Bolton Wanderers)	25	42	14th
1975/76	Ted MacDougall (Norwich City)	23	42	10th
1976/77	Andy Gray (Aston Villa)***	25	42	4th
1980/81	Steve Archibald (Tottenham H)****	20	42	10th

* Joint top goalscorer with Steve Bloomer (Derby County)
** Joint top goalscorer with Harry Hampton (Aston Villa) and George Holley (Sunderland)
*** Joint top goalscorer with Malcolm Macdonald (Arsenal)
**** Joint top goalscorer with Peter Withe (Aston Villa)

After English players, Scots come next with 15 seasons as top or joint top scorers. The 21st century has of course seen overseas players dominate, the exploits of Harry Kane notwithstanding, with France and the Netherlands producing the leading top-flight marksmen five times each. Wales and

Ireland (north and south combined) have contributed four each – all in the latter half of the 20th century.

Aberdeen-born Willie Moir scored over 100 league goals for Bolton Wanderers playing alongside England international Nat Lofthouse. He also scored in the 1953 'Matthews' FA Cup Final which Bolton lost 4-3 to Blackpool. During the Second World War, Moir guested for Aberdeen and Dundee. In season 1948/49 Moir's tally of 25 league goals was seven more than that of Peter Harris, the top marksman for champions Portsmouth.

Ted MacDougall was a bit of a maverick who enjoyed hero status at some of the clubs he played for. In 1975/76 Ted was in top form in East Anglia where his league tally for Norwich City included hat-tricks against Aston Villa and Everton as well as a brace in games against Burnley, Leicester City and Leeds United plus Manchester City in the League Cup. Alas, the Canaries also leaked goals that season, conceding as many as they scored – 58. By comparison, champions Liverpool scored 66 goals with John Toshack netting 16 of them.

Andy Gray's first club after departing Dundee United was Aston Villa with whom he won the League Cup in 1977 before repeating the trick at Wolves in 1980. At Everton he won the FA Cup in 1984 as well as the league championship and the European Cup Winners' Cup the following year. In 1976/77 Andy's Aston Villa were the league's top scorers with 76 goals – 14 more than champions Liverpool.

Steve Archibald arrived at Tottenham Hotspur having started out at Clyde then Aberdeen. At White Hart Lane he collected winners' medals in the FA Cup in 1981 and 1982, and the UEFA Cup in 1984. In the league campaign of 1980/81 Spurs scored 70 goals – just two fewer than champions Aston Villa – however they also conceded 68.

As mentioned earlier in this book, three Scots make it into the all-time top 20 top-flight goalscorers at 20, 15 and ten. The terrific trio are Dave Halliday, from Dumfries; David Herd, from Hamilton; and Bellshill's Hughie Gallacher respectively. Halliday's aggregate total of 211 came about at Sunderland, Arsenal and Manchester City in the 1920s and 1930s. Herd's 222 were achieved in the 1950s and 1960s at Arsenal, Manchester United and Stoke City. Gallacher's prime time was also the 1920s and 1930s when he netted 246 across Newcastle United, Chelsea and Derby County.

* * *

FOOTBALL ASSOCIATION CHALLENGE CUP COMPETITION
CUP FINAL
SATURDAY 19 MAY 1984
KICK-OFF 3.00p.m.
EVERTON
WATFORD
OFFICIAL SOUVENIR PROGRAMME 80p
Wembley Stadium

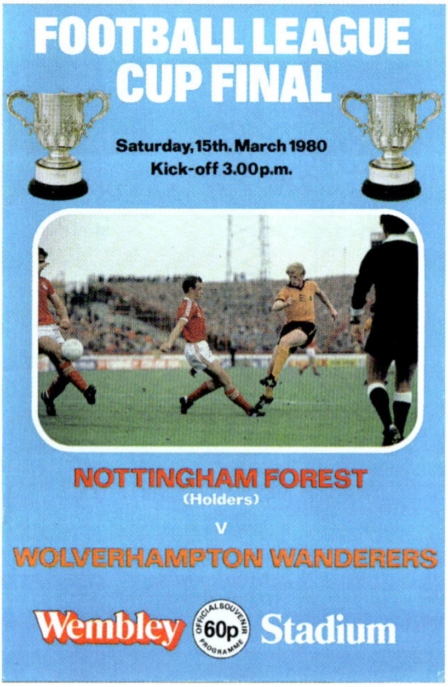
FOOTBALL LEAGUE CUP FINAL
Saturday, 15th. March 1980
Kick-off 3.00p.m.
NOTTINGHAM FOREST
(Holders)
V
WOLVERHAMPTON WANDERERS
Wembley
OFFICIAL SOUVENIR 60p PROGRAMME
Stadium

FOOTBALL ASSOCIATION CHALLENGE CUP COMPETITION
FINAL
LEEDS UNITED
V
SUNDERLAND
WEMBLEY STADIUM
JUBILEE 1923-1973
SATURDAY, 5th MAY, 1973 . . . Kick-off 3pm
Official Programme . . . 15 pence

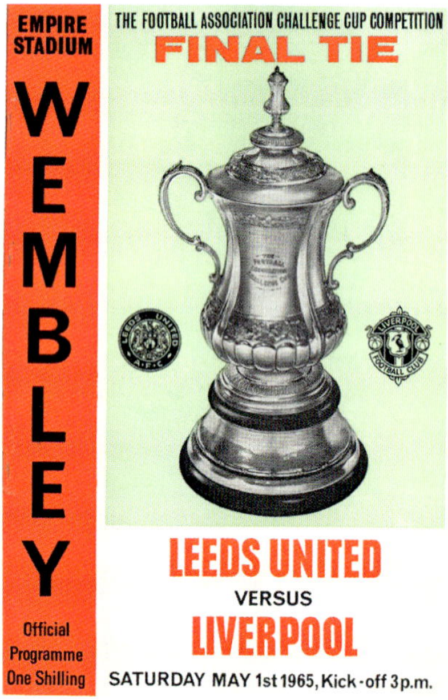
EMPIRE STADIUM
WEMBLEY
Official Programme One Shilling
THE FOOTBALL ASSOCIATION CHALLENGE CUP COMPETITION
FINAL TIE
LEEDS UNITED
VERSUS
LIVERPOOL
SATURDAY MAY 1st 1965, Kick-off 3p.m.

FA Cup Final and League Cup Final goalscorers for winning sides since the Second World War

1946/47: Methil-born former Leith Athletic winger Chris Duffy scored the only goal of the game to give Charlton Athletic victory over Burnley in the FA Cup Final.

1954/55: Ex-Third Lanark outside-left Bobby Mitchell netted the second goal in Newcastle United's 3-1 win against Manchester City in the FA Cup Final.

1955/56: Bobby Johnstone, formerly of Hibernian's 'Famous Five', became the first player to score in successive FA Cup finals at Wembley as his Manchester City triumphed 3-1 over Birmingham City.

1961/62: Ormiston-born winger Bill Punton scored for second-tier Norwich City in their 4-0 aggregate win over fourth-tier Rochdale in the second League Cup Final.

1962/63: When Manchester United defeated Leicester City 3-1 in the FA Cup Final two Scots got the goals for the Red Devils – the opener coming from Denis Law followed by a double from David Herd.

1963/64: Ex-Hibernian inside-left Dave Gibson netted a goal in each leg of Leicester City's 4-3 aggregate win over Stoke City in the League Cup Final.

1964/65: Former East Stirlingshire left-back Eddie McCreadie scored what proved to be the winning goal, an 80-yard dribble to beat Gordon Banks, in Chelsea's 3-2 aggregate win over Leicester City in the League Cup Final.

1964/65: Ex-Motherwell forward Ian St John scored the winning goal in Liverpool's 2-1 victory over Leeds United in the FA Cup Final.

1966/67: Former St Mirren winger Jimmy Robertson hit the opening goal in Tottenham Hotspur's 2-1 win over Chelsea in the FA Cup Final.

1970/71: Lanarkshire's George Graham grabbed the equaliser for Arsenal as his club fought back to win the FA Cup Final 2-1 against Liverpool and in so doing clinched the double.

1972/73: Former Raith Rovers midfielder Ian Porterfield scored the only goal of the FA Cup Final to give Second Division Sunderland victory over much-fancied Leeds United.

1977/78: John Robertson, formerly of Drumchapel Amateurs, converted a penalty – the only goal of the League Cup Final replay at Old Trafford – to give Nottingham Forest victory over Liverpool.

1979/80: Andy Gray of Wolverhampton Wanderers scored the only goal of the League Cup Final against Nottingham Forest and in so doing prevented Brian Clough's side from lifting the trophy for a third successive season.

1980/81: Liverpool defeated West Ham United 2-1 in the League Cup Final replay at Villa Park with the Reds' goals coming from Kenny Dalglish and Alan Hansen.

1983/84: Graeme Souness, formerly of Tynecastle Boys Club, scored the only goal of the League Cup Final replay for Liverpool against Everton at Maine Road, Manchester.

1983/84: Ex-Dumbarton man Graeme Sharp and Andy Gray scored to give Everton a 2-0 win over Watford in the FA Cup Final.

1984/85: The only goal of the League Cup Final came about when Sunderland's Gordon Chisholm, a future Hibernian, Dundee and Partick Thistle defender, deflected a shot from Norwich City's Asa Hartford into his own net. Unlike most sources, however, we're going to credit the goal to the 50-cap international from Clydebank, who was plying his trade in East Anglia.

1986/87: Ex-Celt 'Champagne' Charlie Nicholas netted twice for Arsenal as the Gunners came from behind to defeat Liverpool 2-1 to win the League Cup for the first time having lost in their two previous finals in this competition.

1991/92: Ex-Celt Brian McClair scored the only goal of the League Cup Final in the 14th minute to ensure Alex Ferguson's Manchester United edged out Brian Clough's Nottingham Forest to win the three-handled trophy for the first time.

1993/94: Alex Ferguson's Manchester United romped to a 4-0 victory over Glenn Hoddle's Chelsea in the FA Cup Final with late substitute Brian McClair grabbing the fourth goal in the 92nd minute.

1999/2000: Leicester City became the last club to win the League Cup at the old Wembley Stadium thanks in part to two goals from Wandsworth-born Scotland international defender Matt Elliott as the Foxes overcame second-tier outfit Tranmere Rovers 2-1 in the final.

2000/01: While the new Wembley was being constructed, the Millennium Stadium in Cardiff witnessed Liverpool and Birmingham City play out a 1-1 draw in the League Cup Final before the Reds lifted the trophy by winning 5-4 on penalties with second-half substitute Gary McAllister netting the first of the five.

2021/22: Liverpool and Chelsea fought out a 0-0 draw in the League Cup Final at Wembley. After extra time, penalties settled the issue – 11-10 in favour of the Anfield club with Andy Robertson netting number eight for the Reds.

Appendix 3

Player of the year awards – Scottish successes in England

Season	FWA (started 1948)	PFA (started 1974)	PFA Young Player (started 1974)
1964/65	Bobby Collins (Leeds United)	-	-
1968/69	Dave Mackay (Derby County)*	-	-
1969/70	Billy Bremner (Leeds United)	-	-
1970/71	Frank McLintock (Arsenal)	-	-
1976/77	-	Andy Gray (Aston Villa)	Andy Gray
1977/78	Kenny Burns (Nottingham Forest)	-	-
1978/79	Kenny Dalglish (Liverpool)	-	-
1980/81	-	John Wark (Ipswich Town)	-
1982/83	Kenny Dalglish (Liverpool)	Kenny Dalglish	-
1988/89	Steve Nicol (Liverpool)	-	-
1990/91	Gordon Strachan (Leeds United)	-	-

* Joint winner with Tony Book (Manchester City)

Andy Gray of Aston Villa is the only Scottish winner of the PFA Young Player of the Year award and is one of only three players to have won both PFA prizes in the same season – the others are Cristiano Ronaldo of Manchester United in 2006/07, and Gareth Bale of Tottenham Hotspur in 2012/13. Somewhat surprisingly, Gray won but 20 international caps, netting seven goals, but never made it into any of Scotland's World Cup finals squads.

Kenny Dalglish of Liverpool twice won the Football Writers' Association award as did Tom Finney (Preston North End), Danny Blanchflower (Tottenham Hotspur), Stanley Matthews (Blackpool and Stoke City), John Barnes (Liverpool), Gary Lineker (Everton and Tottenham Hotspur) and Cristiano Ronaldo (Manchester United). Thierry Henry (Arsenal) won it three times.

Gordon Strachan also won the Scottish Football Writers' Footballer of the Year award – 11 years before his English success – with Aberdeen in 1979/80.

FINALE EUROPACUP VOOR BEKERWINNAARS

Officieel Programma — Stadion Feijenoord — Woensdag 15 mei 1963 — Prijs 50 cent

ATLETICO MADRID
BEKERHOUDER

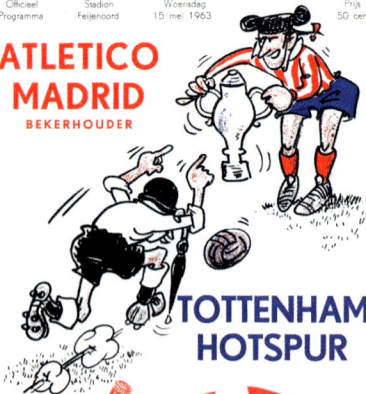

TOTTENHAM HOTSPUR

Cognac **HENNESSY**
„Le plus grand stock de cognac du monde"

EUROPEAN CHAMPION CLUBS' CUP

BENFICA F.C.   **MANCHESTER UNITED**

FINAL

ORGANISED BY THE FOOTBALL ASSOCIATION ON BEHALF OF THE UNION DES ASSOCIATIONS EUROPÉENNES DE FOOTBALL

WEDNESDAY MAY 29th 1968
Kick-off   7·45 p.m.

OFFICIAL PROGRAMME   ONE SHILLING

WEMBLEY
EMPIRE STADIUM

OFFICIAL SOUVENIR PROGRAMME

PRICE 1/-

INTER CITIES FAIRS' CUP   FINAL TIE First Leg

Season 1968-69   No. 53

NEWCASTLE UNITED
ST. JAMES' PARK - NEWCASTLE UPON TYNE
versus
UJPEST DOZSA

THURSDAY, 29th MAY, 1969   KICK-OFF 7.30 p.m.

SEASON 1971-72
Vol. 64   No. 55

Official Programme 5p

U.E.F.A. CUP FINAL
(2nd LEG)
Kick-off 7.45 p.m.

TOTTENHAM HOTSPUR
v
WOLVERHAMPTON WANDERERS

Wednesday, 17th May, 1972

* * *

European postscript – to date, Denis Law of Manchester United in 1964, is the only Scottish recipient of the European Footballer of the Year (Ballon d'Or) award.

* * *

PFA top flight team of the year (started 1973/74)
Season Scottish footballers included in the winning XI

1973/74	Billy Bremner (Leeds United)
1974/75	Gordon McQueen (Leeds United)
1975/76	Don Masson (Queens Park Rangers)
1976/77	Andy Gray (Aston Villa)
1977/78	Gordon McQueen, Martin Buchan, Joe Jordan (Manchester United); John Robertson (Nottingham Forest)
1978/79	Kenny Dalglish (Liverpool)
1979/80	Kenny Dalglish (Liverpool)
1980/81	Allan Evans (Aston Villa); John Wark (Ipswich Town); Graeme Souness, Kenny Dalglish (Liverpool)
1981/82	Alan Hansen, Graeme Souness (Liverpool)
1982/83	Alan Hansen, Graeme Souness, Kenny Dalglish (Liverpool)
1983/84	Alan Hansen, Graeme Souness, Kenny Dalglish (Liverpool)
1986/87	Alan Hansen (Liverpool)
1987/88	Alan Hansen, Gary Gillespie (Liverpool); Graeme Sharp (Everton)
1988/89	Steve Nicol (Liverpool)
1989/90	Alan Hansen (Liverpool)
1990/91	Gordon Strachan (Leeds United)
1991/92	Gary McAllister (Leeds United)
1993/94	Gary McAllister (Leeds United)
1994/95	Colin Hendry (Blackburn Rovers)
1997/98	Colin Hendry (Blackburn Rovers)
2009/10	Darren Fletcher (Manchester United)
2018/19	Andy Robertson (Liverpool)
2019/20	Andy Robertson (Liverpool)

Alan Hansen made it into the winning XI on six occasions, Kenny Dalglish five times and Graeme Souness on four successive occasions. England goalkeeper Peter Shilton holds the record with ten appearances in the PFA top flight team of the year.

On two occasions, 1977/78 and 1980/81, the winning XI included no fewer than four Anglo-Scots.

Appendix 4

League Managers' Association awards

The League Managers' Association (LMA) is the trade union, the collective, representative voice, for Premier League, English Football League and national team managers in England.

The annual LMA awards are voted for by fellow professional managers with consideration not restricted to trophy winners but also including the likes of managers who inherit 'poor' sides or financial difficulties. As such, the Premier League-winning manager does not always win the main Manager of the Year award.

1993: Alex Ferguson (Manchester United), main award

1994: Alex Ferguson (Manchester United), Premier League award

1995: Kenny Dalglish (Blackburn Rovers), Premier League award; Bruce Rioch (Bolton Wanderers), second tier; John Duncan (Chesterfield), fourth tier

1996: Alex Ferguson (Manchester United), Premier League award

1997: Alex Ferguson (Manchester United), Premier League award

1999: Alex Ferguson (Manchester United), main and Premier League awards; David Moyes (Preston North End), third tier

2000: Alex Ferguson (Manchester United), Premier League award; David Moyes (Preston North End), third tier

2001: George Burley (Ipswich Town), main and Premier League awards

2002: Paul Sturrock (Plymouth Argyle), fourth tier

2003: David Moyes (Everton), main award

2004: Paul Sturrock (Plymouth Argyle), third tier

2005: David Moyes (Everton), main award

2007: Alex Ferguson (Manchester United), Premier League award

2008: Alex Ferguson (Manchester United), main and Premier League awards

2009: David Moyes (Everton), main award; Alex Ferguson (Manchester United), Premier League; Darren Ferguson (Peterborough United), third tier

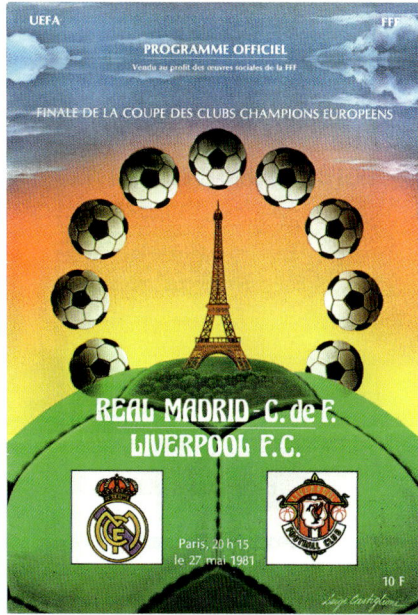

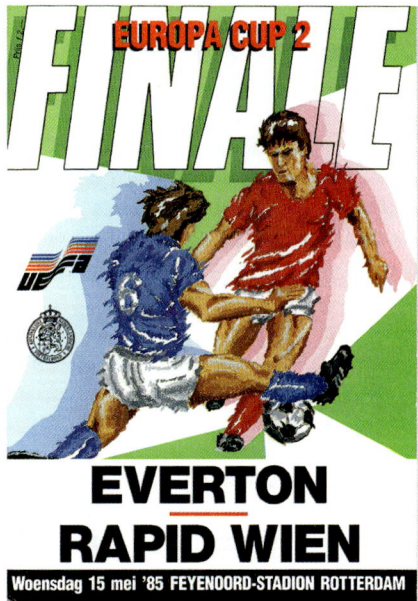

2010: Paul Lambert (Norwich City), third tier
2011: Alex Ferguson (Manchester United), main and Premier League
    awards; Paul Lambert (Norwich City), second tier
2013: Alex Ferguson (Manchester United), main and Premier League
    awards; Malky Mackay (Cardiff City), second tier
2016: Gary Caldwell (Wigan Athletic), third tier

While Alex Ferguson and Paul Sturrock both played all their club football
in Scotland and Paul Lambert played his in Scotland and Germany, it
would be churlish to exclude them from this particular roll of honour
especially in the case of Ferguson whose contribution to English football
has been immense. Fergie is one of the most successful managers of all
time and his English club trophy haul consists of two Champions Leagues,
one Cup Winners' Cup, 13 Premier League titles, five FA Cups and four
League Cups. Not bad for a former East Stirlingshire manager who wasn't
capped for his country – until he was 80 years old. OK, so the belated,
though deserved recognition was in respect of four appearances made
during Scotland's 1967 world tour.

Paul Sturrock enjoyed 15 seasons at Dundee United, playing as a
striker until 1989 and picking up a league winners' medal, two League
Cups and 20 Scotland caps along the way. It's a mere 640 miles from
Sturrock's original home in Aberdeenshire to Home Park in Plymouth
where he guided the Pilgrims to two lower-league titles in the early years
of the 21st century (see also the Seaside Celebrities chapter).

In 2007 Paul Lambert, winner of 40 Scotland caps, guided fourth-tier
Wycombe Wanderers to the semi-finals of the League Cup, defeating top-
flight Fulham and Charlton Athletic on the way before losing to eventual
winners and reigning Premier League champions Chelsea, holding José
Mourinho's Blues to a 1-1 draw at home before losing the away leg. At
Norwich City, Lambert steered the Canaries to the League One title in
2009/10 and then promotion to the Premier League at the end of 2010/11.
The Glaswegian was inducted into the club's Hall of Fame in March 2012,
and as manager of the East Anglian outfit, he also made it on to a Topps
Match Attax trading card! Indeed, he also appeared on a subsequent
trading card as manager of Aston Villa.

Kenny Dalglish's successes are well documented elsewhere in this
book, although it's interesting to think that in 2004 he was touted by some
as a possible successor to Berti Vogts as manager of the Scotland national
team. Another one for the 'What if?' file. In 2023 Kenny won the BBC

Sports Personality of the Year Lifetime Achievement Award, following Alex Ferguson who won it in 2001.

Aldershot's powershot Scot Bruce Rioch, who scored six goals in his 24 international appearances, guided Bolton Wanderers to promotion to the second tier at the end of 1992/93. In 1994/95 he then got the Trotters to their first League Cup Final before losing to Liverpool. However, as a consolation prize they defeated Reading 4-3 after extra time in the First Division play-off final having been 2-0 down at half-time. Two other promotions had also been achieved at Middlesbrough in 1986/87 and 1987/88 to the second and top tiers respectively. Rioch's first signing as manager of Arsenal in June 1995 was Dennis Bergkamp from Inter Milan. Incidentally, Bergkamp had been named Dennis in honour of Scotland striker Denis Law with the additional 'n' being a Dutch custom.

George Burley won 11 Scotland caps during his 13 seasons as a player at Ipswich Town. He later had eight seasons there as a manager during which time he took the Portman Road club to three play-off semi-finals before eventually winning promotion to the Premier League at the fourth attempt via the play-offs at the end of 1999/2000. The following season he steered Ipswich to fifth place in the top flight and a spot in the UEFA Cup.

While in charge at Everton, David Moyes won the LMA main award on three occasions despite never actually winning a trophy with the Toffees. In 2002/03 Everton finished seventh in the Premier League with media attention centred around the exploits of 17-year-old Wayne Rooney. In 2004/05 they finished fourth to make it into the Champions League third qualifying round and in 2008/09 the Goodison club finished fifth and reached the FA Cup Final before losing to Chelsea 2-1, after Louis Saha had given the Merseysiders the lead in the first minute. Earlier in his managerial career Moyes guided Preston North End to the 1999/2000 Second Division title while European success would be achieved with West Ham United in 2022/23.

Darren Ferguson, after five Scotland under-21 caps, has had no fewer than four stints as manager of Peterborough United where he has enjoyed varying degrees of success. He has overseen the Posh winning the Football League Trophy twice, in 2013/14 and 2023/24, as well as four promotions – one to League One and three to the Championship.

Bellshill-born Malky Mackay enjoyed a playing career at clubs such as Queen's Park, Celtic, Norwich (where he helped the Norfolk outfit to promotion to the Premier League at the end of 2003/04), West Ham and Watford. As a manager, he guided Cardiff to their first League Cup Final in 2012 before losing to Kenny Dalglish's Liverpool on penalties. The following season he led Cardiff to promotion to the Premier League.

As a defender, Gary Caldwell won the last of his 55 Scotland caps in 2013. Eighteen of them came with Wigan Athletic, who he became manager of in April 2015, and at the end of 2015/16 he guided them to the League One title and promotion back to the Championship at the first attempt.

In his first managerial stint at Chesterfield, former Spurs and Derby County striker John Duncan guided the Spireites to the 1984/85 Fourth Division title. In his second stint at the Derbyshire club, Duncan led Chesterfield to promotion via the Third Division play-offs in 1995 and the FA Cup semi-finals in 1996/97.

In 2023 the League Managers' Association named a special award in honour of Duncan with the inaugural winner being fellow Scot Lou Macari, winner of 24 Scotland caps and scorer of five international goals, in recognition of his work in creating the Macari Foundation which helps people in Stoke-on-Trent who have been affected by homelessness.

Epilogue

Looking back at season 2023/24 we can see that the English Premier League is really the 'Planet Earth League' with players and managers from the likes of Brazil, France, Spain, Portugal, Netherlands, Denmark, Germany, Argentina and Nigeria featuring prominently. For season 2024/25 the Premier League alone features players from over 50 nations, with Scotland making it into the top 12 in terms of aggregate number supplied. Two are captains, John McGinn at Aston Villa and Tom Cairney at Fulham, with former Scotland defender Russell Martin starting the season as Southampton manager.

If we delve a bit deeper into the 2023/24 Premier League squads we can still find several examples of Scottish influence on the English game. They included John McGinn (209 Championship and Premier League appearances in total with Villa plus 16 goals as at the end of 2023/24), Ryan Christie of Bournemouth (107/4 Championship and Premier League), Aaron Hickey of Brentford (35/0 PL), Billy Gilmour at Brighton & Hove Albion (44/0 PL), Nathan Patterson of Everton (39/0 PL), Tom Cairney (291/41 Champ and PL), Andy Robertson of Liverpool (218/10 PL), Jacob Brown at Luton Town (19/2 PL), Scott McTominay of Manchester United (176/19 PL), Matt Ritchie at Newcastle United (187/20 Champ and PL), Scott McKenna of Nottingham Forest (94/3 Champ and PL) and Oli McBurnie of Sheffield United (146/26 Champ and PL).

In addition, Arsenal defender Kieran Tierney had been loaned out to Real Sociedad in Spain for 2023/24 having played in 91 Premier League games and scoring three goals since joining the north London club in August 2019.

Dropping down to the Championship for 2023/24 we find Ché Adams helping Southampton win a return to the top flight (164/41 Premier League and Championship). Leeds United, who lost to Southampton in the play-off final, featured centre-back Liam Cooper (262/11 Champ and PL) while Norwich, who lost to Leeds in the semi-final, included defender Grant Hanley (178/5 Champ and PL). Southampton also included Stuart Armstrong (191/21 Champ and PL) while Hanley had goalkeeper Angus Gunn (129/0 Champ and PL) and striker Kenny McLean (207/9 Champ and PL) for company.

Still within the Championship we had former Queen of the South and Livingston striker Lyndon Dykes at QPR (156/35). Another 'seaside celebrity' was ex-Rangers striker Ryan Hardie who began his English career at Blackpool in the third tier in 2019/20. Later that season he dropped down to the fourth tier with Plymouth Argyle before helping the Pilgrims to two promotions and Championship football in 2023/24 (172/53 total league football by the sea).

Just for good measure Ché Adams, Grant Hanley, John McGinn, Scott McTominay and Andy Robertson (plus Celtic's Callum McGregor) also appeared in all six Scotland matches across the Euro 2020 and Euro 2024 finals. Furthermore, hopefully Robertson will go on to achieve a century of caps within the next two or three seasons.

Meanwhile, in League One, come the end of 2023/24 Carnoustie-born former Scotland international Craig Forsyth had helped Derby win promotion back to the Championship, totalling 284/10 league games with the Rams at that point.

Looking to the future, the best of luck to those Scots lads and lassies seeking to break through into the big time in England. Some examples include Ben Doak, a teenage striker with the national team and Liverpool (when he's not being loaned out); and Southampton's former Ross County and Sunderland striker Ross Stewart. There's also goalkeeper Cieran Slicker at Ipswich Town, a Scottish youth international born in Oldham in September 2002, and former Hearts midfielder Andy Irving, now at West Ham. There are of course, a whole plethora of Scottish footballers battling away in the Championship trying to help their respective clubs make it into the top flight.

Now while it is all good and well getting your photograph on to the front cover of magazines such as *Time*, *Vogue* or *FourFourTwo* (or having yourself portrayed as a comic-book superhero on the front cover of a Scotland match programme, a la McGinn, Robertson, Dykes, McTominay and Gordon during 2024), there is surely nothing to beat the sense of achievement of having been featured in sticker albums or trading cards collections and having your image sought after and/or swapped around the globe.

Well, I suppose having a statue erected in your honour might rival 'stickermania' and there are a few of them around. At Old Trafford there are statues of Matt Busby and Alex Ferguson, plus Denis Law as part of Manchester United's 'Holy Trinity' that includes George Best and Bobby Charlton. There are also statues of Bill Shankly at Anfield; Billy Bremner at Elland Road; Jimmy Sirrel alongside fellow Notts County legend Jack Wheeler at Meadow Lane; and Hugh McIlmoyle at Carlisle United's Brunton Park. Meanwhile, outside Villa Park, there is a statue of Perthshire man William McGregor, who founded the English Football League in 1888.

In addition, images of Matt Busby, Bill Shankly and Denis Law have made it on to Royal Mail postage stamps, as have Dave Mackay and Frank McLintock. Sadly, the movie *McLintock!* starring John Wayne is a comedy western and not a biopic dramatising the career of the Arsenal double-winning skipper. And then there are the murals – street art recognition at its finest. 'Gable-end glory' is particularly widespread throughout the city of Liverpool with Shankly, Kenny Dalglish and Alan Hansen all featured.

Anyway, they say that history often repeats itself or that it operates in cycles, however it is unlikely that we will see a return to the days when Anglo-Scottish footballers practically dominated the English football landscape – the process of globalisation has seen to that. That's not a complaint, just a recognition of the ongoing social and economic evolution of this planet. So we rejoice in the contribution we Scots have made, safe in the knowledge that we will always be there for our big, wealthier and warmer, next-door neighbour one way or another – to impress or to simply lend a hand. It's quite often what we do best. We play when they ask us.

Acknowledgements

First and foremost, we would like to acknowledge the continued support of our wives, Marion Marshall and Nan Stuart, as well as the team at Pitch Publishing, especially Jane Camillin, Duncan Olner, Dean Rockett, Graham Hales and Alex Daley.

We would also like to dedicate this book to all those young boys who left their native Scotland to follow their dreams.

Bibliography

Bollen, A., *A History of Scottish Football in 100 Objects* (Edinburgh: Arena Sport, 2019)

Boulton, S., *Cult Heroes* (London: BBC Books, 2005)

Brogan, T., *We Made Them Angry* (Chichester: Pitch Publishing, 2022)

Constable, N., *Match of the Day 50 Years* (London: BBC Books, 2014)

Giller, N., *McFootball – The Scottish Heroes of the English Game* (London: Robson Books, 2003)

Hayes, D.P., *Scotland! Scotland! – A Complete Who's Who of Scotland Players Since 1946* (Edinburgh: Mercat Press Ltd, 2006)

Henderson, J., *When Footballers Were Skint* (London: Biteback Publishing Ltd., 2019)

Hugman, B.J., *Canon League Football Players' Records 1946–1984* (Feltham: Newnes Books, 1984)

Inglis, S., *Football Grounds of Great Britain* (Glasgow: William Collins Sons and Co Ltd, 1989)

Keir, R., *Scotland – The Complete International Football Record* (Derby: Breedon Books Publishing Company Limited, 2001)

Lawther, S., *Arrival* (Worthing, Pitch Publishing, 2021)

McCrery, N., *Season in Hell – British Footballers Killed in the Second World War* (Barnsley: Pen & Sword Books Ltd, 2023)

McGovern, J., *John McGovern from Bo'ness to the Bernabéu* (Kingston Upon Thames: Vision Sports Publishing, 2012)

Morgan, W., with Wadsworth, S., *On the Wing* (Liverpool: Trinity Mirror Sport Media 2013)

Potter, D., and Jones, P.H., *The Encyclopaedia of Scottish Football* (Studley, Warwickshire: Know the Score Books Limited, 2008)

Samuel, R., *The British Home Football Championships 1884–1984* (Cleethorpes: Soccer Books Limited, 2003)

Scragg, S., *A Tournament Frozen in Time* (Worthing: Pitch Publishing, 2019)

Scragg, S., *Where the Cool Kids Hung Out* (Worthing: Pitch Publishing, 2020)

Tait, J., *Scotland at 150* (Lerwick: Jicks Publishing, 2023)

Younger, D., *Cult Heroes Newcastle United* (Durrington: Pitch Publishing, 2012)